DAVID STOREY

CASEBOOKS ON
MODERN DRAMATISTS
(VOL. 9)

GARLAND REFERENCE LIBRARY
OF THE HUMANITIES
(VOL. 1293)

CASEBOOKS ON MODERN DRAMATISTS
(*General Editor*, Kimball King)

David Storey
A Casebook

edited by
William Hutchings

GARLAND PUBLISHING, INC. • NEW YORK & LONDON
1992

Library of Congress Cataloging-in-Publication Data

David Storey : a casebook / edited by William Hutchings.
     p.   cm. — (Casebooks on modern dramatists ; vol. 9. Garland
reference library of the humanities ; vol. 1293)
  Includes bibliographical references and index.
  ISBN 0-8240-6887-4 (alk. paper)
  1. Storey, David, 1933–   —Criticism and interpretation.
I. Hutchings, William. II. Series: Garland reference library of the
humanities. Casebooks on modern dramatists ; vol. 9. III. Series:
Garland reference library of the humanities ; vol. 1293.
PR6069.T65Z64   1992   91-48264
822'.914—dc20
                                              CIP

Printed on acid-free, 250-year-life paper
Manufactured in the United States of America

CONTENTS

GENERAL EDITOR'S NOTE

David Storey is one of the most versatile and compelling talents of modern theater, and like every major artist, all of his literary works bear the stamp of his unique personal vision and style. Professor William Hutchings established himself as an authority on Storey's achievement in well-known periodicals and at scholarly conferences even before his definitive book-length analysis, *The Plays of David Storey: A Romantic Study*, was published in 1988. He has selected for this casebook a wide range of articles which focus on language and gender issues in Storey's plays, as well as on their political and social implications. The relationship between the author's drama and his fiction is also thoughtfully explored.

Kimball King

INTRODUCTION

Among the works of the post-1956 English playwrights, the plays of David Storey are remarkable for the diversity of their form, their understated eloquence, and the recurrence of a number of crucial themes and motifs that have become uniquely his own. Although he is best known for such ostensibly plotless works as *The Changing Room*, *The Contractor*, and *Home*—plays whose style he has described as "poetic naturalism"—his works also include a number of more traditionally structured domestic dramas (*The Restoration of Arnold Middleton, In Celebration, The Farm, Sisters, Early Days*, and *The March on Russia*), a history play whose title character never appears (*Cromwell*), and a farce (*Mother's Day*). Yet throughout them all, perennial concerns persist: the nature of the modern family, the effects of social class (not only for those who remain in the class into which they were born but also for those who escape from it), the devaluation of traditional ritual, the dignity of work, and the perennial need to establish oneself (even if only temporarily) as a participating member of a group that transcends and subsumes the self. Because so many of these concerns recur throughout the diverse dramatic forms that Storey has utilized, contributors to this volume have been encouraged to include as many of Storey's plays as they deem appropriate in their essays while focusing on particular aspects of his work.

Like Chekhov's, Storey's plays emphasize "interior action" rather than external events, however crucial the latter may seem; thus, the major battles in *Cromwell*, the wedding in *The Contractor*, and the rugby match of *The Changing Room* occur offstage and between the acts, so that the audience's attention is redirected towards characters' *reactions* to events that remain unseen. Like Samuel Beckett, Storey is

ix

a master of minimalist dialogue and of silences that sometimes speak more eloquently than words. Although there are a few characters in his plays whose tirades are as vigorous as those of John Osborne's Jimmy Porter in *Look Back in Anger*, their views are often not only decidedly unfashionable but also in direct opposition to those that are most commonly associated with Britain's "Angry Young Men": the central character of *The Farm* rails against virtually every social reform that his children's now-adult generation has achieved (he is, in fact, contemporary English drama's foremost Angry *Old* Man); even more disconcertingly, the distraught protagonist of *The Restoration of Arnold Middleton* espouses the value of kingship with an ardor that would seem more appropriate to the reign of Elizabeth I than that of Elizabeth II. More significant than these polemical outbursts, however, is the stoical, sometimes silent accommodation with (or reconciliation to) life's exigencies that is achieved by a number of Storey's less articulate and less educated characters—the coal miners, workmen, athletes, and even the mentally impaired. Theirs is a capability that, for a variety of reasons, Storey's more highly educated, professional, upwardly mobile characters somehow often lack. In an era of often abrasive anger and agitprop, of political theatre and polemical theatre, Storey's plays not only occupy a unique niche but provide a welcome respite; they are characteristically understated and invariably subtle with nuance, avoiding topical allusions as well as didacticism in any form.

From the outset of his career as a dramatist—in fact, virtually from the outset of his literary career—Storey has been closely associated with Lindsay Anderson, who has directed almost all of Storey's plays at the Royal Court Theatre, the specific space for which Storey says they were conceived. The two of them met in 1960 when Anderson directed the film adaptation of Storey's first novel, *This Sporting Life*, for which Storey himself wrote the screenplay. In subsequent years, Anderson directed *In Celebration* (1969), *The Contractor* (1969), *Home* (1970), *The Changing Room* (1971), *The Farm* (1973), and *Life Class* (1974) at the Royal Court; at the National Theatre, he also directed *Early Days* (1980, Cottesloe Theatre) and *The March on Russia* (1989, Lyttleton Auditorium). Their personal friendship and decades-long professional relationship have given

Anderson a unique insight into Storey's works that is reflected in the interview published here. Conducted by Ada Brown Mather in New York in 1984 (when Anderson was directing an American production of *In Celebration*), the interview contains Anderson's most extensive reflections on Storey's works and was brought to our attention by Lindsay Anderson himself when contacted about the plans for the current volume. The interview was originally published in *The Journal* of the Society for Stage Directors and Choreographers, Winter 1986, vol. 2, no. 1; it is reprinted here with permission granted by The Society of Stage Directors and Choreographers, Inc., and by Stage Directors and Choreographers Foundation, Inc. We are grateful to Lindsay Anderson, Ada Brown Mather, and William Martin (president of the Stage Directors and Choreographers Foundation, Inc.) for their cooperation in making this interview available.

As in the works of so many of the Royal Court playwrights of the post-1956 generations, issues of social class, culture, and economics pervade Storey's plays in complex and subtle ways. His characters' families (like Storey's own) are typically working class, although many of his protagonists—the now-adult children of such families—have "risen" into a "professional" and/or managerial class through educations that, through years of personal sacrifice, their parents have devotedly struggled to provide. The result, however, has often been something other than the happiness that the parents envisioned; their sons and daughters neither can feel comfortable in the working-class milieu that they have left behind, nor can be fully "at home" in the new class in which they have arrived. These social issues and others having to do with generational, marital, and religious conflict as well as the decline of traditional social institutions have been assessed by Patricia Troxel in her essay entitled "'. . . We have no turning back': Authority, Culture and Environment in the Dramas of David Storey."

One of the most remarkable aspects of Storey's career has been his ability to achieve popular and critical success as both a dramatist and a novelist; no other writer in the modern era has won such acclaim in both genres. As Storey himself has remarked, however, the plays are more widely known and respected in the United States, while the novels are more acclaimed in England, where *Saville* (1976) won

Britain's most prestigious literary award, the Booker Prize. In many instances, the plays and novels are interrelated, often with characters or incidents recurring in works from both genres; tenting-contractor Ewbank appears in both the novel *Radcliffe* (1963) and *The Contractor*, for example, and the Pasmore family is the subject of both the novel *Pasmore* (1972) and the play *The March on Russia*, though the works are set two decades apart. As Janelle Reinelt's essay entitled "Storey's Novels and Plays: Fragile Fictions" demonstrates, an intertextual demarcation of Storey's "master narrative" provides both a new perspective on his individual plays and new means whereby his stylistic development can be assessed.

Before achieving his literary success, Storey held a number of jobs that would later find their way into his plays, which have won consistent critical praise for the authenticity of his dialogue and the meticulousness of the most technical processes occurring on stage. Thus, for example, the Yorkshire dialect of the rugby players of *The Changing Room* is as meticulously accurate as the idiosyncratic rituals that accompany the players' preparations for the game—knowledge of which Storey gained during his experience as a professional rugby player. Similarly, his stint as a member of a construction crew building tents lends authenticity and technical expertise to *The Contractor*, in which an elaborate marquee is constructed, decorated, and dismantled on stage during the course of the play. Storey's experience as a teacher in a particularly rough school is reflected in the sardonically witty but emotionally beleaguered teachers who are the protagonists of *The Restoration of Arnold Middleton* and *Life Class*; while neither play is autobiographical, Storey's central characters speak with the heartfelt cynicism and frustration of those who find themselves unappreciated and overworked in their provincial academic settings, futilely expounding subjects (history and art, respectively) for which their students have neither aptitude nor even the slightest concern. Nevertheless, in many ways Storey's most intriguing and controversial characters are the artists and writers who occur in surprisingly many of his plays, whether as major or minor characters. Their works—like those of their counterparts in contemporary "real life"—are subject to widely varying critical assessments, both from other characters in their respective works and from viewers and readers of Storey's plays. Accordingly, this volume includes two essays that are devoted to the subject of Storey's artists: Ruby Cohn's "Artists in Play" and Susan Rusinko's "A Portrait of the Artist as Character in the Plays of David Storey." Their views are, in many ways, complementary—and are made all the more provocative and enlightening through their juxtaposition.

As a self-styled purveyor of "invisible events" whose value he alone recognizes, the avant-garde artist/teacher/protagonist of *Life Class* (who is identified only by his last name, Allott) is not only Storey's most complex character but also his most controversial, the enigmatic center of his most intricate and multilayered play, whose central subject is the myriad and complex interrelationships of art and life. At the play's startling climax, the nude model who poses before a class of art students appears to be raped by two of them; though the incident is subsequently revealed to have been a hoax, its dire consequences raise issues about the nature of art, of "life," and of theatre as well. *Life Class* is also the play in which Storey's own theatrical doctrine is expounded at greatest length. The aesthetic of "invisible events" that Allott propounds is no less applicable to Storey's "acts of theatre" than to the avant-garde art works that the beleaguered artist creates for (and/or describes to) an uncomprehending audience. A more detailed definition and assessment of the implications of that doctrine is the subject of my essay, "David Storey's Aesthetic of 'Invisible Events.'"

From virtually the outset of his career, the nature of the modern family itself is also among the foremost of Storey's recurrent concerns, though his characters' assessments of it have often ranged from bewilderment to harsh recrimination. That the modern family is "in crisis" is hardly news, of course, and it is often conjoined with issues of "madness," particularly in *The Restoration of Arnold Middleton* and *Home*; Storey's delineation of the problems thus raised is—in a unique way—both unsparing and understanding, coruscating and compassionate. His views have often been compared to those of R. D. Laing—whose influence Storey has long denied. In her essay on "Madness and the Family in David Storey's Plays," Laura H. Weaver explores this topic in further detail and introduces major new evidence on the issue of Storey and Laing, which she found in the unedited transcript of an interview with Storey conducted by Bernard Bergonzi for the BBC in 1968; the remarks in question did not appear in the edited version of the interview that was subsequently broadcast.

Although it is obviously an important issue, the characterization of women in Storey's plays has received relatively little sustained critical and/or theoretical attention heretofore, apart from considerations related to the aforementioned crisis in the modern family. Lois More Overbeck's essay on "'What It Is to Be a Woman' in the Plays of David Storey" thus provides the first detailed analysis devoted wholly to this topic, which is in fact central to so many of his works, despite the fact that, as Overbeck points out, "most of [his] central characters are male." Her essay is intended to invite further and more theoretical discussions of the women in Storey's plays.

Amid considerations of the complex and serious issues with which the foregoing essays deal, the fact that there is much humor in Storey's plays as well should not be overlooked. In fact, it comes in a remarkable variety of forms: the antic disruptiveness of Arnold Middleton's behavior in both his home and classroom; the often-bawdy double entendres of the workmen's banter in *The Contractor*; the Beckettian humor of the characters in *Home*; the bombast of the beleaguered father in *The Farm*; the black, Ortonesque farce of *Mother's Day*. In "'Insuring People Against Disaster': The Uses of Comedy in the Plays of David Storey," D. S. Lawson contends that Storey's comedy "arises mainly out of an element of parody" and demonstrates a number of the plays' intertextual traces.

In "Another Storey: A Reappraisal of *Mother's Day*," Phyllis R. Randall undertakes a reassessment of the play that is in many ways Storey's most controversial—a wild, bizarre, and deliberately "disquieting" farce that received scathing reviews when it opened in 1976 but is still resolutely defended by Storey himself. Though its style is wholly the antithesis of the "poetic naturalism" for which he has become renowned, the playwright has resolutely insisted that *Mother's Day* is wholly consistent with the concerns raised in his other plays. After detailing the full range and types of Storey's humor, Randall offers a provocative analysis of the play as both an inversion of the specific values that Storey has created in his other works and a unique parody of his other plays.

Alongside such literary and contextual considerations, the unique theatricality of Storey's plays also deserves particular attention. Accordingly, in his essay on "Space, Language, and Action in *The Contractor*," William J. Free analyzes one of Storey's best-known and most innovative but allegedly "plotless" plays in terms of practical issues that arise in production: the use of on-stage space, the implications about off-stage space, and the consequences of both for the action and dialogue of the play. His discussion of the stage space and the larger "domain" of the play, as well as the directional "paths" that connect the two, provides an innovative analytical methodology, and the insights that it yields are quite germane to Storey's other plays as well.

Kimball King's essay, *"The March on Russia,"* is the first scholarly assessment of Storey's most recently produced play, which opened at the National Theatre in 1989. King's detailed description of the play will be of particular interest to those who have not yet had an opportunity to see or read it—and his comparison of it to certain plays by Eugene O'Neill seems particularly apropos.

The volume concludes with a complete list of Storey's works (citing both British and American editions, including reprints and paperbacks), followed by an annotated bibliography of secondary sources *other than* individual production reviews, which are by now too numerous for inclusion. Readers are advised that a selected list of such reviews published from 1967 through the mid-1980s can be found in my book, *The Plays of David Storey: A Thematic Study* (Southern Illinois University Press, 1988), 196–200.

Finally, I would like to express my gratitude to David Storey, not only for the plays and novels that have inspired the critical considerations collected here, but also for his cooperation in the preparation of this volume, his encouragement, and his generous permission for us to quote from his works.

CHRONOLOGY

1933   David Malcolm Storey is born in Wakefield (Yorkshire) on 13 July; he is the third son of Frank Richmond Storey, a Yorkshire miner, and Lily Cartwright Storey.

1943–51   Attends Queen Elizabeth Grammar School.

1951–53   Studies at the Wakefield Art School.

1952–56   Plays professional rugby-league football for the Leeds Rugby League Club.

1953   Goes to London to attend the Slade School of Art, where he becomes a prize-winning student; at the same time, he commutes weekly from London to the north to play professional rugby.

1956   Marries Barbara Rudd Hamilton. Receives diploma from Slade School of Art

1956–60   Works at a variety of jobs, including as a postman, a bus conductor, a workman on a crew erecting showground tents, a farm worker, and a teacher in a secondary school in the East End of London.

1960   *This Sporting Life*, winner of the Macmillan Fiction Award, is published in New York by Macmillan and in London by Longman; his second novel, *Flight into Camden*, is also published by Longman.

1961   *Flight into Camden* published in New York by Macmillan; winner of the John Llewelyn Rhys Memorial Prize

1963   *Radcliffe*, novel, published in London by Longman; *Flight into Camden* wins the Somerset Maugham Award. Film version of *This Sporting Life*, directed by Lindsay Anderson from a screenplay by Storey, is released. Directs two documentaries for the BBC, "Death of My Mother" (on D. H. Lawrence) and "Portrait of Margaret Evans."

1966   *The Restoration of Arnold Middleton* is produced in Edinburgh.

1967   *The Restoration of Arnold Middleton* opens at the Royal Court Theatre (London) on 4 July and transfers to the Criterion Theatre in the West End on 31 August. Storey wins the *Evening Standard* award for the most promising playwright.

1969   *In Celebration* opens at the Royal Court Theatre on 22 April; *The Contractor* opens at the Royal Court on October 20.

1970   *The Contractor* transferred to the Fortune Theatre in London's West End on April 6; wins the London Theatre Critics Award. *Home* opens at the Royal Court Theatre on 17 June and transfers to the Apollo Theatre on 29 July. *Home* opens at the Morosco Theatre in New York on 17 November. Award from the London Theatre Critics for Best Play (*The Contractor*). Drama Award from *Evening Standard* for *Home*.

1971   *The Changing Room* opens at the Royal Court Theatre on 9 November, transferred to the Globe Theatre (London) on 15 December. Writer of the

Year Award from the Variety Club of Great Britain (for *The Contractor*). Award from the New York Drama Critics Circle (for *Home*); nomination for Antoinette Perry (Tony) Award from the League of New York Theatres and Producers (for *Home*).

1972   *Pasmore*, novel, published by Longman.

1972–74   Storey serves as associate artistic director of the Royal Court Theatre.

1973   *Cromwell* opens at the Royal Court Theatre on 15 August; *The Farm* opens at the Royal Court on 26 September and transfers to the Mayfair Theatre (London) on 1 November. *A Temporary Life*, novel, and *Edward*, a work of children's literature, are published by Allen Lane. *The Changing Room* opens in New York at the Morosco Theatre on 6 March; wins the New York Drama Critics Circle Award; nominated for Tony Award for Best Play. *The Contractor* opens in New York at the Chelsea Theatre Center, Manhattan, on 9 October. *Pasmore* wins Geoffrey Faber Memorial Award.

1974   *Life Class* opens 9 April at the Royal Court Theatre, transfers to the Duke of York's Theatre (London) on 4 June. Storey becomes a fellow at University College, London. Writes teleplay based on James Joyce's short story "Grace" for the BBC. Wins Obie drama award for *The Contractor*.

1975   Film version of *In Celebration*, directed by Lindsay Anderson from Storey's screenplay, is released in the American Film Theatre series. *Night*, a play about actors in rehearsal (unproduced and unpublished), is planned for production at the Edinburgh Festival but is withdrawn by Storey, who offers *Mother's Day* instead; the latter is declined by Edinburgh authorities.

1976   *Mother's Day* opens 22 September at the Royal Court; the same week, *Saville*, novel, is published by Jonathan Cape.

1977   *Saville* wins the Booker Prize for Fiction (for 1976).

1978   *Sisters* opens 12 September at the Royal Exchange Theatre, Manchester.

1980   *Early Days* opens at the Cottesloe Theatre (National Theatre) in London.

1981   An adaptation of *Early Days* is shown on London Weekend Television.

1982   *A Prodigal Child*, novel, published.

1984   *Present Times*, novel, published.

1985   *Phoenix* (unpublished) is produced by the amateur group Ealing Questors and subsequently staged by Century Theatre in Huddersfield and Rotterham.

1989   *The March on Russia* opens at the Lyttleton Theatre (National Theatre) on 6 April, directed by Lindsay Anderson.

David Storey

CELEBRATING GOOD PLAYWRIGHTING: A TALK WITH LINDSAY ANDERSON HELD AT NEW DRAMATISTS ON NOVEMBER 9, 1984

Ada Brown Mather

Lindsay Anderson is here to direct the first major production of *In Celebration* in New York at the Manhattan Theatre Club. I have read that David Storey himself felt that his work had been misunderstood because people took it at its face value. Would you like to talk about this?

LINDSAY ANDERSON:

I think most people do take things at their face value. It's only a happy few—the minority of any audience—who can receive a poetic or complex work with the kind of understanding that it needs and deserves. As a matter of fact, David's first play was very well received. It was called *The Restoration of Arnold Middleton*. I didn't direct it, although there had been a plan for me to do so after we'd worked together on *This Sporting Life*. He had written the play before we made the film. He'd written it for television, but it was rejected by the television companies

Originally published in *The Journal,* Winter 1986, vol. 2, no. 1. Permission granted by The Society of Stage Directors and Choreographers, Inc. and by Stage Directors and Choreographers Foundation, Inc.

because it contained an episode in which the hero went to bed with his mother-in-law. In the innocent days of the early sixties, this was enough to ban a work from television. The play was eventually staged at the Royal Court after being premiered at the Traverse Theatre in Edinburgh and it was, as I said, very well received. I don't think David would disagree with me if I say that it wasn't fully achieved as a play. It had two relatively realistic acts and then a third act which went into a sort of subjective extravaganza. In other words, the hero went mad. It was full of ideas which then preoccupied David—the myth of the artist as hero-victim, and all sorts of other very personal mythic themes which I found difficult to sort out. It's a great tribute to David's writing that *Arnold Middleton* was so critically successful. It won him an award, the *Evening Standard* "Most Promising Playwright of the Year," simply by the truth and vivacity and imaginative promise of the writing.

Having made the film of his first novel, *This Sporting Life*, and, rather to my surprise, I was invited to direct his second play by the Royal Court, from which I had been more or less excluded when William Gaskill took over as artistic director after George Devine retired. Bill wanted to have a clean sweep at the Court, which meant the exclusion of some of the people who had been working there regularly. But he got into trouble, because his new broom fell to pieces rather quickly. Anyway, he invited me to direct *In Celebration*, just when I was finishing my second feature film, *If.* . . .

At that time David was producing an extraordinary flow of work. He's always been a writer who just sits down and writes; he doesn't plan. He sits down in the morning and starts writing, like a coal miner who goes down the pit and starts digging out coal and can never be sure what he's going to produce until he's produced it. That was the time he wrote—and I can never be sure in what order—*The Contractor* and *In Celebration* and possibly, *Home*, all in a very short space of time. He has said that he took about three days to write a play, and I think that's more or less true. When he tried to re-write, it was often not very successful. *In Celebration* may have been written after *The Contractor*, which was the second of his plays I directed—in fact David says so.

They are certainly very different, with *In Celebration* much more novelistic in style.

As David went on writing his plays and his novels, he developed a much barer and less traditional style. But different as they were, the plays were all well received. Of course they weren't always fully understood, particularly by the people whose job it was to write about them; but that would be asking rather a lot. *In Celebration* did exceptionally good business at the Royal Court—although it was the policy of the theatre to change its program every five or six weeks, there wasn't another play to follow it and it ran for twelve weeks. It didn't however achieve a West End transfer. All the other David Storey plays I directed after that did go on into the West End. *In Celebration* certainly should have, but in London, in the West End in particular, there is a persistent prejudice against what the middle-class audience and critics label "working-class" plays. I think that's something that does not happen in New York, because the American class system is quite different from ours. Unfortunately, the British remain morbidly fascinated by class and helplessly entrenched in their class system. One of David's difficulties in finding an audience has always been that, although he writes what may be called "working-class plays," (i.e., they are generally about working-class people and set in the North of England), they aren't what the bourgeoisie—and very often the working class themselves—expect working-class plays to be. They're not plays of protest; they're not plays of scandal or squalor; they are subtle, poetic plays. Of course his style developed from *In Celebration*; he acquired a reputation for naturalism, although I don't think that's a word that accurately describes his writing. He does not really write naturalistic plays. If you want to use that kind of label, I would prefer to say that he writes poetic and realistic plays. He has written plays in other styles, which I haven't directed. He wrote *Cromwell*, which is not a realistic play, and he wrote *Mother's Day*, which is a black, somewhat Ortonian comedy. But the plays I have directed I would call poetic and realistic.

ADA BROWN MATHER:

Is it right that you approached David Storey about doing a film of *This Sporting Life*, and that it was you who encouraged him to write plays?

LINDSAY ANDERSON:

The story of how any film gets made, particularly any serious film, is almost always strange. I remember quite clearly reading in the book pages of *The Sunday Times* about the forthcoming publication of a book called *This Sporting Life*. I had just finished directing a musical play at the Royal Court called *The Lily White Boys*, and I went to Paris for a few days relaxation. I was sitting in a café reading the morning paper and was attracted by the sound of the book, although it was really misleadingly reported. The report suggested that this was emphatically a social work, with some kind of connection (to speak in cliché) to the Angry Young Man or "protest" theme. In fact, *This Sporting Life* turned out not to be like that at all. But I ordered the book and read it. I must have been one of the first people to read it, because it came to me immediately on publication.

To be honest, I cannot remember anything specific about reading *This Sporting Life* for the first time, but I know I liked it and thought that perhaps it was a film I could make. I knew Tony Richardson, who was George Devine's co-director at the Royal Court, where he had directed John Osborne's *Look Back in Anger*. When this finally succeeded, Tony was invited to film it, so he and John Osborne formed a production company, Woodfall Films—Woodfall Street being where John Osborne had his house in Chelsea. The company prospered. Tony had often said to me, "Why don't you make a film for Woodfall? What would you like to do?" And this was a time, largely through the theatrical renaissance centered on the Royal Court, when the British cinema was beginning to stir after a long period of fossilization, of quiescence after the war. One of the films that caused the ice to break was Woodfall's *Saturday Night and Sunday Morning* directed by my friend, Karel Reisz. So it was all beginning and young actors were starting to appear in British cinema, which had never till now had much use for new faces—actors like Albert Finney and Peter O'Toole. The prevailing climate can be judged from the fact that the first play I directed at the Royal Court—it was called *The Long and the Short and the Tall*, in which Peter O'Toole acted with great success—was filmed by Ealing Studios and I wasn't allowed to direct it, and Peter O'Toole was not allowed to appear in it. His part was given to Laurence Harvey.

Anyway, the success of *Saturday Night and Sunday Morning*, which by some miracle Woodfall managed to get financed, changed all that. So I put my idea up to Tony Richardson and he said, "Well, I'll read it." I spoke to him about a week later and he said, "I've read *This Sporting Life*, but I don't think it's the right kind of film for you." I said, "Oh, all right. Perhaps I'll find something else." And about a week later I found that Woodfall had in fact put in a bid for *This Sporting Life*, which Tony had decided was a film for him. However, the ways of providence are mysterious: Woodfall didn't have enough money to buy the rights and they were acquired instead by the Rank Organization, for not a very large sum—but enough. Rank was interested because Joseph Losey wished to direct it and Stanley Baker wanted to play the lead. Then the producer who got the book said to Stanley Baker, "Well, fine, I'm delighted for you to play this part, but I don't wish to make another movie with Joseph Losey." They had worked together once and he didn't want to repeat the experience; I know no more than that. Anyway, Stanley Baker, in all honor, said, "Well, I'm committed to Joe so I'm out." So then they approached Karel Reisz because he had directed *Saturday Night and Sunday Morning*. But Karel did not want to make another film with a Northern, working-class milieu, though he did think he would like the experience of production. So Karel asked me if I would be prepared to direct the film if he offered to produce it. I said, "Well, you can try. I don't see any reason why they should agree, but have a go." And he came back the next day and, somewhat to my astonishment and trepidation, said, "Well, they've agreed." So I said, "I suppose I'd better do it then."

And this is how I got to know David Storey. Karel said, "I think we should get the author to write the script," because he'd worked very successfully with Alan Sillitoe on the adaptation of *Saturday Night and Sunday Morning*; so we met David Storey. We were both immediately taken with David, who is a very fine and impressive person besides being a good writer. When we were making the film, because I'd been at the Court, I did ask him, "Have you ever thought of writing a play?" And David said, "Well, as a matter of fact, I've got one." This was *To Die with the Philistines*, and we planned to do it at the Royal Court with Richard Harris.

But *This Sporting Life* was a success, Richard Harris got an Oscar nomination, and naturally his American agents got hold of him and told him he should stop messing about with art and get out to Hollywood and do a film with Doris Day. So he did that instead. The project to do David's play fell through, which was probably a very good thing. The script sat on a shelf, until an assistant from the Royal Court who was now running the Traverse Theatre in Edinburgh asked if he could produce it. I really feel that this was the best thing for the play because, as I said, I never felt it was quite fully achieved. I was very conscious of what I felt were its faults, whereas the director in Edinburgh was not impeded by any such doubts and did a very successful production. As a result, the Royal Court asked the Edinburgh company to come down and show it to them. The Edinburgh company came down guilelessly, thinking they might be invited to present *To Die with the Philistines* at the Royal Court. Of course what actually happened was that they showed their production and then one of the Court directors decided he would like to do it himself. So he managed to get the play away from the people who had launched it and he directed it. Again, it was a good thing it was done by a director who was not particularly aware of the faults of the play, because he just did it. If you do a play feeling it is faulty in certain respects, you are likely to end up not doing it very well. So I'm glad I didn't direct the play. I'm sure it did better than if I had. However, Bill Gaskill did invite me to direct David's next play, *In Celebration*. We were very lucky: we had a brilliant cast, the play was very well received, and I was then asked to do *The Contractor*. So it began.

ADA BROWN MATHER:

Could you talk a little about the problems of plays like *The Contractor* and *The Changing Room*, where some complex physical event takes place onstage?

LINDSAY ANDERSON:

Every play presents its own kind of challenge. The three plays I did after *In Celebration* were interesting because they were autobiographical in a different way from *In Celebration*. This, of course, David had written out of his own emotional family experience. I would say it has the same relationship to him, is as close to him as *Long Day's Journey Into Night* was to O'Neill. In plays like *The Contractor* and *The Changing Room*, he again drew on his own experience, though on a different emotional level. As a schoolboy on vacation, he had worked on the erecting of tents, he had been for a period a professional Rugby League player, and he had studied at art school, where a lot of *Life Class* came from. So these plays were also autobiographical, but in a different way.

For those who don't know it, *The Contractor* is a play of which the central event is a wedding. At the start of the play, five workmen arrive to erect the tent in which the wedding reception is going to be held. The play begins with a bare stage, grass-covered, on which three poles have already been erected. The workmen arrive, with all the impedimenta—the canvas, the ropes—and in the first act, through all the dialogue, they erect the tent. In the second act, they put down a floor and bring in flowers and decorations and chairs and tables. All this action, too, has to be integrated with the dialogue. In the interval before the third act, the wedding has taken place. When the curtain goes up, we see that the beautifully appointed tent has been reduced to a shambles by a riotous celebration. The workmen arrive, look around, find a few bottles with some champagne in them, glasses and furniture scattered around, and proceed to tidy everything up, take out the dressing and the floor, let down the tent, roll up the canvas, until we're left at the end of the play with the empty stage again . . .

Looking back, I'm not sure how we did it. I certainly couldn't have done it if David hadn't been there, because he knew from experience how tents were erected. I had the feeling—I don't really know how correct this was—that the actors needed to discover the play and the physical practical activity at the same time, so we had one preliminary day when a professional came down from the firm who supplied the tent and showed us how it was done. From the start of the play, the actors with their books in their hands had to carry out all the business of erection, furnishing and dismantling. It drove them nearly mad. I really don't know how we did it, but in the end the action and the dialogue were perfectly integrated. Of course there's a very strong choreographic element in a play like that. There is a choreographic element in every play, except that in a more conventionally structured work the choreographic element is not so observable; actually most audiences and most critics do not see that there is any. They're not receptive to that element in a production. Whereas, if you have something spectacular like the erection of a tent—or a battle or a scene in a crowded street—they begin to see, and to realize that there is some kind of pattern unfolding before them.

In *Home*, which followed *The Contractor*, there were only five characters. In the first act there were only two, sitting on chairs in the middle of the stage. David has described how the initial idea of *Home* was the image at the end of *The Contractor*. The workmen have finished their work: one table is carried back, and their boss brings in some champagne and glasses, pours it out and they all drink a toast before they go home. So there's just this single white table on the stage, and that gave David—who is also an artist and trained as a painter—the image of a man sitting on a chair, with a table, on a bare stage, and another man comes in and they start talking. I quite believe David when he says that initially he didn't know who the men were or why they were there, and it was only when he had reached the end of the first act that he realized they were in a mental hospital. As you can imagine, that situation offered very few moves indeed. There were two actors and two chairs. Of course we were incredibly lucky to have John Gielgud and Ralph Richardson play the two men. I think each of them probably had two moves—they got up, walked around a little bit and sat down again. And that was that. But to do that is just as difficult in its way as to erect a tent—or at least demands just as much precision. The movement is just as important if there are only four moves in the act as if there are three hundred and fifty.

ADA BROWN MATHER:

There is something which we do not discuss very much, it has become unfashionable, and yet it seems to me that it is at the very core of everything—would you like to talk about the magic of the rhythm of dialogue?

LINDSAY ANDERSON:

I agree it is unfashionable to the extent that people really don't perceive it, and that's very nice. If an audience becomes aware of the rhythmic structure of the dialogue, it usually implies a destructive self-consciousness—they start admiring instead of experiencing. (The famous "Pinter pauses" for instance.) I think the kind of work that I have tried to do—or the only kind of work I am able to do really—is to discover within the text the rhythms and the movement that is most expressive of that text. If I've been able to bring out those elements in a production, I'm extremely pleased. I'm gratified that it should be recognized, but I think it's very important to realize that the rhythms, patterns, and moves derive from the text—exist, so to speak within it. If you haven't got a text with the necessary thoughts, feelings, rhythms built into it, of course you can't do this. You can only then trick it. And a great deal of virtuoso direction is trickery. It's something I've never been responsive to, and have never been good at anyway.

During all of that period, I was extremely lucky to have a writer as talented, to put it mildly, as David, and to have the opportunity to direct those plays. From time to time I would make a film and afterwards I could go back to the Royal Court and do a new play by David Storey. That was a great, great stroke of luck.

For me, rhythm of dialogue, rhythm of movement, shape of movement on the stage is very important, very satisfying and very much a part of the expressive quality of a production—a vital part of one's function as a director. As I say, it is an element often not consciously recognized. It is something that audiences are not very aware of, or helped to be aware of, by people who write about the theatre. In general, those people are extremely literary in the way that they experience plays—literary rather than theatrical. The literary person or critic will judge a play primarily in terms of its dialogue, maybe its characterization, and then in terms of any sort of *coup de théâtre* that the director may produce, which is so striking that even they can't help seeing that something is happening on the stage. Often it's heartbreaking. I remember at the Royal Court, which is a little theatre, I could look down from the side of the Upper Circle and watch, for instance, the venerable Harold Hobson, the influential critic of the *Sunday Times*. So often, in moments which were treasurable and expressive on the stage, he'd be looking down and writing in his program and not seeing them at all. Unaware of the expressive quality of what was being performed in front of him, he was only just listening.

[There followed a brief discussion of Anderson's London production of Chekhov's *The Cherry Orchard*, which has been deleted here.]

[W]hat critics [also] want [is] a conceptual production. In other words, a production in which the director's concept can be seen and discussed, as distinct from the play which the author has written. My formation— apart from any temperamental qualities I may have been born with— was at the Royal Court. At the beginning, when George Devine and Tony Richardson started it in 1956, the Royal Court was called a Writers' Theatre. It wasn't a Writers' Theatre in any literary sense, though; it was a Writers' Theatre in that the aim was to conceive and execute productions which would realize what the author had written. That was very different from the intellectualized theatre that has become the tradition of, say, the Royal Shakespeare Company. The RSC has developed a tradition of intellectual theatre, which often involves, at the beginning of rehearsals, the director sitting with the actors and giving them a long talk about the play and then having a long discussion about the play in which the actors all try to behave like intelligent people instead of being content and happy to be intelligent actors. Actors can be very intelligent, but with their own kind of intelligence, which is often, as far as the theatre goes, much more valid than the intelligence of the intellectual. (When they try to be intellectual, the result is usually disastrous.) So, although I have felt frequently that it's a great disadvantage not to be what Michael Billington calls a conceptual director—and it is a particular disadvantage today—I have to accept the fact that I'm just no good at it. I'm unable to form concepts which are distinct from an intuitive, and I hope intelligent, apprehension of the text.

ADA BROWN MATHER:

Would you talk a little about how you felt having to approach *In Celebration* fifteen years later—not a long time, but time has passed. Did you have to think differently, did you have to take account of the fact that the world was fifteen years further on, did you think about being in America?

LINDSAY ANDERSON:

No. It may sound unimpressive, but I just went ahead and did it. The play had never been presented in New York, though I think there have been quite a few productions around the U.S. I didn't know anything about these; but I did know, from the critical reception of the film version which we made five years after the first production at the Royal Court, that the themes and emotions of the play were perfectly comprehensible, even familiar, to Americans. So I thought it should certainly be done in New York. I was, of course, a bit apprehensive in that, for the first production, we had been extremely lucky with our cast. I don't need to say how important it is to have the right actors for a play like this—especially when you are presenting it for the first time. Casting was always given great importance at the Court, and for *In Celebration* we searched long and hard. We were successful, and we found a group of actors who not only suited the roles perfectly, but worked together most happily. We even had the extraordinary experience, five years after the first production, of filming it, with exactly the company we had in the theatre. This gave the film, I think, a quite unique quality, because the actors knew not only the play, but each other so well. When the opportunity came to do it in New York, I started off thinking, "Well, I don't suppose I can do it as well as before." I was also somewhat intimidated by the disadvantage of coming to a country where I don't know the profession, the actors, as well as I do at home. It's more difficult in America, too, because of this terrible split between New York and Los Angeles, the capitals of theatre and television, which of course is something we don't experience in London.

But once again we were lucky. I was particularly lucky in having two actors I had worked with often before. Malcolm McDowell was able to come to New York and do it, and Frank Grimes, whom I've worked with on two other David Storey plays at the Royal Court, is now living in New York. So I began with two familiar talents whom I knew I could work with. I feel I was incredibly lucky with the other casting and I think we have a production that is absolutely as valid and as good as the first one—with inevitably different qualities—but in no way inferior. As a matter of fact, when I've done productions again, I've never found the experience repetitive or boring. It's the actors who recreate the show.

ADA BROWN MATHER:

I noticed that one of the characters [Mr. Reardon, a sixty-eight-year-old neighbor of the elder Shaws—*Ed.*] had been cut.

LINDSAY ANDERSON:

Quite right. When we came to do the film, I thought that one of the characters somewhat diluted the concentration—particularly from the point of view of a movie. We weren't adapting or reconstructing the play for the screen, we were filming the text, so I felt that it was extremely important to maintain tension. And it worked so well, the play gained so much in concentration, that I suggested to David that we should use that text for the New York production, and he agreed.

ADA BROWN MATHER:

When you first worked with David Storey, did he do any rewriting of his plays?

LINDSAY ANDERSON:

Only at the start. He rewrote a lot of his first play, which I didn't direct, trying to get the last act right. *In Celebration* was considerably cut, and had a little bit of rewriting. I made a suggestion of reconstruction which David carried out with great reluctance. He is very emotional and subjective about this—almost superstitious. He would always feel that rewritten scenes didn't have the validity of the original, which really was not true. Since then I'd say the plays had very little rewriting. *Home* was considerably cut in rehearsal, because David felt he needed to hear the initial, too-long dialogue before he could be sure where to cut it. *Early Days* was considerably worked over, from the first text which was quite long and not very formed, to the final version as performed by Ralph Richardson, which was concentrated into two acts of about forty minutes each. As a result it became much more poetic and less naturalistic.

ADA BROWN MATHER:

When you come to doing Shakespeare, of course you have a text, but you also need to find a physical world in which to make this work, in the way that David Storey supplies you with a very strong physical world.

LINDSAY ANDERSON:

Well, as far as David's plays go, neither *Home* nor *Early Days* really present one with a strong physical world. And even in *The Contractor* or *The Changing Room*, although the physical action gives the plays a strong framework, one must never forget that this framework is poetic rather than purely naturalistic. The action-scenario is rather like the pretext of a ballet: the staging has to be choreographic rather than simply naturalistic. In fact, I am not too fond of the word "naturalistic"—or at least as it applies to these plays. I would rather call them "realist." Shakespeare is also a realist, particularly in a play like *Hamlet.* I've only directed *Julius Caesar* and *Hamlet* and they are both realist plays in a way that I find congenial—and somehow familiar. Even their rhetoric is dramatic rather than literary. I'd be very intimidated if I had to stage *Love's Labour's Lost,* say, or *Richard II.* I'd be very wary of *Romeo and Juliet*—or of *Coriolanus,* because so much of it is so difficult to understand.

[A brief discussion of direction of *Hamlet* which ensued has been deleted here.]

ADA BROWN MATHER:

Now that you're visiting America, it would be very interesting to hear what you think of the theatre in England at the moment. There's no place like the old Royal Court where young playwrights can have their work performed.

LINDSAY ANDERSON:

I find this difficult to talk about because I'm not a critic, and this means that my opinions are very personal, very subjective. Certainly, since the early days of the Court, it is much, much easier for young and new playwrights to get their work performed. Sometimes it's a bit too easy. Very often the plays are not worked on as carefully as they should be, and as they would have been. New playwrights tend to be over-indulged and over-praised. After the first fifteen years of the Court, I personally found myself out of sympathy with the new young generation of writers. This is the generation of what I call the university wits: intellectual left-wingers, generally university educated, like David Hare, Howard Brenton, Howard Barker. I find their plays much too theoretical, written not with experience but with "concepts." Unfortunately this became the ruling fashion in Britain. Of course, critics favor this kind of writing, because (like a "conceptual" production) it is easy to write about. It's also not emotionally challenging.

So far as the general picture goes, I think the big subsidized companies are pretty disastrous. It's a sad irony that the idea of a National Theatre, which seemed so necessary, which was so tenaciously fought for, should have occasioned such errors. In the euphoria of the sixties, of course, the economic situation was completely misread and, partly as a result of that, the fatal decision was made to go for size. And so, instead of a living National Theatre, we got an oversized, soulless white elephant. Theatre subsidies in Great Britain have been hogged by the National Theatre and the Royal Shakespeare Company to a quite unjustifiable degree. And over-subsidy has resulted in over-expenditure. Scenically, for instance, we are almost back to the era of Beerbohm Tree: the technology may be modern, but the extravagant display and the conspicuous expenditure are fully eighty years old. These productions represent a great waste of resources as well as being bad theatre art; but unfortunately, the public tends to like circuses and so do the critics. Shakespeare said that there were no tricks in "plain and simple faith," but I'm afraid plainness and simplicity are not popular. They require too much attention. I don't go to the theatre much in London.

FROM THE AUDIENCE:

You must be an actor's dream, because you make them act so well.

LINDSAY ANDERSON:

I don't make them act well. I try to help them to act well. But it's a common critical cliché and a great fallacy to say that a director *extracts* good performances from his (or her) actors. Really this is nonsense: a director is not a Svengali. It may be that the *actors* have extracted a good production from the director. That can happen just as easily; many an inadequately directed production has been saved by the actors. It is the responsibility of the director, as far as the acting goes, to first of all cast the play correctly, and then to provide an atmosphere in which the

actors can be confident and relax and achieve the best performances of
which they're capable. Of course he can help by giving them an
understanding of the play and of their relationships to each other, and by
finding the right choreography and rhythm to express these. And, if you
can give them technical guidance along the way, so much the better.

FROM THE AUDIENCE:

Jonathan Miller was recently in New York and said that he was fed up
with directing plays in England. He said that occasionally he'd direct an
opera because Peter Hall doesn't control all the opera in England. I am
curious about your opinion of Jonathan Miller's work. Who really does
control theatre in England, and how might things change?

LINDSAY ANDERSON:

My opinion of Jonathan Miller's work is not particularly relevant, and
anyway I haven't seen an enormous amount of it. I always think of
Jonathan as a "conceptual" director. I believe he has done simple
productions, and I've been told they are excellent. But I can find his
intellectualizing temperament very irritating; intellectuals tend to relate
ideas to other ideas, instead of to life. As a result, they offer illustration
rather than experience. Of course Jonathan has been in charge of
producing the BBC Shakespeare series for television, which has been an
Anglo-American enterprise, part-financed from the States. I personally
feel this whole enterprise has been unfortunate, most particularly
because of the decision that the productions should be entirely British.
It is fallacious to suppose that the English, and no one else, know how
to present Shakespeare. I myself find the English way of doing
Shakespeare at the moment emotionally inadequate and over-pictorial—
technical rather than truthful. I cannot watch those BBC versions even
if, certainly through Jonathan's influence, they are more handsome and
more intelligent than they were.

    Who controls theatre in Britain? Well, Jonathan Miller is
paranoid about Peter Hall—even if with some justification. But really,
he should have known better. He became one of the artistic directors at

the National Theatre when Peter Hall took over, and did some productions there. And then both he and Michael Blakemore had a row and left. It was naive of Jonathan not to have known what the place would be like—you know the proverb, "He who sups with the Devil must use a long spoon." Of course Peter Hall does not control theatre in Britain. As head of the National Theatre, he exerts a powerful influence; he is an accomplished politician and knows how to manipulate the media. But he has been too busy with his own career, making the considerable amount of money he needs, to give the National Theatre a strong sense of style or ensemble. There isn't really a style at the National. You'll see on the back of their programs a list of "The National Theatre Company," about ninety names, but this is mostly window-dressing. All it means is that those are the actors who are working at the National Theatre at that particular moment. A lot of them will only have been engaged for one production, and maybe towards the end of that production will only be working once every ten days. There is an unfortunate lack of overall policy at the National Theatre—perhaps the place is just too big.

But after all, you've got the Royal Shakespeare Company too, which is powerful and well-subsidized, and not part of the National Theatre empire. They have their own empire. They have a strong house sense, a marked technical style, and a demand—in a rather schoolmarmish kind of way—for what they like to call "loyalty." Loyalty from the actors, that is, which generally means the actors putting themselves at the disposition of the management. Then there is the mini-establishment of the Royal Court, which is conventionally leftish in its policies—the alliance with Joe Papp is significant. And of course there is still what is called the "commercial theatre," (which perhaps ought to be known as the "independent theatre"), West End producers who can do more or less well with more or less conventional work. The West End is going the way of Broadway, though it hasn't gone so far, so fast. There's a flourishing fringe theatre in London of various kinds, performing in clubs, in little theatres, doing lunchtime theatre—a lot of that. There are repertory theatres around the country, which are mostly run (of course there are exceptions) by fairly mediocre directors appointed by the Arts Council. Generally I think the British theatre is probably about what Britain deserves, as must be the case of any theatre. I suppose the New York theatre is what New York deserves.

FROM THE AUDIENCE:

I wonder if you'd tell us something about *Home*: the stage and television version. I saw both several times, and it seemed to me that, in essence, it was a play on television. Would you elaborate on that?

LINDSAY ANDERSON:

Well, you're quite right, that was the intention. It was interesting, and depressingly significant of English attitudes, that although *Home* was very well received, both in London and on Broadway, we could not persuade a British television company or the BBC to record it. I was extremely annoyed about this, which I thought both shameful and ridiculous. Finally, we did get Channel 13, WNET to finance the taping. I really wanted to preserve the quality of the production and, particularly, the performances of Gielgud, Richardson, and the other members of that wonderful cast. I don't think the problem of setting the play was really solved in the television production. Jocelyn Herbert, who had done the design in the theatre, was not available and we were given a television designer who didn't have the necessary sense of style. So, unfortunately, we ended up with a not very clever, pseudo-naturalistic decor for the play, but I hope that's not too important. We rehearsed the play again and I shot it. Actually I was given a television director who was supposed to call the shots, but by the time we got halfway through the taping, I realized that he didn't understand the material. He was trying to record it like an anecdotal television play. To be honest, I think I was terribly naive not to realize the extent to which the performance was very subtle and original and needed to be handled with great finesse and accuracy. It was an impossible assignment for someone who didn't know the play intimately. And so he dropped out, and I finished it. Of course I would like to have had the accuracy of film—film is more accurate than video. Nor was (or am) I really experienced in video. However, it was as good a transcription of the stage production as we could do.

FROM THE AUDIENCE:

I saw *Home* here in New York on its opening night and it was wonderful. And afterwards I saw a television interview with Sir Ralph and he was asked about the play—Sir John was on the program as well—and he said that when he was given the script, he didn't understand a word of it. He didn't believe he could commit it to memory, and didn't see how he could possibly do it. He was eventually convinced by his friend, Sir John. I wonder if he was kidding.

LINDSAY ANDERSON:

He wasn't wholly kidding. But what he said was not quite true. I did send the play first of all to John Gielgud. John Gielgud had, at about that time, allowed himself to become a bit "elderly," a bit stuffy, frightened of young people and new things. I think this was largely because of the kind of people he was associating with, and had long been associated with, in the West End theatre. Then he changed course and became much more venturesome: he was in Alan Bennett's play, *Forty Years On* and in Tony Richardson's film, *The Charge of the Light Brigade*. He discovered for the first time that he could play in the cinema—he's a marvelous screen actor, but he never thought he could do it. Changes took place in his personal life as well, and, really, he's been young ever since and getting younger. When we sent him the play, to my amazement, the very next day the casting director at the Court came in with a big grin on her face and said, "Gielgud wants to do it! We've had a call from his agent and he's said he'd like to do it. He thinks it's terribly funny!" Then David and I met Gielgud and found that he just instinctively wanted do the play. He did think it was very funny and that's about it. He hadn't really gone into it a great deal or realized how tricky it was—but perhaps that's how the best decisions are always made. It was he who suggested Ralph Richardson, whom I hadn't worked with before. I knew of course that Ralph was a wonderful actor, but I did think that he often gave performances so eccentric that I couldn't really relish them. Ralph's eccentricity was so colorful that people tended to say, "Isn't he wonderful? Isn't Ralphie marvelous?," and the truth is that often he did act badly—as a fine actor can. When he wasn't sure what he was doing, when he felt uncertain about the material or the direction, he'd fall back on tricks, which were to a great extent defensive. Anyway, I went to see him and he was intrigued by it and also by the prospect of working with his admired old friend.

We got on very well together and he said he'd like to do it. And then I remember he said, "When are we going to start," and I said, "about seven weeks ahead." The Court had a program and the next play was already scheduled to go into rehearsal. Ralph said, "Oh, I can't wait that long. If I have to wait that long, I'll take something else because I can't bear to sit around waiting." So I went back to the Court and we did manage to re-jig the program. Thank God the other actors were free and we were able to start rehearsing *Home*. It was during rehearsals that both John and Ralph became extremely frightened: they realized what they'd let themselves in for. They were great actors, but this was a new thing and it was naturally scary. I remember Gielgud would suddenly say, "I just sit here. I say, 'Yes, yes. No, no.' What am I supposed to be doing? Aren't they all going to be terribly bored?" And I would say, "Now John, it's marvelous and it's going to be great. It's perfectly all right. Don't worry." And he'd say, "Well, I suppose you know what you're talking about. I'd better leave it to you." Ralph would come into rehearsal taking off his crash helmet (he rode his motorbike down to the Court) and he would announce, "Oh, I decided to withdraw from the play. I woke up in the middle of the night, I was having nightmares. I can't possibly do it. But my wife said, 'Go on, don't be an old fool. Go on. Get down there.' So I'm here." Their fears were perfectly genuine. It's a great tribute to their instinct, to their great feeling and respect for David—who was there, of course, all the time—that they rehearsed the play without a moment of disharmony or recalcitrance. It was really only in the last week of rehearsals, I think, that they began to believe we might pull it off. We opened the play in Brighton, but in the last week of rehearsals at the Court, we had a run through and I invited the cast of *The Contractor* to come and watch it, and also the cast of the company then performing at the Royal Court, a company from La Mama. I was a bit apprehensive about this, because I thought this American avant-garde company would probably think this a load of old-fashioned rubbish. But fortunately, all the actors, American and British, responded with wonderful enthusiasm. That was the first time that Gielgud and Richardson felt that, "This can work." Really, they did it on faith. It was a great act of courage.

"... WE HAVE NO TURNING BACK": AUTHORITY, CULTURE AND ENVIRONMENT IN THE DRAMAS OF DAVID STOREY

Patricia M. Troxel

In 1964, as David Storey was composing his first play, Susan Sontag opened her essay, "Going to the theater, etc.," with the observation that "the best modern plays are those devoted to raking up private, rather than public hells." She continued with the observation that "the public voice in the theater today is crude and raucous, and, all too often, weak-minded."[1] While the principal object of her criticism was Arthur Miller's new drama, *After the Fall*, her equally vehement attack on Rolf Hochhuth's *The Deputy* led her to conclude that "the worst offense is the refusal to dramatize anything really painful to watch."[2] What Sontag wanted was theater that offered "self-exposure" not "self-indulgence."[3]

From his earliest dramas such as *The Contractor* to his most recent play, *The March on Russia*, David Storey has instinctively created such dramatic works of self-investigation, self-awareness, and self-exposure. To present works with this focus, Storey has enhanced two elements within his dramas. First, Storey blends his depiction of character with an analysis of social conditions. While as Richard Dutton points out, these characters share a distortion of communication and emotional antagonism typical of Pinter's creations, Storey's characters can be understood in terms of a British class system that has made them the way they are.[4] Second, Storey's plays deny the reader a central dramatic event, a development in his dramatic work that has often led to charges of "plotlessness." As William Hutchings describes it, "by placing the ostensibly important and 'dramatic' events offstage, the playwright effectively shifts the audience's attention to the *impact* or *consequences* of such events on the individual characters' lives."[5] Hutchings continues with the observation that this shift "reveals insights into not only the lives of the characters but the life of their times as well."[6]

Storey's dramatic techniques and his determination to understand the culture and the authority that shape modern man are inseparable. They must be inseparable because, as Raymond Williams explains, the very essence of art lies in its cultural and social expression. As the definition of "art" changes from "skill" to "imaginative truth," so the understanding of culture changes from "a process of human training" to "a way of life, material, intellectual, and spiritual."[7] Yet in offering this definition of culture, Williams emphasizes that any successful "way of life" must resolve the inherent conflict of the observed or prejudicial "mass culture." If the culture speaks to a community, a democracy in which the term "mass" is understood as "majority," then its expression of the democratic way of life can be acknowledged as an objective and valued aspect of our social and political existence. However, if the culture speaks only to class democracy, a democracy in which the term "mass" is taken to mean "mob" rather than "majority," then it must be rejected.[8] Williams's ideal culture is what he describes as "common culture." It is a culture based on equality of access, equality of participation, and equality of life and production.[9] It is also a culture which must constantly evaluate its inherited tradition; each culture must strive for a balance, what Williams calls "a shifting attachment," between its "strength, vitality and richness" and its common experience without straying into questions of superiority, uniformity, or value.[10]

This striving for balance is also present in Frederic Jameson's concern for the place of literary art in a changing cultural/social context. Jameson argues that the drive for "realistic" modes of discourse and portrayal in the novel is tied to "a properly bourgeois cultural revolution."[11] Jameson further asserts that this revolution will produce a transformation of literary work from an expression of life habits to a reflection of all aspects of market capitalism.[12] As a result of this transformation, the literary work must strike an uneasy alliance with its traditional form of "closed" adventure or *recit*; endings can no longer be defined or definite as was once assumed.[13]

As part of his analysis of realism in the eighteenth-century novel, Jameson describes the significance of antinomy or a double bind; this juxtaposition of elements should replace the traditional notion of contradictions.[14] In terms of Storey's plays, the double bind juxtaposes off-stage events and off-stage authority with on-stage verbal and physical energies of language and action. This juxtaposition creates a multi-level dialectic rather than a series of contrasts or contradictions. Such double bind realism is what Richard Cave has termed David Storey's "poetic naturalism." For Cave, Storey's plays offer a "working through inferences and nuances of meaning rather than with articulate statement—a technique that requires the audience to respond creatively to ambiguity and illusion."[15]

While Jameson limits his discussion to the novel, his points are equally applicable to the drama, especially since Storey's plays are grounded in explorations of class and economics. But to explore this new realism in that political context requires further consideration of culture. In his opening chapter of *Culture and Society*, Williams explains that culture and art in that culture "merges two general responses—first, the recognition of the practical separation of certain moral and intellectual activities from the driven impetus of a new kind of society; second, the emphasis of these activities, as a court of human appeal, to be set over the process of practical social judgement and yet to offer itself as a mitigating and rallying alternative."[16] In other words, culture is both a product of its social and authoritative context and a commentary on that context; it encapsulates both a reaction to a public world (one of political, social, economic events) and an enhancement of a private world (one of habits, thoughts, and individual experience).

Culture is concomitant with artistic expression because it combines both transmission and reception or response. However, because communication relies on transmissions and receptions that are colored by historical, social, and political biases, culture will by its very definition reflect a specific "way of life," a particular aesthetic that will always carry its own ideology. Williams describes his history of the idea of culture as "a record of our reactions, in thought and feeling, to the changed conditions of our common life" and "a record of our meanings and our definitions . . . to be understood within the context of our actions."[17] In tracing stages in, or aspects of, culture, we reveal our understanding of the authorities and controls which influence environment, behavior, language, and artistic expressions of these elements.

Frederic Jameson supports this perspective on culture and authority when he argues that as writers and critics we are participating in "a single vast unfinished plot" and that our critical liberation comes from our recognition that "there is nothing that is not social and political."[18] What Jameson sees in the struggle between literary and political ideologies of the text is a historical dialectic. This dialectic may address both the historical awareness within the text (the individual voice of the work itself) and the historical context of the text (the class voices which battle for dominance over that text).[19] For Jameson, this battle centers around an "antagonistic dialogical structure,"[20] what Jameson goes on to define as "a dialogue of class struggle . . . in which two opposing discourses fight it out within the general unity of a shared code."[21]

When translated into traditional Marxist terminology, this idea can be expressed as "a ruling class ideology [that] will explore various strategies of the legitimation of its own power position, while an oppositional culture or ideology will, often in covert and disguised strategies, seek to contest and to undermine the dominant 'value system'."[22] In other words, when considering culture and authority in Storey's plays we should explore: how his work reflects the dominant British class system and its attempts to maintain that dominance through control of language, rituals, and institutions, how he expresses the dialectic of competing notions of culture or artistic discourse, and how these choices contribute to the "unfinished plot."

In his plays, Storey explores the nature and influence of culture and authority on modern British life through specific dramatic choices.

The following pages explore these features through a consideration of four plays, *The Contractor*, *Cromwell*, *Early Days*, and *The March on Russia*. In each dramatic work, our awareness of authority is initially sparked by Storey's use of exterior powers who seldom appear on stage yet control the on-stage action. It may be the title character of *Cromwell*, who as "The Big One" controls the battlefield, condones the rape and pillage of the Irish countryside and its inhabitants, and contributes to the disintegration and destruction of Joan and Proctor's family. The authority may also appear as an institution—church, political party or coal mine—that has controlled and dominated the lives of the Pasmore family in *The March on Russia*. In both cases the families have "accepted the social structures in which they were absorbed."[23] Even when those authorities do appear on stage, their dominance is the result of their superior position in the off-stage world; through his status as Board Director, employer, and financier, Benson of *Early Days* controls Bristol. Benson also dominates his father-in-law, wife, and daughter through repeated use of the legal, financial, and medical authorities of a 1980s' Great Britain.

This dominance of position and environment is linked to class. In each Storey play, the authority figure is opposed to the working class, characters who people the stage world. And those authority figures use their positions to influence the dynamics within the working class family unit, a situation Storey discussed in a recent interview. Storey stressed how important those family dynamics were to his work; "the peculiar history or nature of my own family seemed to illuminate the degree to which family experience governs us throughout our life."[24] Storey described his family as a balance of "disturbance and harmony" and acknowledged that "the conflicts of family activity have never left [him]."[25] These family conflicts, as Storey embodies them in his dramas, mirror the battle for dominance in the larger social structure, the exterior playworlds, and as such mirrors they reflect Storey's own domestic training as a combatant in an environment where "challenge[s] had to be met" and "a world had to be overcome."[26]

These worlds to be overcome are quite specific in each of the four plays. In *The Contractor*, we are presented with preparations for a

traditional society wedding. The Ewbanks are only one generation
removed from the working class background of the family's patriarch,
Old Ewbank, while Maurice and Claire, characters whose very names
suggest their social class, are a doctor and nurse—"bloody aristocrats"
(TC, 28). Even their jobs are professional ones, not blue collar. If *The
Contractor* celebrates the success of the upper class, the stage activities
reveal the working class. Their work, the raising of a marquee,
reenforces class distinctions. They are the workmen labouring to create
the perfect artifact which simultaneously celebrates the transformation
of the Ewbanks from "artisans" to "aristocrats" and the perpetuation of
the traditional social institution, marriage, which facilitates that
transformation. Significantly, we see neither the marriage ritual nor the
communal celebration in the tent. We see only "the work" that makes
those celebrations possible. In the play's own terms we see the
economic "contract" that is enacted between employer and employee
but neither the audience nor the workmen participate in the social or
personal contract enacted between husband and wife.

In *Cromwell* the dominant authority is a British general who
never appears on stage, yet controls the military, political, and
economic life of an occupied Ireland. As "The Big One," he represents
the brutalization of a native population by a superior military invader.
As an "Englishman," he stands for the historical usurper of Irish rights
and certainly in Storey's context, the contemporary British usurper of
rights in an annexed Northern Ireland. And as a historical figure,
eventual Lord Protector, he becomes a symbol of the working man
transformed to Protestant aristocratic oppressor of a Catholic agrarian
peasant class.

If *Cromwell* presents authority overtly tied to political and
religious affiliation and dramatic enactment of sectarian racism, then
Early Days is an exploration of authority and "ageism." As Stephen
Wall noted, "the old, whoever they are, are too like us for comfort."[27]
The conflict of age and youth appears in the battles between Kitchen
and his family in which various combatants and various intellectual and
emotional strategies vie for dominance. While Storey is not especially
concerned with the specifics of Kitchen's diplomatic/espionage past, he
is at pains to contrast Kitchen's memory of political battles for

dominance with Benson's struggles for economic and social dominance. Kitchen's encapsulation of his son-in-law's rise reflects both Kitchen's hostility and Benson's changing status. "He was a doctor. Then he went into business. He became a research scientist, discovered a pharmaceutical drug, and was taken on to the board of directors. Subsequently he was appointed chairman of an organization which I heartily despise" (ED, 14). Kitchen's own penchant for viewing himself as the working man in contrast to Benson the chairman or Steven the artist reveals another aspect of this battle for authority. Kitchen asserts that "Art is a commitment to self-aggrandizement" (ED, 37). In contrast, Kitchen views his work as purposeful and necessary; Steven's work is self-interest and self-ish. Yet despite Kitchen's assertions, *Early Days* offers its audience a series of struggles for power that reveal the increasing political, economic, artistic dominance of a younger generation. Kitchen may serve as the play's principal character but he is not its most powerful. What little authority of class and age he holds over others is subordinate to the isolation and loneliness of his few remaining months.

The March on Russia also introduces us to generational disputes and like *Early Days* is concerned with a weight of past political, military, and economic choices. However, the question of authority or dominance is shifted from the family members to the social institutions which control their lives. In the other plays, professional positions impart status and upward social mobility. In *The March on Russia*, those same professional positions restrict their practitioners. Wendy's life as a politician is one in which she tries to serve the women of "broken . . . mind, broken . . . spirit" (MR, 45). But she admits that she gets "no satisfaction—except that of knowing that, if I didn't do it, someone else might do it worse" (MR, 45). Colin finds his professorial position equally stultifying. Despite the family's change in "class," no Pasmore child finds fulfillment or satisfaction in his/her new upwardly mobile life.

Authority in this dramatic world is embodied in the social structure and institutions—the political party that Wendy must reject to find independence, the college and its publishing craze that has extenuated Colin's "dementia," the local shopkeeper who will deal with

Mr. Pasmore's shoplifting. Even the past was controlled by institutional authorities—the town council, the mine or the military who gave us the failed but inspirational march of the title. *The March on Russia* offers its audience the clearest example in Storey's dramas of "worlds to be overcome."

To accentuate the power and dramatic impact of these authorities, Storey enhances our knowledge and awareness of the off-stage worlds in which those dominant characters make their lives. In *The Contractor* we learn as much about the "estate" (house and grounds) we can't see, as the tent and the wedding reception paraphernalia that are within our field of vision. And not only does Storey supply vivid portraits of those off-stage worlds that match the visual power of the on-stage details, but he also makes us aware that those on-stage environments are the product of off-stage events.

Because the stage environments are dominated, even generated, by off-stage authorities, their very composition, their list of ingredients, is essential to our understanding and awareness of political, social, and cultural conflicts of the plays. As Katharine Worth has pointed out in relation to *The Contractor*,

> Out of the rough old jumble of the stage scene—the noisy, confused effect of men at work, the fights, the swearing, the broad jokes, the simple animal behavior . . . out of all this comes the lovely, delicate thing, the marquee, with its white ironwork tables, its pots of flowers, its air of elegance and festivity.[28]

The contrast of the workman's physicality and the marquee's ornate beauty, the Ewbanks' concern for the grass and the damage to their estate, to the tattered appearance of the marquee following the celebration foregrounds the class and social distinctions between the upwardly mobile generations of Ewbanks.

In each play, the battle for authority and the individual, ideology or institution which achieves the dominance makes us conscious of three things: class and its impact on culture/way of life, the mediocrity or failure of the inherited culture, and life as it has been lived and will be lived as process not progress. In *The Contractor*, class and culture *are* the event at the center of the play. Across three acts, we watch the raising, decorating, and disassembling of the marquee for the Ewbank wedding reception. Storey's detailed set descriptions make certain that the setting itself is character and culture simultaneously. This marquee stands as the new generation's way of life, a decorated idealization of marriage to be trampled and mangled by the celebrants of that new way of life only to be disassembled by those who have been excluded from the celebration (the workmen)—particularly those whom that rite has failed (Bennett's wife has left him for another man).

The failure of marriage for Bennett leads to a fight with Fitzpatrick and the loss of his job (TC, 102). The de-construction following the de-molition suggests the failure of the "refined" classes to exercise the style or control that is traditionally associated with the "aristocracy." To call attention to this failure of behavior, Storey gives Mrs. Ewbank's concern about the workmen's treatment of the grass and the house. Yet from an audience perspective those workmen behave with a great deal more control than their "betters." They also take a great deal of pride in their class and nationality (TC, 47). Ewbank is uncomfortable with his own. This discomfort has been passed on to his son who, rather than apply himself to a profession, studies and spends his father's money. Paul's failure to find a profession anticipates this family's inability to find a secure and prosperous niche in the new class. And this failure mirrors others in the play, including the generational conflict between Paul and Ewbank as well as the personal failings that culminated in Kay's embezzlement. These problems suggest an emptiness, a lack of culture, beneath the facade of celebration. And in the final moments of the play, the stage itself drives home this point: "Empty: bare poles, the ropes fastened off" (TC, 108).

While the final image of *The Contractor* is a space from which most objects have been removed, *Cromwell* offers us a space that has been stripped bare. This drama reveals a series of environments where the invading armies and the defenders have resorted to pillage and destruction as part of a military campaign. The battles for dominance between Catholic and Protestant, English and Irish, deserter and recruiter, are enacted in an increasingly ruined landscape. Bare fields and woods, a cart on a road, a ruined farmhouse, a burning farm and a stream separating a dark land from "one darker still" (C, 78) are all

striking images of such destruction. Joan and Proctor's effort to create a
haven, a way of life on a new farm, is destroyed by yet another battle in
Act III. Flight to a new and unknown land is the only option for
individuals who find no creation, no procreation, no culture in war.

While the play's physical landscape reflects the conflicts of
class, religion and nationality, the journeys enacted within it emphasize
the transition of culture. In *Cromwell*, culture literally becomes "a way"
of life. To live, to survive, one must move constantly. And since
nothing is permanent, sustainable, or maintainable, the failures and
mediocrity of this world seem almost self-evident. There are no winners
in the military battle; none serve in the army long enough to affect any
change. Joan and Proctor's new life is taken from them; both their child
and their farm are destroyed when the troops arrive looking for the
insurrectionists. Even the spiritual battle is a failure; debate over
political or spiritual reform between Proctor and Cleet the
insurrectionist is resolved by the arrival of troops, not by reasoned
discourse.

The failure to create or sustain any culture in *Cromwell* is
transformed into a debate between alternative views of culture in *Early
Days*. For Bristol, Kitchen, and Kitchen's family, the world is reduced
to a static environment of chairs and country life. The landscape of the
play is static antinomy or double bind. The class distinction of Kitchen
and his family and Bristol's "servant" background are juxtaposed
against the landscape of Kitchen's memory played against the "way of
life" of his wealthy, artistic, and intellectual family. To the family,
Kitchen is an interference, a disruption, and an anomaly because he
insists that his perspective, his memory is the environment all others
must recognize.

And because Kitchen manipulates successfully his mental
landscape, other characters cede to him control of subject or control of
action while still attempting to limit the destruction he can wreak in the
"real" world of the play. In this battle for control of environment,
Kitchen represents this family's history and Britain's history, the failure
of the domestic unit and political unit, family and country. Not only has
he distanced himself from his immediate family, but Kitchen has also
destroyed his wife, the one woman he loved. Gloria claims:

> The one person who loved you callously destroyed, by
> doing those very things you accuse my father of, with your
> obscene phone calls and grotesque abuse and promenading
> of your genitals in the village street (ED, 38).

He also destroyed his political career by "opening [his] mouth too much" and by failing to pass on the ideals and values of his generation (ED, 32).

His failure as both an effective communicator and an effective force for change are in someways reflected in the familial world that now surrounds him. His caregiver, Bristol, is working for Benson because his wife has left him for another man and he is isolated from his family and previous connections. Gloria has abandoned Kitchen's traditional ideals of "God and country" for personal pleasure and a life of "art" with a poet whose work, "Samson," de-constructs and de-mythologizes the heroic man. In this poem, Samson is newly-shorn and sapped of strength rather than the leader who defeats Philistines. Even Mathilde sees her father as one "who grasps at us. At times I feel he'll never let go" (ED, 43). Her entrapment by this parental figure may be mirrored in a marital entrapment where she is forced into domestic life and an interest in the local doctor. But in each of these relationships we see the specter of failed communication, apathy, and self-destruction. As authority has failed to provide nurture, role models, and purpose, the basic elements within the society have abandoned progress for mere process—the living of life. Gloria's revelation in the final scene—Kitchen's impending death—is almost an afterthought. That this revelation carries not the sense of finality but instead a sense of inevitability suggests that Kitchen's final failure—his death—will have little impact on the financial or political world.

If *Early Days* provides authority as a specter of failed communication, apathy, and nostalgia for destruction not creation, *The March on Russia* offers authority as the driving force of the past, a past which challenged men to survive in economic and politically repressed conditions only to destroy those aspirations with its failure to transform ideologies into practical actions. While the Benson/Kitchen family occupies static environments, the Pasmores of *The March on Russia* are trapped in a claustrophobic one. Throughout the play, the five characters are enclosed by the confines of the parent's house. This restricted stage space serves as a powerful visual reminder of the enclosed and restricted environments of the family's emotional past and present. This bungalow is the only secure world for Pasmore and his wife for when they leave it for some activity in the off-stage world, disasters follow. Pasmore's forays into the backyard lead to flirtation and accusations of sexual impropriety with the next-door neighbor. His trips into town reveal his habit of shoplifting, and his anniversary trip leads to excessive drinking and aggressive behavior. While the house represents security (it was Colin's gift, purchased for his parents after years of deprivation to reward their support of his education), it also represents enclosure and restriction. Within this house, the parents enact their games of hate and love separate from their children's lives and homes, their past friends, and work environments. The Pasmores have separate bedrooms, a symbol of their growing isolation from each other. The trust and love that makes "house" into "home" is not present despite the stage props and mementoes that are attempts to humanize this space.

It also contrasts with descriptions of past family life. When they occupied a squalid counsel house, there was a sense of unity and determination despite the poverty. But now, deprived of purpose and struggle, the family has disintegrated. The children experience divorce, anxiety, and frustration. Colin will never advance in the academic world because he writes histories of popular figures. Wendy is divorced and a working mother who has lost interest in the concerns of the political party she had embraced. Eileen's world is centered around her husband who is only limitedly successful. While the children have exceeded their parents financially and intellectually, they will never succeed beyond limitations imposed by social and political institutions.

The failure of the family mirrors the decline of all the important institutions in the dramas—the military, the government and the industrial estate. The campaign to free the Czar, the march of the title, ended in defeat at the hands of women with pickaxes. Wendy realizes the government is unable to provide even basic services for the very constituents she was elected to serve. Colin's description of Jonathan Wroe, the Last Evangelist, reminds us of the ultimate failure for those who attempt to change the status quo; Wroe's campaign against "the despoliation, the conformity, the dilution of feeling—the despiritualization" of the Pennines by the forces of the Industrial Revolution ends in his own destruction and that of his family (MR, 21). "To add significance to their execution, they [Wroe and his mother] were hanged successively, the mother before the son, a few feet apart, and face to face" (MR, 21). Wroe's campaign of civil disobedience is futile, leads to death, and has no impact on the authorities. In fact, the campaign even taints Wroe's would-be biographer Colin, whose history of Wroe leads not to tenure but to his condemnation as a popular historian.

While in each of these plays it is important to recognize the relationship between the on-stage environment and the dominant authorities, it is equally important to see how the failure of those authorities and the individuals they effect is reinforced by the play's emphasis on process rather than progress. Because Storey's plays are concerned with the nature of culture and how that culture or way of life is influenced by the various authorities who may or may not control it, there is a dialectic or perhaps one might say a collision in his dramas between the impetus toward progress driven by the dominant authority in each dramatic world and the reality of process, the essence of being not doing, impelled by the bond of work, of activity rather than dramatic action that each play offers at stage center. In other words, Storey's plays may project a sense of "plotlessness" because they are more interested in showing us precisely how characters change what they are, not only what they do; they en-act rather than re-act.

In *The Contractor*, progress is suggested by the wedding celebration. The Ewbank family is moving up and out with their changing social status and their financial success. While there is a gap between the workmen on stage and the family predominantly controlling from off-stage, the class distinctions emphasize the possibility of achievement and the potential for any one to change his/her economic circumstance. This possibility conflicts with the on-stage action of the play which reveals only a dramatic process, men at work. Each man is part of a successful team that in the course of three acts can create and disassemble a complete set. The changes we see are those of work well-done but work that does little to change any social or economic situation. In fact, the comraderie of the work will lead to personal revelations which in turn lead to economic deprivation, unemployment. As this play proceeds, we see the completion of the work but we do not see that work rewarded with significant respect or financial recompense. And the most valued event of the drama belongs to an off-stage world in which neither the workmen nor the audience play a part.

And while the off-stage marriage of Claire and Maurice gives the couple a change of class and a future with financial security, it is separate and untouched by the sheer manual labor that makes it possible. In this play, Storey's insistence on stage activity restricted to one class and one gender bonded by the necessity of and pride in its work ethic, drives home to an audience the failure and repugnant dominance of a capitalist oligarchy that controls by economic and social power without regard for integrity, comraderie, or honesty.

In *Cromwell*, those issues of honesty, integrity and comraderie are raised in the environment of war. The controlling force of the play is neither cognizant of nor seemingly concerned with the cost of a determination to seize power and control of land and religion. Because the destruction in this world is so dominant, process is represented by those characters who attempt to nurture and sustain life even if they must eventually flee the land to protect that life. Proctor and Joan so desire life that they will even feed and protect Cleet the insurrectionist. They are the builders of culture and they are always in process, preserving or creating because they believe in life as the essence of being and to attain that life they will risk all. The progress of the play, on the other hand, is the military battle, the desire to win by absolute and arbitrary destruction of the opposition. The collision of progress and process can be expressed by the ideologies of Cleet and Joan. While Cleet argues for an idyll, a political and religious utopia, Joan argues for a stoicism. The men of the play struggle, try for an ideological future, while the women try to survive. The process for Joan and Proctor becomes a transformation of the fear of destruction into a force for action. Thus, at the end of the play, we see them enter the boat

for the darker land, there may be no sense of improvement but there
will be no looking back.

For *Early Days*, action or process becomes the field of memory
where, as Kitchen says, "throughout our lives we stand, looking up at a
multitude of faces, not one of which we shall ever know "(ED, 29). The
process is juxtaposed with Benson and Gloria's world of progress.
"New art," new chemicals, new and better lives and tastes counter
Kitchen's fragmented memory. While we never learn all there is to
know of his past life and activities, we do see the power and destruction
it wrought on those around him. And if *Cromwell* gives us some sense
of the integrity to be gained by action, change, and movement, *Early
Days* makes us aware of integrity gained through admission. In his
memory, Kitchen is brutal, enchanting, and alive, while in the physical
world he is isolated and dying.

The March on Russia is punctuated by an inversion of the
principles of *Early Days*. In this new work, memory is an effort toward
progress while the playworld's activities are the process. In the
Pasmores' past, there was a belief, indeed a conviction that progress
and transformation of political and economic situations were possible.
The Russian ruler could be saved to transform the communist
revolution; the Pennines could be saved from the advance of
industrialization; the Pasmore family could be lifted from squalor and
physical disease to a life of economic success and physical ease.

While this conviction was once strongly held, none of these
events comes to pass. They were moments of glory which still attract
the interest of Pasmore and Colin, but they do not change the family's
economic and political lives, nor do they change the real physical
destruction which both experience in later life. Pasmore is clearly
suffering from "black lung"; his coughing fits and the play's stories of
his ulcers and weeping sores show his general physical decline. His
sacrifice of health for economic gain produced a house not a home,
upwardly mobile children he seldom sees, and a wife who reminds him
constantly of the price they have paid for their better life. Colin, the
symbol to all the family of their changing status in modern Britain,
suffers from severe and debilitating anxiety attacks which make it
impossible for him to function as a teacher, writer, or man. He is

distanced from his own wife and children, resented by his sisters, and misunderstood by his parents. In this house, he is relegated to the cold trundle bed upstairs where insomnia brought on by an anxiety attack matches that of his father downstairs—whose nightly pacing is a product of his lung disease. In these physical and mental declines we see that few of the traditional ideals have been achieved for either children or parents, and the desire to continue the struggle to maintain those old objectives is gradually disappearing from this world.

Thus the environment, the failures and the conflict of process and progress which reveal them draws our attention to the battles over authority and culture that are at the heart of Storey's plays. A crucial component of this collision of authorities and cultures is the reinforced power and dominance of the masculine voice. While Storey creates strong female characters from Joan in *Cromwell* through Gloria in *Early Days* to Wendy and Eileen of *The March on Russia*, none of these women has significant control over her environment in on- or off-stage worlds. They must accede to established authorities, although Storey allows us to watch their struggle with repression or suppression. Yet while Storey seems willing to provide the feminine voice space and time to articulate frustrations, in each play he gives the climactic moments and the final lines to a masculine speaker. Thus, while the issues of power and dominance are raised in an increased audience and authorial awareness of gender status and position, once raised, the issue is retired by a return to the ostensibly masculine world of post-war British society.

The feminine appears to exist in these plays as a reminder of the domestic world, the procreative possibilities and the role that it can or cannot play in the changing political and social environment. Because the majority of environments are domestic, we assume a dominance of feminine parlance and activity. Instead the feminine voice is restrained and subordinated to overarching issues of class. Storey seems more interested in the political struggle than the gender one. In *The Contractor*, the primary activity of the workmen is an exclusively male enterprise. Mrs. Ewbank and Claire visit and comment on the work but have nothing to say about its assemblage, its disassemblage, or the process of the work. They can inhabit certain spaces, but they have little to say about the activities in the play. They are also very traditional in their roles; they are wives first and foremost. Though Claire is a nurse, that profession is clearly subordinate to her husband and his occupation. The woman who has attempted to change this dominance, Bennett's wife, does so not to gain independence, but to exchange one man for another. The power in both on- and off-stage worlds belongs to men; in final moments of the play, Mrs. Ewbank is resigned to the change in the family, while her husband is concerned about Kay's embezzlement, the loss of a daughter, his family's future and his own social and professional position. When he does return to the house with his wife, it is his choice, not hers.

As Ewbank controls the end of *The Contractor*, so Proctor controls the end of *Cromwell*. His determination, his ability to overcome his own fear, makes Joan and Proctor's final deliverance from the brutality of the known (war-torn Ireland) to the ambiguity of the unknown (the darker land) possible. Even the intellectual debates of the play belong to its male characters. While Joan assumes a stoic acceptance of what life deals out, Cleet, Proctor, and even Logan and O'Halloran argue the religious, political, and social aspects of power and change. While the men strive for understanding, the women try for acceptance. And despite the intellectual arguments offered by the opposing forces, the brutality and violence practiced by the men toward all others question the comraderie, power and value of war. The flight of soldiers from both sides, the deserters, and the draft-dodgers further undercuts the intellectual idealism. Yet that war continues and destroys the nurturing and procreative world of Joan, the farm and her child. The future may be articulated by Proctor, but it will only be possible if Joan brings it into being. Because the play questions the values of the masculine and yet denies the possibility of a strong feminine, it does suggest that the only possible future is beyond a dark river, beyond the present conflict, perhaps beyond death.

In *Early Days*, the brutality of the relationship between the two genders appears in Kitchen's destruction of his wife and Bristol's divorce. It also appears strongly in Kitchen's distinction between himself and Mathilde:

> I've had enough of your passivity ... That's Mathilde's
> philosophy: that's the creed of your long-suffering wife
> who's borne you a child and stood by you all these years. I
> have no patience with her. She become immobilized ...
> I'm a man of action. (ED, 26)

While Kitchen no longer acts, Mathilde or Gloria have never begun to act. The actions of the play relate to Steven as a writer, Benson as a breadwinner and head of the corporation, and Bristol as a caregiver. This play replaces the traditional female role of nurse with a hired male and reinforces that passivity which Kitchen readily asserts is the forte of the opposite gender.

The play also suggests that despite Gloria's articulate defense and rejection of her grandfather's tradition, his definition of culture is far more precise and supportable than hers. As Kitchen makes clear to his doctor, "I'm interested in culture" (ED, 31). For him, culture is selecting and controlling the art and artifacts of the household and most importantly being the "best." From Kitchen's perspective, culture is what lasts and what is fought for; those like Steven and Gloria who make art by describing only disintegration will never be the best.

In *The March on Russia*, the feminine appears in two generations who repeat a pattern of dissatisfaction and disillusionment with the authorities that control their lives. While both Pasmore and Colin have taken domestic roles and Wendy and Mrs. Pasmore have taken on that of worker, none are satisfied in the new roles. Wendy was the caregiver for her father and brother as a young child; she was forced to forgo advantages and education so that Colin could succeed. Now she faces the same demands from her political party and her aging parents who insist that she remain married, vote Labour, and generally subscribe to their vision of happiness. But as Wendy indicates, she has gone independent. She voted independent in the last elections, and, while divorcing her husband, is using her caregiving skills to aid the disenfranchised and abused women of her district. But despite this rejection of her parents' values, Wendy has found little satisfaction in her new job.

Mrs. Pasmore also expresses dissatisfaction. She finds that after a life of hardship and domestic servitude to husband and family, she faces an old age with a husband who "had an eye for the women" (MR, 44) and despite all her best efforts, continues to drink. While she admits that she loved and respected Pasmore and worked with him to provide for their family, she refuses to accept his present retirement or her children's dissatisfaction with the lives she and her husband have built for them. She does not understand what has happened to her children's sense of duty nor how they could feel rejected or oppressed by their parents' expectations. Mrs. Pasmore also resents the failure of her ideals to provide the sense of fulfillment and satisfaction in old age. She is left with a husband who reminisces about the war, misses his children, and steals second-hand rings. She has always led a vicarious life and at the end of the play we see her continuing that pattern.

These dramatic elements and choices in regard to authority and gender provide one-half of Storey's dialogic structure. The other half is provided by Storey's shifts in physical and verbal language. These shifts enhance the audience's awareness of Storey's specific concerns with culture and authority and his London audience's sensibility toward the exploration of its entangled personal and public histories as modern British citizens. In both sides of this dialogic structure Storey acknowledges an understanding of history in the drama as an exploration of what we desire but what we can never achieve. As Jameson indicates:

> History is . . . the experience of Necessity, and it is this alone which can forestall its thematization or reification as a mere object of representation or as a master code among many others. . . . [I]t is therefore a political narrative in the enlarged sense of some properly narrative political unconscious. . . . History is what hurts, it is what refuses desire and sets inexorable limits to individual as well as collective praxis, which its "ruses" turn into grisly and ironic reversals of their overt intention.[29]

In Storey's plays we find this "History," this political unconscious with a series of ironic reversals of event and action. For Storey creates a dialectical process between on and off-stage events, characters and worlds in a process which is distinct from either Samuel Beckett's obsession with form as the content or Harold Pinter's absorption with

language as both form and content. For Storey, the predominant choice
lies in an awareness of class in language and form coupled with a
determination to work inside both.

When Storey does focus on language, it is for him both physical
and verbal. In his character's speech, Storey makes direct and pointed
use of class distinctions, political obfuscation, and cultural expression
to present in his dramas not imaginative or intellectual worlds but the
semblance of a life lived—the cultural form preferred by Williams's
analysis of that artistic construction in our contemporary political
environment. In physical language, Storey makes a clear distinction
between the Aristotelian notion of physicality as action and/or plot, and
creates instead a world where not much happens but a great deal takes
place. The individual's actions and reactions are highlighted; much of
the character's personalities are revealed through physical action and in
each play an activity is the center of the stage action. While all of those
elements do little to "move" or "forward" a plot, the physicality of the
stage is predominant.

The verbal shifts in Storey's plays call attention to our cultural
choices by collision of class and dialect, by language that does not
complete, and by narrative passages describing past events which are
invested with great power. For *The Contractor*, Storey offers us three
distinctly different classes and several dialects. The chatter of the
workmen is distinctly different from the bride and groom, though
Ewbank's own speech is a combination of both his background and his
new social status. He punctuates moments of emotion with the
expletive "bloody" and he reverts often to northern dialect in words
such as "aye" and "you recken."

So in addition to our awareness of the working class, the
nouveau riche and the aristocrats, we also expand the linguistic
horizons of this play with Glendenning's stutter and the Irish accent of
 Fitzpatrick. Language reveals class, nationality and the inherent
stereotypes of behavior and authority assigned to both. Language is
also a reflection of confidence. Ewbank's insecurity about the future is
reflected in his disjointed and incomplete thoughts at the end of the
celebration. This pattern of incomplete expression or fractured dialogue
is also enacted repeatedly among the workmen. Marshall and

Fitzpatrick play out this sequence in their humorous discussion of why they might work for Ewbank. Underlying this banter is an awareness of Kay's dishonesty, the inequality in the business and the tenuous quality of their employment (TC, 85–87). Fractured logic and fractured sentence structure are covers for the disease and dissatisfaction that lie just beneath the surface of the comraderie and bravado in the work environment.

This disjunction of language is enhanced in *Cromwell* by the addition of narrated histories through which we learn what has happened beyond our field of vision. Because Mathews functions in this play as the destroyer of family and future, yet is unable to speak or cogently express the reasons for his actions, the description of those events is filtered through the words and actions of another, Joan:

> The day they came I found one lying in the hedge . . . he'd got a pipe . . . It was the smoke I saw first . . . rising . . . a thin blue cloud . . . it settled round the twigs and leaves . . . 'ther's a fire over ther' I thought . . . when I went across I saw a boot . . . It was sticking out . . . and when I looked between the leaves I saw en eye . . . (C, 24).

For Joan, the trauma of the recollected vision together with the demand and desire to speak of it publicly fractures her language and causes it to be composed of momentary visual images, pieces of a puzzle rather than a complete and well-thought out description. Only Moore speaks in those complete phrases and this may be because each aspect of his plan has been rehearsed. His attempt to bury the trooper in the coffin and to disguise the purpose of their journey is well-conceived and, were it not for the priest's flight, would have succeeded. But once his plan is revealed, he is reduced to silence and then dies.

As the play progresses, and death and destruction increase, Joan and Proctor search for another way to "go into the darkness." If assurance and confidence in speech can be reduced to the eventual silence of death as in the case of Moore, then the only possibility for survival is to transform the verbal debates of Cleet and Wallace into the new plan, a new action which Proctor describes, "My toil, my labour . . . I carry revolution in my head and heart . . . not streaked along a sword, or buried with the dead" (C, 66). As Proctor reminds

Wallace, "oppression makes reflections of itself—and calls it revolution
. . . change . . . the end to discontent and the change is . . . the beggar
usurps the horseman and tackles the whip himself" (C, 66). Once
Proctor learns to articulate the need for change, he can begin to put that
desire into action, and he can also transform bombastic speech into
poetry.

By shifting from prose to blank verse and then rhyme in the final
moments of the play, Storey calls attention to Proctor's changed
sensibility. It is also important to note that this final poetic command
speaks not of "reality" but of dreams. "I dreamed I took conviction
down to hell . . . cleansed and bathed its empty shell . . . and when I
drank I found its contents full of blood" (C, 78). In this last step,
Proctor transforms the narratives of death and destruction that have
proliferated in this play into a prophesy of his own complicity and his
own need for change. Conviction is destruction and from that cause he
must turn away. So rather than despair or be destroyed, he joins with
Joan in a voyage to where there is no turning back. Proctor uses verbal
language to create a new sensibility, a new vision of the future, still
inarticulate but motivated by the need to escape destruction and silence.

If *Cromwell* offers verbal language as a transformation of
destruction into some action, some choice for the future, in *Early Days*
language is an expression of the disintegration of man and society. Art
and culture have come to be lifestyles of the younger generation rather
than paintings and quality objects selected with an eye for the best and
for tradition. As a result, Kitchen's language reflects not the novelty
and vitality of youth but the despair and frustration of old age. In this
drama, language plays between class, between spheres of influence, and
between transmission and reception. The first instance is evident in the
distinctions of Bristol's and Kitchen's speech. Bristol is deferential,
precise and reticent. Kitchen is aggressive to the point of offense,
expansive to the point of excess, and ambiguous to the point of
obfuscation. Yet, each man's speech reveals much of the past pain and
frustration that typified the restrictions imposed on their behaviors and
language by class, rank, and age. None of these restrictions occur for
Benson, Gloria, or Steven. And as class and position shape language, so
does the sphere of influence. Benson speaks with the precision and

determination of a self-made man, Mathilde speaks with the frustration and repression of a bored and brooding housewife, and Gloria and Steven speak with the unnerving and aggressive power and confidence of the newly educated. They often assert rather than explain, demand rather than ask, and use insults as a badge of independence where they might accede and gain control through silence and observation. This is also a play shaped by an overabundance of characters readily offering opinions and information but rarely willing to listen or receive information. As Mathilde so aptly indicates, "I shan't sit and talk if you refuse to listen" (ED, 17). Only Bristol is attentive to his charge and Storey's presentation of the subordinate as the most compassionate character indicates which class and attitude Storey respects.

he's paid to

While Kitchen is the most vocal and virulent of the speakers in the play, the final scene reminds us that his approaching death will soon silence his voice. Thus for both audience and other characters he becomes "full of contradictions with a good deal of sense in them" (ED, 24). As we play through his memories and his despair, we also see the future of his world and family. They are lost in a mass of contradictions that reveal their love for tradition, but they refuse to allow that tradition to interfere with their pleasures and routines.

In *The March on Russia* verbal language becomes an expression of nostalgia, a means to call attention to the continuing distinction of class in the workplace and the never-changing desire to rediscover an empire that represented the heroic, the adventurous, and a release from the monotony and drudgery of a life down the mine. This nostalgia surfaces in Pasmore's description of his Royal Naval Air Service time, the title's foray. The excitement of the chase is encapsulated in Pasmore's enervated description of his induction, training, and participation in the battle for Sebastopol, in the descriptions and exotic terminology used to invoke the fleeting memories of Empire from Gibraltar to Indian Gurkhas, and in the tempo and rhythm of a speech composed of short bursts of scene setting, quoted commands, and narrative driven by geographical references (MR, 4–5).

wrong word

However that nostalgia is colored by his awareness of the arbitrary authority of a service that "takes o'man's [sic] name for spitting on the deck," that surrenders power and control to a weeping

Russian general, and eventually launches a suicidal rescue attempt of the Czar and his family. While this authority offers release from the cruelty and destruction of the pit, it is also likely to sacrifice its serving men for a failed ideal. That Pasmore cannot sustain his speech is indicative of the failure of that Empire and the ideals for which it stood. His freedom was momentary and the harsh reality of economic survival returns at the end of his narrative to be punctuated by the cough that reminds both the speaker and audience of precisely what he gained from "forty-five years i' the coal-bin" (MR, 5).

If the narrative passage reveals the failure of authority to create a better way of life for common man, the bickering and fragmented communication among the children and their parents reveal that their private dream of retirement in peace and harmony with a financially secure and loving family is also a failure. The generational conflict and dissention in this family mirror the failure of the Labour Party's socialization and public aide schemes. The lack of economic satisfaction and social advancement has led even a traditional working woman like Mrs. Pasmore to vote Conservative. That this is a northern family, the backbone of Labour politics and working class aspirations, drives home the failure of contemporary British politics and policies. With the failure of these traditional attitudes comes a subsequent isolation of individuals which is reflected in the linguistic and regional distinctions between the educated Colin's description of Jonathan Wroe and his father's nostalgic recollection of World War I.

If Storey's speech choices reveal his awareness of failed authority and unfulfilled aspirations for a common culture, his physical choices extend that awareness. While the events of each play are contained within a single task or action, if we consider that situation carefully we will recognize that none of those tasks or actions is ever completed. Moreover, in each play, Storey calls attention to the inappropriateness of the task in the cultural context of the play.

In *The Contractor*, the drama's events are framed by the raising and lowering of the marquee. However, at the end of the play, the basic supports, ropes, and tenting remain on stage; only the details, the wedding paraphernalia are removed. And while the wedding may bring together Maurice and Claire, it does little to change the isolation of

Ewbank from his workers and his children, the economic and social situation of the workmen, or the hierarchy of prestige and power in contemporary society.

For *Cromwell*, the war, the continuous action of destruction which encompasses all characters in the drama, is never completed. While Joan and Proctor flee to another land, Ireland remains in the throes of Civil War. And as the play progresses, the actions of this play are centered less on the environment than on the objects that environment contains. The disenfranchisement and reduction of property and power are mirrored in the diminution of physical goods. The only object that remains is that cart which, within the play's context, reminds us of the necessity of movement and the physical struggle that movement entails. It also serves as extra-textual link to Brecht's wagon in *Mother Courage*, a symbol of economic struggle, failure and inevitable suffering in that work as well.[30]

The physical action of *Early Days* is contained within the experiences of Kitchen's last few months of life. None of these experiences is ever completed; conversations remain unfinished, walks are never taken, escapes to the village are never successful, and the retelling of memories is fragmentary. The play offers us loss and isolation in a static space, and a sense of the family and the society's failure to deal with the inevitability of decline, the cantankerous old age that Kitchen represents.

This stasis is extended in *The March on Russia* where the anniversary and the sixty years of the Pasmore marriage, the ostensible action of the play, are never satisfactorily or happily celebrated. What we see is the isolation of the two spouses from each other and from their children, their dissatisfaction with the future, an ambiguous nostalgia for the past, and a minimal and fragmented celebration of a significant moment in their lives. These elements are played out through a series of movements and actions that continually separate husband and wife, parent and child. Throughout the play there is constant interruption of any sustained conversation by the entry and exit of various characters. Separation of spouses, parents, and children is emphasized through location of activities within individual bedrooms. We are not here to celebrate the success of marriage, only its survival; we also see that the future holds even less to celebrate as the Pasmore children abandon the ideals and values of their parents.

Finally, Storey denies us closure or recit in these dramatic worlds by neither resolving stage conflicts nor privileging them. Once the play has presented the political, familial, cultural, or social conflicts that make up each particular dramatic world, Storey maintains that dynamic until the final curtain. He denies us resolution, and he also denies us confrontation. Each play completes an activity, but not one play resolves the conflicts precipitated by that activity or previous events that may in some way shape that activity. In essence, I would argue that Storey's plays offer their audience what Jameson has described as "fantasm." We experience:

> an unstable or contradictory structure, whose persistent actantial functions and events (which are in life restaged again and again with different actors and on different levels) demand repetition, permutation, and the ceaseless generation of various structural "resolutions" which are never satisfactory, and whose initial, unreworked form is that of the Imaginary.[31]

The dialectic of culture and authority is always in play, but it continues beyond the time and events of each Storey drama. Thus, in the dramatic worlds of David Storey, the search for common culture, a common way of life as articulated in Williams and Jameson, becomes a comment on that which we want in modern times but can never achieve—unity, completion, and satisfaction. For Storey himself, this failure is expressed as an ambivalent attitude toward the evils and virtues of the family and the society; as he puts it, "there's a degree to which it destroys us, and a degree to which it makes us, and the irony or the tragedy if you like, or the comedy, is that you can never separate the virtues from the disabilities."[32]

Notes

1. Susan Sontag, "Going to the theater, etc.," in *Against Interpretation* (New York: Anchor Books, 1990), 140.

2. Sontag, 141.

3. Sontag, 141.

4. Richard Dutton, "*Home* by David Storey" in *Modern Tragicomedy and The British Tradition* (Norman: University of Oklahoma Press, 1986), 151.

5. William Hutchings, *The Plays of David Storey: A Thematic Study* (Carbondale: Southern Illinois University Press, 1988), 3.

6. Hutchings, 3.

7. Raymond Williams, *Culture and Society: Coleridge to Orwell* (London: The Hogarth Press, 1987), xvi.

8. Williams, 299.

9. Williams, 303.

10. Williams, 322.

11. Frederic Jameson, *The Political Unconscious: Narrative as a Socially Symbolic Act* (Ithaca: Cornell University Press, 1981), 152.

12. Jameson, 152.

13. Jameson, 154.

14. Jameson, 166.

15. Richard Cave, *New British Drama in Performance on the London Stage, 1970–85* (Gerrards Cross: Smythe, 1987), 134.

16. Williams, xix.

17. Williams, 334.

18. Jameson, 20.

19. Jameson, 172.

20. Jameson, 84.

21. Jameson, 84.

22. Jameson, 84.

23. Mick Martin, "Family Feelings," *Plays International* April 1989: 15.

24. Martin, 15.

25. Martin, 15.

26. Martin, 15.

27. Stephen Wall, "Kitchen Agonistes," *Times Literary Supplement* 2 May 1980: 495.

28. Katharine Worth, *Revolutions in Modern English Drama* (London: G. Bell and Sons, 1973), 28.

29. Jameson, 102.

30. For a further discussion of this issue see Hutchings, 32–4.

31. Jameson, 180.

32. Martin, 15.

STOREY'S NOVELS AND PLAYS:
FRAGILE FICTIONS

Janelle Reinelt

'It's amazing,' he said, 'how quickly everything drops to
bits.'—*Pasmore*

Examining the relationship between David Storey's novels and plays
illuminates what might be called the master narrative of Storey's work.
This relationship also entails the technical and stylistic features through
which Storey constructs his fragile fictions. In this essay, I will point
out the main features of Storey's "master narrative" through an
intertextual reading of the novels and plays, and then discuss the novel
Pasmore (1974) and the play *The March on Russia* (1989) in order to
specify the attributes of Storey's form and technique. By a master
narrative I mean a recurring set of situations, characters, events and
images which taken together constitute a dominant pattern in Storey's
work. While each "piece" has its own specificity and meanings apart
from the others, the connections among them bring strength and clarity
to the corpus of work, taken as a whole. Not each novel and play has all
of the elements discussed here, but most of them display a fair number
of them.

One advantage of this intertextual reading is the opportunity it
affords to avoid the critical attribution of realism (or naturalism) to
Storey's evolving style. Realism is actually the least fruitful stylistic
term for describing Storey, because he often works to undermine its
efficacy in the novels and plays, and because recognizing the

underlying anti-realistic techniques makes other thematic and structural features visible. Realism here means representing a cause-and-effect set of events, psychologically coherent and unified characters, and space and time as shared objective correlatives of a predictable, knowable social world. While it is unquestionably possible, even perhaps unavoidable, to consider Storey's novels and plays as instances of this paradigm, doing so underestimates the unexplainable occurrences, the unprepared or deferred "closures," the partial and inadequate motivations, and the pointedly formal and therefore arbitrary organization of space and time which mark Storey's work. Character is less a representation of unified subjectivity than a certain position in the narrative; plot is less a series of unfolding events leading to a crisis than the juxtaposition of one particular event against the more general flow of ordinary life. Storey himself provides an intertextual and anti-realistic gloss on his work by deliberately repeating certain characters, situations, and literary tropes. *Pasmore* and *The March on Russia* deal with the same family. The central event of *In Celebration* and *The March on Russia* is a wedding anniversary. In *Present Times*, Storey's protagonist watches a rehearsal of Storey's play, *The Farm*, and in the course of the novel, comes to write Storey's play *The Changing Room*. Such self-referentiality also implicates the author, who as writer/artist/athlete/teacher, occupies the same subject-position as his protagonists. If the following discussion sacrifices an emphasis on the richness of the variety and specificity of detail which characterizes Storey's work, it is in order to call attention to a mode of representation which is more figural than mimetic, more composed than transcribed, more philosophical than social.

Charting the Master Narrative

The narratives of David Storey's novels and plays put before the reader/viewer certain philosophical issues about the relationship of ordinary tasks to the structure of meaning, and about the longing for transcendent meaning in the face of what William Hutchings calls the "desacralization" of contemporary life.[1] While the plays are usually organized around a central formal or semi-formal event, the novels are organized around an episode or rite of passage in the life of the protagonist. In both cases, a separate spatio-temporal order breaks the hegemony of the ordinary. Unlike the novels, the plays sometimes feature a group rather than an individual protagonist, although even in the most communal (*The Contractor* or *The Changing Room*), an implicit male subject-position underlies the narrative. Thus the novels and plays share more than they differ from each other. The major recurring narrative features are the following: (1) The protagonist has an interior experience or crisis which marks out a period of change or reassessment; (2) The subject position is male and the narrative is Oedipal—that is, marked by transgression of sexual codes, involvement with "older women," emphasis on mother/son bonds, encounters with paternal injunctions, threats, and struggles with authority; (3) Certain literary and visual tropes emphasize the constructedness of all meaning and its transitoriness. These are often taken from art (painting, sculpture, theatre, writing); and (4) Closure is inconclusive. The events end, but the dilemma is not resolved; or alternatively, the crisis passes, but the change is minimal and not adequately explained.

The emphasis on the domestic and Oedipal in Storey's work is, of course, embedded in a specific post-war experience of working-class life in northern England, and is, to that extent, socially grounded. Storey's protagonists, like himself, are those sons who by education and talent extend themselves beyond the ideological limits of their class background, and find themselves confronted with the futility and empty promise of the middle-class life their parents endorsed. Brought up to feel obligated to provide a kind of redemption for their parents' lives of poverty and struggle, as adults their own inadequacy to this impossible task brings them to crisis. In response, they seek first to return, somehow, to the womb, to retreat from the world—sometimes moving, literally, into a smaller, darker "space." Their behavior becomes more infantile; they take less responsibility for their actions; they become rebellious, or turn inward and isolated. They cling to older women, or behave as children with their wives, struggling over thresholds and doors to their "homes."[2]

The philosophical aspect of these familial struggles enters Storey's narratives by way of religious associations with traditional

Christianity. Again and again, the boys are characterized as little saviors (e.g., Arnold Middleton, Steven Shaw, Colin Pasmore, Allott, Alan Morley). In Storey's first play, *The Restoration of Arnold Middleton*, the verse monologue which Arnie delivers to a wall clarifies the psychological structure of this savior trope:

> When I was young, my mother said to me:
> Never drown but in the sea—
> Rivers, streams and other dilatory courses
> Are not contingent with the elemental forces
> Which govern you and me—
>   and occasionally your father—
> So remember, even if the means are insufficient, rather
> Than die in pieces subside by preference as a whole,
> For disintegration is inimical to the soul
> Which seeks the opportunity or the chances
> To die in the circumstances
> Of a prince, a saviour, or a messiah—
> Or something, perhaps, even a little higher—
> You and me and several of your aunties,
> On my side, though working class, have destinies
> Scarcely commensurate with our upbringing:
> I hope in you we are instilling
> This sense of secret dignities and rights—
> Not like your father's side, the lights
> Of which, I hope, we'll never see again,
> Who have, I'm afraid, wet blotting-paper for a brain!
> Please, please my son,
> Don't fail me like your father done.[3]

Storey's sons often bond with the mother rather than the father (Arthur Morley perceives Alan as belonging to his wife [*A Prodigal Child*]), and receive both a perception of being special and an injunction to redeem the past. The fathers' generation has had its own notions of heroism, seen in Mr. Pasmore's repeated if inconsistent account of his "march on Russia," or in Mr. Shaw's vicarious pleasure in western novels (*In Celebration*). Storey's sons are sent out as their parents "own private army" (*Pasmore*) or "our protagonist . . . our crusader" (*The March on Russia*). The crisis of Storey's "story" comes when the sons become conscious of the impossibility of the task and the ludicrousness of its rhetorical terms.

These protagonists are artists, athletes, writers, teachers—in short, exemplars in some way. They create models of meaning, beauty, excellence, or "model" the way. The drawing room in *Life Class*, the technique of the rugby players in *This Sporting Life*, *The Changing Room*, or *Present Times*, the books about evangelical idealists (*The March on Russia* and *Pasmore*) and modern society (*In Celebration*), even the artisanal mastery of tent-making in *The Contractor*—all these "creative" activities are analogous with the constitutive activity of making meanings. When the protagonists are in crisis, they cannot write (*Pasmore*) or paint (*Life Class*) or play (*This Sporting Life*). When the crisis passes, they get on with it.

The closures in Storey's work are never solutions, nor are they real remedies. When *In Celebration* or *The March on Russia* ends, the specific event—the anniversary celebrations—ends, but no resolution of life is implied for any of those involved, even less in *The Contractor* and *The Changing Room* where the tent and game are finished only until the next one. In novels like *Pasmore* or *Present Times* something has changed for the better—the characters experience some sense of relief or hope, but without any substantial motivation or tangible result. Thus the novels and plays deny closure, in the sense of resolution, while providing formal endings which mark the arbitrariness and constructedness of all narrative shapes.

These general remarks on Storey's master narrative will perhaps become clearer when seen in light of the discussion of the stylistic features of the novel *Pasmore* and the play *The March on Russia*.

Pasmore and Narrative Voice

Pasmore (1974) is the fourth of Storey's seven novels published since 1960. He considered it, at the time, "a kind of interim statement" of his thematic concerns.[4] Indeed, both the novels and plays which precede it and those which come after often bear direct relationship to this slender, almost minimal novel, which may be Storey's most experimental. A highly controlled third-person narration results in undermining the seeming objectivity of the novel. Instead, it stresses an intense experience of reality controlled by the central consciousness of the protagonist. Space, time, and character are deployed only insofar as they function for Colin Pasmore, without verification of various "facts" or other aspects of his experience. Thus, through scrupulous objectivity, "objectivity" itself is deconstructed.

Pasmore's central crisis could be called a nervous breakdown. Like so many of Storey's characters, Colin Pasmore loses his ability to function in his already-existing set of everyday structures: he cannot work, cannot maintain his personal relationships, experiences existential dread. In fact, the inadequacy of merely psychological terminology (i.e. "nervous breakdown") is apparent as soon as one tries to describe Pasmore's experience—it requires religious and philosophical language. In his review of *Pasmore*, Martin Price likened Pasmore's experience to Colin Wilson's description of Henry and William James's "vastation" experiences. Both the Jameses describe experiences of terror and threat. Henry James Sr. wrote, "The thing had not lasted ten seconds before I felt myself a wreck, that is reduced from a state of firm, vigorous, joyful manhood to one of almost helpless infancy. I felt the greatest desire to shout for help to my wife."[5] These experiences are made up of acute anxiety, a falling apart of the taken-for-granted world of everyday, and a presentiment of nothingness. The quotation from James Sr. is apt for Pasmore's experience because it ties psychological symptoms to the general collapse of a world-design and links them to the Oedipal motif.

In *Pasmore*, the experience which impells him to change his life develops through a variety of images, most clearly in a recurring nightmare that leaves Colin in a state of terror: "He was running in a race, not unlike those races he had run, stoically though with no great enterprise, at school, when he had begun to be overtaken not merely by the runners, but by all those idlers and dullards who jogged, or even walked along at the rear. Quite soon, despite all his efforts, he'd been left behind; each time he woke up with a sense of terror." He tells his wife, "But it's not just the feeling . . . of being passed that I find so awful, so much as the feeling that, despite being last, I don't want the race itself to finish."[6] He also begins each night to make whimpering, moaning noises of which he is unaware, but which are so excruciating that Kay, his wife, covers her head with a pillow to avoid hearing them.

These feelings grow out of Pasmore's perception of the incongruousness of his style of life in an "era of disintegration." He feels himself to be out of step:

> Almost furtively, and with decreasing resistance, he had begun to see how everything that was good in his life, his peace of mind, his modesty, his reliability, his self-effacement, even his sense of achievement, was irrelevant to the kind of life which he felt obliged to live. How meaningful was his existence if he could not transpose himself into the world of individuals whose experience, patently, all around him, was lacking in those self-validating certainties which made up all he knew of himself as an individual? (20)

This sense of incongruity informs a simple explanation of his recurring dream. In the race he is passed by everyone, even idlers and dullards who are clearly not of the same moral convictions and fiber as Pasmore, yet his virtue avails him nothing. The sense of being out of step with the world is very strong: his fear of the race finally ending is a fear of death while in a condition of bewildered defeat.

The intense experience of this lack of meaning results in Pasmore's retreat from his "constructed" life. Leaving his wife and children, moving to a small room, he does no work on his book on evangelical idealists, eventually retreating to his bed. In the course of things, he has a brief affair with an older woman. After a time, he returns to his home and takes up his life once again.

This "vastation" experience is not just Colin's; all the males in the novel apparently experience it in one form or another. Emblematic of this crisis is artist Bill Newsome's canvas: blank except for a single speck of red paint. After months, he is unable to go beyond it. When Pasmore asks what holds him up, he replies:

> I don't know, . . . To paint anything, I suppose you need a sense of space that, at one level, you can presume is secure. And yet, these days, what is there that can promise that? All I've got is a single blob of paint: I'm beginning to feel that

> beyond that it's become more or less impossible to
> go.... It's amazing, isn't it ... how quickly everything
> drops to bits. (87)

The other male characters in the novel also seem to recognize and share Pasmore's experience, although each functions as a variation on some aspect of the basic theme, which is only fully articulated in Pasmore himself. Thus Coles, for example, links only minimally to the major experience of the novel. When Pasmore discusses his Oedipal question, "How to accommodate adultery within the conventional framework of marriage," he assumes Coles does not share his problem:

> 'No doubt in Clapham they have ways of dealing with
> it.'
> Coles hesitated, then said, 'No," shaking his head.
> 'I see.' Pasmore watched his friend intently, 'You
> think I should face up to myself and these things would
> vanish.'
> 'Not vanish.' Coles' smile had disappeared. (16)

The implication is that Coles understands and himself participates in the problems with women that Pasmore describes. By itself, this does not seem like a remarkable detail in Storey's design. However, when Pasmore goes home to visit his parents and two sisters, his brothers-in-law provide additional testimony. Eileen, whose life is exactly like Pasmore's mother's or Kay's, is threatened by her brother's actions. She wants her husband to reassure her:

> 'Don't you think he's being very foolish, Jack?' his sister
> said. He didn't reply for a moment. He gazed intently at the
> fire. Then without raising his eyes, he said, 'No, I don't
> think so.'(109)

Eileen responds with great anxiety and finally begins to shout. Jack is quite capable of feeling what Colin has felt, and Eileen of fearing it. The other sister's husband makes up a story about a friend who is in love with a young girl who works in his household. When Colin asks why "he" doesn't just get rid of the girl, he responds, "The damage's

been done. The fissure's open. Get rid of her or keep her: he sees now
what a complete crack-up the whole business really is" (119).

Fowler, who becomes involved with Kay, is himself an artist
who has separated from his wife, had a mental breakdown, and has
taken up with another woman. Even Pasmore's father, the least likely to
participate in the experience, exposes his true feelings in his insistence
that Pasmore has been chasing women: "Do you think I was born
yesterday?. . . For God's sake. Don't you think I don't know what it's
all about?"(192).

Surely it has not been "all about" chasing other women. Yet each
of the men in the novel can now be accounted for in terms of the central
elements in Colin Pasmore's experience: meaninglessness, collapse of
life-design, extramarital desire. The novel becomes a closed structure,
almost a nightmare state where the central experience is distributed
through the characters. They become positions or functions rather than
"realistic" representations of discrete individuals; the subject-position is
clearly male-gendered.[7]

The women, as well, can be seen as interchangeable positions
within the novel, although the women are in no sense subjects.[8] They
appear only as they are seen by and as they function for the men—as
mothers, mother surrogates, possible sources of comfort and
acceptance. Helen, with whom Pasmore has a short affair, is older, self-
possessed, a mother of two children. He experiences an urge to tell
Kay's mother about his affair while she is visiting them. He kisses
Kay's mother instead of Kay one day when he leaves the house, "an
embrace which, carried from one woman to the other, [Helen] united all
his worlds, bringing together at long last the extremes of his existence"
(51). This merging of the various women, (wife, lover, mother-in-law)
clarifies the function of women for the male protagonist. The last
description of Pasmore's relationship to Helen includes his views of
women in general:

> Theirs was an instinct for what was 'for life,' fed from their
> own flesh and blood, and from their own outpouring: with
> it they loved, with it they bore children, with it they died,
> locked in a communion of spirit. What came out of their
> wholeness, this sense of life, was something which men

> could only compose for themselves by edict, that moral
> order which they fitted onto life like a suit of armour,
> hoping to contain from the outside what could only be
> directed from within. So it seemed to him that women were
> little less than gods, drawn here to love and be loved, to
> praise and be praised, the whole illumination of men's
> struggle to exist. (67–68)

Storey attributes the contrast between women's wholeness and men's fragmentation to a generalized distinction between women and men. For Colin, the desire for women is a desire for recovery of wholeness, of a world-design; it is also an elegaic wish for the lost state of connectedness before the world cracked apart—an Oedipal wish.[9]

Storey's technical choices with regard to space and time reinforce the dominant interior experience, displacing any fluid social reality. Space comes to signify Pasmore's inner state, or more precisely, a series of the phases of his inner state, while time is represented as personal and subjective rather than as objective and verifiable.

In *Pasmore*, three crucial spaces, correlating to three stages of Colin's experience, organize the material: the room to which Pasmore retreats (first in order to be with Helen, later to live alone), his childhood home, and his home with Kay, where the novel begins and ends. Colin spent much of his time before his current experience renovating and repairing his home with Kay, which is spacious, clean and well-lit. Following his "experience," one of the first things Colin considers is looking for a "room" someplace. The second space, the room he finds after beginning his assignation with Helen, is small and poorly lit. Storey places continual emphasis on the womb-like properties of the space and Colin's desire for darkness. When he has completely collapsed, he lies for hours on his bed, or even curled up on the floor; he refrains from turning on the single reading-lamp.

His visit home, by train, continues the light and womb imagery:

> Trees, like squat spiders, slid out of the wilderness of
> waste that began to open up on either side. Rows of
> factories and chimneys covered the horizon. It was like
> moving into a cavern. A dark and massive gloom settled
> round the train.

> It slowed. Wedges of black and orange rock enclosed
> the tract. It was like a room. The thick flakes of snow
> vanished. The train ran into a tunnel. (90–91)

If the trip is metaphorically regressive, the actual house is important
mainly for the representation of Colin's parents and their life, as a prior
structure of order and meaning from which he is now irrevocably
alienated.

Significantly, all three spaces are linked to the image of a door
fastened against him. When he returns home, he walks in without
knocking, much as he does when he returns to his parental home. When
Kay changes the lock on the door, Colin is outraged and starts hanging
out in the street watching the house.[10] With Helen, Colin sprang the
lock and bolted the door the first time they made love in the "room."
After Helen's husband beats Colin and Helen telephones to suggest
they not meet any more, "It was as if, somewhere, a last door had
closed" (74).

The representation of time as well as of space constructs the
subjective experience of the protagonist. This subject-time emerges to
compete with or replace a model of everyday time in a socially defined,
clock-time universe. The length of Pasmore's "vastation" experience
literally determines the length of the book. It is a clearly marked, yet
strangely unmeasurable time—a lapse from some other order of
temporal sequence. Storey stesses both the integrity of the experience
and its connection with other temporal orders. The last passage of the
novel, for example, deals explicitly with the temporal organization:

> In the winter he returned to teaching. Outwardly, despite
> the events of the preceding year, little had changed. He still
> had a regular job, a home, a wife and children; the
> apparatus of his life from his books to the commerical van
> was virtually the same. (201)

The accent is on the difference between the inner experience and the
outward appearance. Because the experience had been confined within
a term, and because he had a leave to study independently, some
external order was left unchanged during the course of Pasmore's

strange "illness." Yet a personal sense of time shapes the entire novel until this last passage.

The lapse of time is relative to Pasmore's awareness or lack of awareness of it. Although he visits his children on an ordinary clock-time Sunday, the interminable duration of the experience obliterates clock-time:

> He drove them from park to park. At each deserted playground they got out, were encouraged to climb onto swings where, motionless, they were pushed to and fro, their faces white, their eyes red and swollen, gazing sightlessly around. From the wet swings he led them to the wet slides, to the wet roundabouts and rocking horses, then back to the van. At each park the same ritual began, pushing and coaxing, a kind of terror running through him at their incapacity to be reassured. (130)

The monotony and futility of Pasmore's actions make the Sunday afternoon seem a long, drawn out nightmare, which is how Colin experiences it and Storey, through a third-person dispassionate account of the action, represents it.

The duration of any given sequence of events is not established in the novel. For example, when Colin's father visits Pasmore's room, Colin insists Kay and Fowler are on vacation while the father insists they have been back for weeks. The reader is not able to verify the truth. Indefinite syntax deliberately obscures measurable time: "Some days he didn't eat at all." "There were periods, too, when he could do nothing but weep." "One morning he opened the street door and found his father waiting on the pavement" (163–65). Since the expression "They've been back for weeks" carries the imprecise character of hyperbole, especially in the mouth of Colin's angry father, who couples it with the outburst, "I could fair kill you now," the validity of the remark is questionable. There is no way to ascertain how long Colin has lain in his room or how long Kay and Fowler have been back.

The motif of mental collapse facilitates the special uses of space and time discussed above. Thus Pasmore's physical world takes the shape of his inner experience. Time intervals blur, so that one experience lasts an indeterminate period. "Breakdown" provides an opportunity to examine how space and time function as coordinates of a world-design that is not stable, but mobile; not objective but highly idiosyncratic. Mental crisis results in the collapse of the operative temporal order: a conventional intersubjective order may be superceded by an idiosyncratic obsessive order. Thus while these vastations are important in Storey's work because he wishes to represent the impossibility of fulfilling obligations from a social and familial past, they also afford the opportunity for technical experiment with spatio-temporal orders which juxtapose realistic and solipsistic dimensions.

The March on Russia and Fourth Wall Realism

Sitting in the Lyttleton Auditorium at the National Theatre in the summer of 1989, I was struck by the way Jocelyn Herbert's set for *The March on Russia* seemed to quote itself. For at least three decades of contemporary British theatre, audiences have observed designs which feature deliberately sketchy, rapidly changing spatial representations that overtake the detail and solidity of the 19th-century box set. To provide a perfect cut-away of the Pasmore bungalow is now, in 1990, not to assert it as realistic mimesis of an actual bungalow, but to remind the audience of the constructedness of such notions as "realism" in the first place. The set seemed hyper-real—it commented on the conventions governing its construction; it was, like a painting, *framed.* In Storey's novel, *A Temporary Life*, the eccentric art school principal Wilcox paints "Pre-Raphaelite" highly symbolic, realistic compositions controlled, as he says, by "will." He is sure that the public will return to his kind of pictures, and reveals his epistemological orientation in his fervor:

> "They'll come back to pictures by people who put down
> exactly what they see, but in compositions created by good
> taste, tradition, by the instinct of the eye and hand, and by
> the intelligence which is the natural and inevitable outcome
> of a good digestion." (124)

Thus empirical knowledge is shaped by good taste and tradition: without realizing it Wilcox undoes his own sentence, asserting the social shape of knowledge at the same time that he claims it is based on instinct and nature. Ideological, one might call him. In a similar way, *The March on Russia* reveals the ideology of realism, as it re-works many of the themes of Storey's master narrative.

Although linked to all of Storey's work in various ways, the play invites strong comparisons with *In Celebration* and *Pasmore*. Like *In Celebration*, the play is structured around a family celebration of the parents' wedding anniversary. Three grown children come home, take their parents out for a meal, confront some family strife, and leave. In both plays, the anniversary event functions as a spatio-temporal disruption of the ordinary, unconfronted life of the family. As for the novel, the play can almost be seen as a sequel, since it continues to trace the characters of the family beyond the "time" of Colin's breakdown. His children are grown, his life with Kay seems stable, and he has finished his book, *The Last Evangelist*. His sisters also reappear. Wendy and Arnold are now getting a divorce; Arnold has been chasing younger women, something foreshadowed in the novel. They did not adopt children after all, and Wendy has pursued her politics, although she has switched parties. Eileen is still with Jack, and her children are seemingly grown. Colin, for his part, functions, although he is still afflicted from time to time with the old traumas:

> The other morning I woke so terrified that all I could do was cry for help: in the middle of a bedroom, in a quiet house, in the middle of a sedate neighbourhood near the heart of London. . . . When you're in the grip of this thing every second becomes an hour. And then, in the wake of this feeling, comes despair."[11]

If reading the novel and the play intertextually reveals how the characters "continue" in time while remaining the same, reading the two plays in this fashion reveals the alignment of the different characters in nearly identical positions or functions. Steven Shaw, like Colin Pasmore, is a history professor. They are the silent central male characters in the plays; Steven is in the midst of a breakdown similar to Colin's (this is a fortieth anniversary and Steven is said to be in his thirties). Andrew Shaw, like Wendy Pasmore, is the "angry child" who finally provokes and even attacks the family mythology, especially the mother. Colin Pasmore has bought his parents a retirement home near the coast; Colin Shaw has offered to buy one for the family when Shaw retires. Both plays feature a middle child who attempts to straddle two classes—Colin (Shaw) as a labor negotiator for management and Wendy (Pasmore) as a corporate executive's wife who serves as Labour Party councillor.[12] The parents' relationships, both Shaws and Pasmores, are fraught with tensions based on traditional gender roles and past disappointments. Given the brilliant performances by Bill Owen and Constance Chapman as both the elder Shaws in the original production of *In Celebration* (1969) and as the elder Pasmores in 1989, the temptation simply to superimpose the plays is strong.

However, two differences between *In Celebration* and *The March on Russia* stand out. The earlier play is clearly "about" the bankruptcy of the family mythology for the children who have been asked to live it out, while Storey's latest play is clearly "about" the parents' confrontation with the inadequacy of their own lives. The children's distress was central to *In Celebration*; the parents' distress is central to *The March on Russia*. Domestic tension and bickering mar the marriage, even after sixty years—for instance, Mrs. Pasmore becomes overly upset when Mr. Pasmore polishes his shoes with the kitchen towel. Part of the problem is age itself: the most painful struggle for them now is coping with Mr. Pasmore's tendency to steal things from the shop. As his wife says, "He puts things in his pocket. A life of honesty thrown away. We've never taken a penny—not a halfpenny—not from anyone. We've always paid our way. Now this" (48). This shoplifting has Mr. Pasmore so worried he cannot sleep nights. It underlies the unfortunate argument between husband and wife over the ring he bought her at an antique market: partly, Mrs. Pasmore rejects the gift because it is second-hand; partly, she is afraid he stole it. In addition, they do not understand their children's lives, especially Wendy's divorce, and find the world bewildering and upsetting. Mrs. Pasmore has voted conservative in the last election after fifty-five years of supporting a socialism which she feels is "worn out." At several different points in the play, Mr. Pasmore expresses his disorientation: "I don't know where I am" (38). "It's nought I understand" (48). "I don't know what's happening to me. I don't know where I am any more"

(49). The last image of the play is the couple sitting together, after the children have left. Quoting the defeated Russian General from his past, Pasmore says, "Oh where are we going to, my love?" (60).

In Storey's other work, the fragility of life-structures or world-design is represented by a crisis, usually emotional, which precipitates collapse of the operative pattern of meaning. In this play, no literal crisis occurs or is threatened (the shoplifting is not treated as monumental, only as matter-of-fact). Rather, the fragility of the Pasmores' life-structures is mostly represented by the central attention to daily rituals which accompany the action.[13]

From one standpoint, the play is full of innumerable cups of tea. The brewing of a pot, the way the various family members drink it, the doing of it for others—these repetitions and variations may be "realistic" detail, but when foregrounded as they are in *The March on Russia*, they become formal elements in a design of ordinary details which establish and re-establish a fabric of security and meaning. Bringing in the coal and lighting the fire, locking the doors to secure the house, doing crossword puzzles, keeping watch on the neighbors— these are the tasks that structure the Pasmores' "daylies." Mrs. Pasmore must have a glass of water by her bed at night in order to take a swallow when she wakes up. Mr. Pasmore listens to the radio news when he wakes up at night. The repetition of certain cliché phrases insures not that they make new meanings when said, but that they keep meanings in place: "Nothing beats hard work" (36). "A house wi'out a fire is like a home wi'out a woman" (36). "A little goes a long way in my book" (44). "On with the dance" (48).

This, then, is another major difference between *In Celebration* and *The March on Russia*. While a central event (the anniversary) provided an occasion for the disruption and examination of the family's life in *In Celebration*, the realism of the play was not itself in focus. Perhaps, as I suggested above, the way spectators view realism and its alternatives has changed, making "realism" more visible now than in 1969 as an aesthetic construction. However, *In Celebration* also retains a more traditional revelation-based plot structure which builds toward a crisis, a *scène à faire* between parents and children which, while never fully occurring, ensures the basic well-made play conventions. Hidden secrets and urgent searches for self-knowledge mark that text while their absence marks *The March on Russia*.

The characters are sketched as positions or perhaps "situations" rather than as agents of action or change. The parents, especially, gain definition as they banter and bicker with each other. They are a mutually constructed dyad, defined in reference to and in difference from each other. Storey has used this technique in both *The Contractor* and *Home* to represent the tacit complicity in social interaction. The Irish workers Marshall and Fitzpatrick operate as a unit, or at least as a linked pair, mitigating their outsider status in *The Contractor*. The emotionally disturbed dyads in *Home*, based on similarities of class and gender, break down when they attempt to interact. Similarly, the Pasmores define and limit each other through their rigid gender roles and habitual patterns of communication, a source of both solace and suffering:

PASMORE:	We're hanging on until we die.
MRS. PASMORE:	We're not hanging on at all.
PASMORE:	We're not hanging on at all.
MRS. PASMORE:	That's right.
PASMORE:	We accepted each other for what we are.
MRS. PASMORE:	We did.
PASMORE:	I'm not sure what that is. But whatever it was—I accepted it. (16)

In light of these representations, notions of unified autonomous subjectivity seem as quaint as A.C. Bradley's notion of "character." In terms of composition, character consists of a set of functions or coordinate points; in terms of individual experience, character is an interdependent and often contradictory set of social roles and practices.

David Storey's novels and plays, then, display strong continuity of both content and form. While Storey's master narrative explores the failure of human subjectivity to conceive and design solid, secure structures of meaning, his style choices reinforce the constructedness of artistic form as well as of lived experience.

A Personal Coda

When I first wrote about the work of David Storey I was in my twenties.[14] Before the second wave of feminism, before I had any politics but liberal humanism, I identified with his lonely protagonists in spite of their gender, and especially with the dilemma of being the child charged with making parents happy. I recognized myself as a daughter of the working class, educated to a professional class from which I felt equally estranged. In Storey's style, I appreciated the attempt to represent discrete counter-realities to that of the "normal" status quo, to that, I supposed, of realism.

As I encounter Storey now, I am in my forties, unable to read his work apart from a gender critique which by now has become automatic in my own critical discourse. Disturbed by certain reactionary elements I think I see in Storey's politics, especially in his most recent novel *Present Times* (1984), I have found it difficult to write about this work. However, my parents are now in their eighties, and, like the Pasmores, they struggle to understand a perplexing world and wonder why their daughter isn't quite what they expected. I, for my part, am sadly troubled by the fragility of the tissue of existence and meaning and, of course, by the approach of their deaths. I find now, more than ever, that realism represents a sham, the thin veneer of familiarity which cloaks the ever-present possibility of nothingness and the necessity of confronting it. Storey's latest work continues to move me because it seems to attack, or at least to undermine, an aesthetic style which lies about loneliness, about politics, about truth. Perhaps we do not need to share many specific views in order to share aesthetics.

Notes

1.   William Hutchings, *The Plays of David Storey: A Thematic Study*, (Carbondale: Southern Illinois University Press, 1988). "Desacralization" is a major term in Hutchings's analysis of Storey's plays.

2. The trope of a door closing, of being locked out, of struggling at the threshold with wife/mother is central especially to *Pasmore, In Celebration, Present Times,* and even *Home*.

3. David Storey, "The Restoration of Arnold Middleton," *New English Dramatists* 14 (Harmondsworth: Penguin Books, 1970), 85.

4. Storey has described a large novel from which he abstracted *Pasmore.* "I've written several novels on or around this theme. Three of them are virtually—not the same novel, but they involve the same situation and characters in three different conceptions." Interview with David Storey in Ronald Hayman, *Playback* (New York: Horizon Press, 1974), 7.

5. Henry James Sr., *Society the Redeemed Form of Man* (Boston: Houghton, Osgood & Co., 1879), 43ff.

6. *Pasmore* (New York: E.P. Dutton and Co., 1972), 18. All quotations are from this edition.

7. The term "subject position" here connotes not only the point of view of the narrative, but also the experiential space of the spectator or reader encountering the text. The psychoanalytic term for this process of identification is "suture." See, for example, Kaja Silverman, *The Subject of Semiotics* (New York: Oxford University Press, 1983), Chapter Five.

8. The women do not occupy subject positions in any of Storey's work, for that matter. Even in novels where the women are more central—Margaret in *Flight Into Camden* or Yvonne in *A Temporary Life*—the subject position is reserved for the male. Similarly in the plays, male experience provides the entry to the narrative. Thus *The Farm* is more about the returning son than the three daughters and *Sisters* represents women in relation to men, structured, in feminist terminology, by the male gaze.

9. The reference to women as god-like, as well as royalty is common in Storey's work, e.g., *A Prodigal Child, The March on Russia, In Celebration.*

10. The metaphor of being barred from the house also appears in *In Celebration,* in which Andrew stood locked outside his yard and cried for his mother.

11. *The March on Russia* (London: Samuel French, 1989), 30. All quotations are from this edition.

12. Actually, she is divorcing her husband and switching to the Independent Party at the present time of the play.

13. For an insightful discussion of the role of ritual in Storey's work, see Hutchings, especially 17–25.

14. See my dissertation, "The Novels and Plays of David Storey: New Solutions in Form and Technique," Stanford University, 1978; and "The Central Event in David Storey's Plays," *Theatre Journal* 31 (1979): 210–20.

ARTISTS IN PLAY

Ruby Cohn

Artists are notoriously difficult to dramatize, as opposed to satirize or parody. Thus, Aristophanes could stage Aeschylus and Euripides as bickering boasters in *The Frogs*, and Molière in the *Impromptu de Versailles* presents himself as a nervous Nellie, but Shakespeare in *Pericles* restricts Gower to a narrative function. Despite this Western heritage of recalcitrance to artists in the theatre, contemporary English playwrights have been remarkably hospitable to them. Tom Stoppard lampoons Joyce and Tzara in *Travesties*. Howard Brenton admires Shelley and even Byron in *Bloody Poetry*, and Adrian Mitchell praises Blake in *Tyger*. John Arden contrasts three kinds of poet—Merlin, Taleisin, and Aneurin—in *The Island of the Mighty*, and he mocks himself in *The Bagman*. *Total Eclipse*, an early play of Christopher Hampton, focuses on Rimbaud and Verlaine, but several refugee Central European writers people his *Tales from Hollywood*. Edward Bond contrasts the bourgeois Shakespeare, the feudal Basho, and the working-class John Clare as writers in their respective plays. Other contemporary English playwrights invent fictional writers: John Osborne in *West of Suez*, Simon Gray in *The Common Pursuit* and *Hidden Laughter*, David Hare in *Map of the World*, Peter Nichols in *Piece of my Mind*, and Harold Pinter fashions a trio in *No Man's Land*. David Mercer, Yorkshire-born like David Storey, composed a television trilogy about a fictional Nobel Prize novelist. Storey himself belongs to the inventors, and, an art school graduate himself, he stages not only verbal but visual artists.

Storey's first dramatic protagonist, Arnold Middleton, punctuates anecdotes of catastrophe with the confession: "You know, I've always had the ambition to be a writer. The things I'd write about would be fairly rhetorical in manner" (260).[1] Middleton's first sentence is a weary cliché, but his second sentence posits a curiously skew connection between subject and predicate. "Things" is not only the subject of Arnold's sentence but the promise of subject matter for writing; yet *"fairly* rhetorical in manner" is sheer style. To leap from Arnold to his creator, it is by style that David Storey has distinguished his own plays, grouping them as poetic naturalism, traditional literary plays, and overt stylization (Ansorge, 32). But if subject were to dictate the grouping, Storey's drama bifurcates into his realistic North Country family plays, on the one hand, and his several fragile communities, on the other (tent workmen, asylum inmates, rugby team members, seventeenth-century army units, and life class art students). Critics (including myself) tend to favor these undramatic dramas of community, which are "rhetorical in manner" and symbolic in resonance.

With one main exception. *Life Class* (1974) has elicited small praise, despite Lindsay Anderson's direction and a cast studded with Alan Bates, Bob Peck, and Brian Glover. (Harold Hobson, exceptionally, pronounced the play "a blazing masterpiece.") *Life Class* deserves close examination as the most explicit rendition of a pervasive if minor Storey theme—the role of the modern artist—and William Hutchings alone has scrutinized the play through that lens, but we differ on certain key points.

Storey first consigned his concern with the role of the modern artist to fiction, in his novel *A Temporary Life*, which preceded *Life Class* by a year. The protagonist of the novel, like that of the play, teaches a life class in an art school, whose principal in both works is a non-smoking miser obsessed with diet and digestion. In the novel, students not only draw from a live model, but they also sculpt in clay, and telltale fingerprints on the model's body disclose their extracurricular activities. Unlike the dramatic character, the protagonist-narrator of the novel actually paints, and he also responds sympathetically to the creation of his colleague who manipulates lightbeams. He is aware that contemporary artists work with events: "There are no artefacts of any sort. . . . They don't make objects any more" (90). However, he has a different name and a more active temperament than the corresponding dramatic character, refusing to theorize about art. (The only onomastic carryover from novel to play is Mathews, transferred from a sympathetic working-class student to the most philistine student of the life class on stage.) More central than art in the novel is the assault upon the protagonist of the ruthless rising bourgeoisie. Finally, the first-person narrator-protagonist salvages a simple life, however temporary, from the several pretensions of art.

Less ambitious socially but more tightly focused dramatically, the play *Life Class* is set in the eponymous life class of an art school. With good will, one might view the eight life class students—five men and three women—as "artists," and that term is attractive to the four faculty members—all middle-aged men. The word "artist" is heard most often in the speech of Storey's protagonist, Allott, self-described as a leader of the avant-garde. Actually, Allott's artistic stance wavers, but schematic attitudes toward art are embodied by others; the loathsome headmaster Foley preaches classicism; the commercial designer Philips espouses passionate daring; the student Catherine is aware that "study of natural objects isn't very popular today" (162), and the student Saunders seeks "something dispassionate in human nature" (221). The other students accuse Saunders of talking, looking, and smelling like Allott; together they taunt him: "*He is Allott!*" To some extent, they are correct, even though Saunders eventually betrays Allott. The student, like the teacher and unlike his fellow-students, *thinks* about his art, and he tends to verbalize those thoughts in comparable abstractions. Although Allott and Saunders both praise impersonal art, we witness their respective very personal reactions to rejection by a woman, Allott by his (offstage) wife and Saunders by the (very much onstage) model of the life class.

As a member of the avant-garde in the mid-1970s, Allott no longer draws or paints, and, extolling the artistry in events, he sounds like a conceptual artist as well as a happener: ". . . the contemporary artist creates his work out of the experience—the events as well as the objects—with which he's surrounded in his day-to-day existence"

(188). Yet Allott is so addicted to epigrams that he sometimes enunciates verities that sound curiously classical in the mouth of a self-proclaimed revolutionary: "What is true will last" (167), "All true art is impersonal" (198). More often, Allott inclines toward Romantic tenets, such as organicism: "Unless you are constantly relating the specific to the whole, Mooney . . . a work of art can never exist" (176). "The problem, Catherine . . . isn't to pin-point . . . nor even to isolate . . . it's to incorporate everything that is happening out there into a single homogenous whole" (184). Or he evokes anti-utilitarian inspiration: "we are life's musicians . . . its singers . . . and what we sing is wholly without meaning" (176–77). "Feeling creates its own form, form its own feeling" (191). Moreover, Allott reiterates the outworn Romantic belief: "The artist, after all, has no real life outside his work" (188). On the other hand, Allott sometimes speaks disparagingly of art as a substitute for life. Insisting that his students draw scrupulously from the nude model, he himself prefers to pontificate about art.

Storey himself does not lecture about art, but he has nevertheless issued a statement about the art of drama: "The purely literal level [of drama] has to work first. And perhaps work only at that level" (Ansorge, 35). Although Storey has a fine arts degree and presumably is well acquainted with schools of art, credibility falters at the literal level of *Life Class*; how and why should a conceptual artist teach a life class? Even more troubling at the literal level is Allott's basic misconception of happenings, which sought to dissolve the distinction between actor and audience. Allott's onstage happening, if we can call it that, preserves the traditional divorce between actors and onlookers. And it is not carefully conceived, like those of Allan Kaprow (in which I happen to have participated). Allott's happening rushes on its own momentum after that instructor offers to pose for his life class. The offer itself seems like an escapist ploy by Allott, who has been abandoned by his wife, ridiculed by the duet of his colleague Philips and his student Mathews, and confronted with two students about to come to blows.

No sooner does Allott volunteer to pose than the bellicose Mathews enthusiastically precedes him to the platform, undressing as he mounts. Urged on by another male student, decried by the women students, resisted by the nude model, Mathews appears to rape that model. Unlike the invisible events in many Storey plays, this violent scene happens center-stage, and in the heat of the moment we are scarcely aware of Allott's spectatorial passivity at what proves to be a simulated rape. Not only does the instructor fail to intervene, he reduces the event to aesthetics, and, after regretting the inevitable personal element in art, Allott directs his class to "return to the job in hand . . . I to instruct, you to be instructed" (227). On the complaint of "impersonal" Saunders, however, Allott is discharged by the hypocritical headmaster Foley.

At the literal level, rape in a life class—real or simulated—is as difficult to credit as a live cadaver in an anatomy class. What is not difficult to credit is Storey's own preoccupation with the boundary between art and life. Storey may have transferred that preoccupation to his protagonist, and reviewers were divided on how much sympathy to accord Allott, a name that encapsulates possible puns on allot, all out, or a lot. As originally played by Alan Bates, that master of the polysemic pause (in, for example, plays by Pinter or Gray), the artist's arrogant brilliance elicited admiration, and yet Storey seems to me anti-Allott. As Stoppard travesties Tzara's Dada in *Travesties*, Storey travesties esthetes and happenings in *Life Class*—but more ponderously, and far, far less affectionately.

Life Class traces Allott's several failures.[2] A self-proclaimed artist, he disdains its several media. A teacher of embryonic artists, he expresses scorn both for them and their work—"Leonardos" (166). At the beginning of the play Allott treats the student Saunders like a servant, asking him to hang up his hat and coat, and to chalk off the platform. In themselves these tasks are harmless, but they are followed by the instructor's barbs at a student couple, and then by a generalization about the whole class: "All these *aficionados*—myopic . . . disingenuous . . . uninspired—are images of youth no longer: pubescent excrescences on the cheeks of time" (161–62). What may at first be interpreted as banter grows increasingly hostile as Allott continues to vilify the students and their drawings, sometimes in Latin or a Latinate lexicon. Although Allott addresses the male students by their surnames, he patronizes the women with Christian names.

Although he claims impartiality in the stage skirmish of the sexes, his sexism is consistent: "You could say that women have never had the *consciousness* to become artists—there are exceptions but I mean as a general rule" (181). He is sardonic, too, about lower class art: "The education of the working class of course is still something of an anomaly" (181).

Obsessed with his own problems, Allott shows no consideration for his students. He leaves a blot on Catherine's drawing, and he does not object to Mathews's gossip about the model or the headmaster. He allows Mathews to collapse with fatigue as he draws him, but when the instructor's pad is examined, "There's nothing there." Finally, it is Allott's offer to act as a model that prompts Mathews to behave pornographically at the expense of the real model. Far from regretting his irresponsibility, Allott indulges in self-pity to his students. To his colleague Abercrombie, he boasts of refusing to barter with the headmaster, and to the headmaster he brags: "I've achieved some of my best work, I think, in here" (236). The whole play—especially the startling Storey climax of a simulated rape—gives him the lie.

Although Allott spurns the traditional materials of the artist, he indulges himself in the materials of another art—words for verse, which we hear in performance. To the amused admiration of the students, Allott composes cynical quatrains about love. While Allott is absent from the studio, Mathews and Philips read aloud his jingle of self-pity, and this prepares us for the more guarded self-pity, which Allott seeks to conceal when he leaves the life class, perhaps for life: "My next work may be something altogether less commendable . . . That's to say, more . . . substantial . . . if not altogether more extravagant than what I appeared to have achieved today . . . I shall have to see . . . sans means . . . sans wife . . . sans recognition who's to know what I . . . what I might rise to . . . " (234–35). Such self-pity precludes our own.

Neither before nor after *Life Class* was Storey to focus a play so centrally—and overexplicitly—on the delicate balance between art and life. His other artist figures are confined to his North Country family plays, beginning with *The Restoration of Arnold Middleton* (1959, but not produced until 1967). In that first Storey foray into drama, it is a very small family—the titular protagonist, his wife Joan, and her mother Edie. And the art aspired to is very embryonic indeed. Yet I believe that it is crucial to an interpretation of the play, which was originally entitled *To Die with the Philistines*, ending on Arnold's suicide.

William Hutchings has admirably summarized the links between *Middleton* and *Life Class*:

> In each, the protagonist is a teacher whose marriage is failing, whose students are . . . unappreciative, whose values and beliefs are not shared . . . by those around him, and whose recourse becomes an increasingly untenable withdrawal into his subject and a cynical disparagement (often in doggerel) of the outside world (60).

But whereas Allott has achieved some recognition as an artist, Middleton is not taken seriously as a writer.

Arnold Middleton is a history teacher who strews both home and classroom with miscellaneous artefacts of the past. Since his wife keeps an obsessively orderly house, the arrival of a suit of armor signals the playlong marital tension. From Arnold's first appearance, literally barking, he seems to be seriously maladjusted. After the canine performance, he treats his mother-in-law to an enactment of stamping his pupils into oblivion: "*He growls and roars as he drives the imaginary child into the floor*" (204). Then husband and wife quarrel about the visible suit of armor, which he claims is a gift for his parents, whose visit is expected. Glaringly anachronistic, the armor is at once an emblem of the chivalry that Arnold lacks, and the past for which he apparently yearns. With tensions high, the little family go together to the cinema—and return drunk. Increasingly, mother and daughter vie for Arnold's affection, and finally for his home.

Act 2 consists of Arnold's party with his colleagues (and an improbable student) whom he insults in a drunken rage. During his absence from the stage-room, his wife Joan maintains that her husband is God, and her mother drunkenly denies that Arnie wants her to leave their household. The next morning Joan invites Arnold himself to leave, but he refuses, hoping instead to go mad: "The insights that irrationality brings. . . . Cleavages. Cracks. Fissures. Openings. Some little aperture of warmth and light" (264). But no openings are visible in the next scene a few days later, with Arnold's artefacts absent from the "immaculate" living-room. There remains, however, a fissure in Arnie's mind, which seems to be associated with his mother-in-law, whom he has perhaps seduced, and whose existence he has started to deny. After again insulting colleagues, after assenting to his mother-in-law's seemingly voluntary offer to leave their household, Arnold labors through the birth of some unnamed agony in his head. Finally, with his wife's support, Arnold Middleton is restored—to the placid middle tone literalized in his name.

Not an artist, this boozer in anger is nevertheless an embryonic poet. At school, Arnold has composed a play in quatrains about Robin Hood, whom Arnold pronounces "a refugee . . . from the proper world" (212). Arnold woos his mother-in-law with a quatrain and insults his wife with a limerick. Drunk, he pours out nonsense quatrains, and drunkenly out of character his wife recites a moving poem—author unnamed—on the birth and death of love, which contrasts markedly with Arnold's facile quatrains and limericks. When Arnold seeks refuge in madness, however, he recites a longer poem, about a mother who urges her so to submerge himself in "the elemental forces / Which govern you and me," rather than in the mediocrity of his father. The elemental force of Arnold's lyric shades Middleton's restoration with irony, but the more immediate reaction to his own poem is Arnold's flippant couplet of self-blame:

> Oh. Oh. Oh.
> When I was young, when I was young,
> There were so many things I should have done. (88)

The wild, inventive, and rebellious Arnold seems to depart with his mother-in-law, whereas his wife dominates the restoration of middle-toned immaculacy. In this neo-Romantic conflict between wild art and domestic order, restoration is accomplished by the destruction of the embryonic artist.[3]

We never learn the geographic location of the Middleton living-room, but we know that Arnold hasn't seen his North Country working-class parents in years. The three sons of Northern working-class parents

in *In Celebration* (1969, dedicated to Storey's parents) make a point of
returning to the family home to celebrate their parents' fortieth wedding
anniversary. Educated to succeed, they have apparently fulfilled their
parents' ambitions: "Getting these three into the world, setting them up
in life" (35). Sons of a coal miner, the youngest Steven is a teacher, the
middle one Colin is a labor mediator, but the oldest Andrew has given
up his law practice to be an artist. Although his (offstage) painting may
be abstract—"not a sign of human life" (26)—Andrew's lashing tongue
would serve a barrister rather than the solicitorship for which he
trained. It is Andrew who sneers at the brothers' supposed
accomplishments, including his own art.

As a child, Steven showed the most promise, and later he hoped
to be a writer. During the play several characters inquire about his
book, which is once called an "artistic endeavor." But Steven has
abandoned his book, and after the family's offstage celebration, this
man in his mid-thirties lies in bed and cries like a child. Spurred by
Steven's sobs, Andrew analyzes their family: "Forty years of my
father's life for a lady like my mother, . . . for getting her with child at
the age of eighteen . . . on the back of which imprudence we have borne
all our lives, labouring to atone for her sexuality. . . . We—*we*—are the
inheritors of nothing . . . totems . . . has-beens, wash-outs,
semblances . . . a pathetic vision of a better life" (74–75). Andrew has
found the vision so hollow that he has sought escape in art. Steven,
with four children, sticks to his teaching, but he is plagued with
nightmares. Only the middle son Colin has adjusted to the class for
which his education has prepared him.

Their father, bewildered by Andrew's post-celebration outburst,
worries that the accusatory voice might waken his wife, but Steven
broods about the brothers' "crushing, bloody sense of
injury . . . inflicted, as he says, by wholly innocent hands" (77). Yet
Andrew does not view the maternal hands as *wholly* innocent, and his
brothers fear that he may terminate the celebration in vengeful
laceration of their mother. At the last, however, Andrew limits his
vengeance to a personal question, which he does not press upon his
mother. Although Steven jokes that they'd all be artists if they were as
maniacal as Andrew, the oldest brother actually views his abstract art as

a liberation from his predicament—"Not a sign of human life"—
welcoming its very insecurity.

Richard Cave faults Storey for relying on Andrew as he did on
Allott "to articulate and explain the theme" (138), but the theme is
explicitly articulated in neither play. Allott's preaching and practice of
art (sometimes at odds) are implicitly condemned in *Life Class*, but in
the earlier *In Celebration* art is secondary to the family and class
conflicts that dissolve in compassion—at least for the moment.

So, too, in *The Farm* (1973), where compassion is diluted. The
crusty hard-drinking patriarch of this play is a farmer, and of his four
children only one is a son. As the male heir, Arthur is a disappointment
to his father, but he is the darling of his mother who believes him to be
a poet: "Thought he was bloody Shakespeare before he'd even opened
his bloody mouth" (333). Unlike his three sisters, Arthur has fled from
the farm, returning occasionally and surreptitiously when in need of
money. On the day of the play, however, he returns to announce his
prospective marriage—to an ex-actress twice his age, with two
children. To his sisters, mother, and finally father, one by one, Arthur
communicates his matrimonial intention. He has, moreover, brought his
fiancée to the nearby town, with the intention of introducing her to the
family. Although the family dress up for the meeting, the bride-to-be
never appears, and Arthur explains: "I brought her here . . . hoping that
time might have changed, if not your character, at least your
manner . . . It seems that nothing's got better . . . if anything, it's got far
worse. I don't know why I troubled even to think of coming back"
(349). Livid with disappointment, the father accuses the son of
hastening him toward the grave. The next morning Arthur flees before
anyone is up, but the play ends on laughter as the old patriarch
welcomes an acquaintance of his youngest daughter to the family
breakfast. Perhaps "nothing's got better," but Arthur fails to appreciate
the warmth of family meals on the farm.

For a farm family, the members are curiously intellectual. Even
the scornful patriarch interjects polysyllables between his "bloody"
tattoo—paradox, immortalize, clandestine, octogenarian, brontosaurus.
His wife undertakes extramural studies in sociology and psychology.
The older sisters Wendy and Jenny are avid readers. Young Brenda is a

political radical, who composes aphorisms on public posters, but in the privacy of her room she dedicates herself to continuous prose, which her mother considers lewd. Incontestably, however, the family artist is Arthur—sometimes called Art. Although his sisters refer to him as "poor old Arthur," Wendy asks whether he is still writing poetry. "Yeh," is the shrugging answer. Despised by his father—lying on his back . . . composing bloody sonnets" (333)—Arthur is also misunderstood by his doting mother, who expects poetry to pay—"Did it sell well, then, the poem?" (326).

The poem has not sold well, but it *was* printed, and with some effort Arthur recites it for his mother—and us. Entitled "Evening," the brief free verse lovers' dialogue ends on a faint promise of warmth. By the end of the play, however, Arthur's mother has found an older poem by her son. Without a title, it poignantly commemorates a brief human impact upon the earth. Earlier, Arthur's sister Jenny recalls one editor's verdict on his poems—"a parody of Yeats" (339). There are worse poets to parody, and Arthur's two lyrics are redolent of turn-of-the-century symbolism, with a harder edge. It is not as a poet but as a man that Storey's Arthur lacks promise; torn between conflicting ambitions of father and mother, ill suited to farm life but unadaptable to any other, he seeks love outside the farm that nurtures it in its own rough way.

With *Life Class*, composed the year after *The Farm*, Storey temporarily halted his run of artists and would-be artists whose names start with the letter A—Arnold, Andrew, Arthur, and Allott.[4] It seems probable that they wrestle with problems that have afflicted their creator: Arnold smooths over the fissure of an irrationality that might prove creative, smothering the embryonic artist in himself. Andrew escapes from philistinism to an art that does not demand his commitment, whereas Arthur remains committed to his poetry but is unable to function in any practical world. In Allott, Storey creates an artist whose dedication has trickled down to discourse; at once self-aggrandizing, self-pitying, and socially irresponsible, Allott weights Storey's *Life Class* too ponderously toward theory. But he seems to have freed Storey himself to pay only cursory attention to artists in two later plays.

Early Days (1980), written for Ralph Richardson, inspired a memorable performance of the old actor. Richardson gloried in the role of a lovable old rogue, but the character of Sir Richard Kitchen, retired politician, is also related to Storey's other volatile, old disempowered men—Shaw of *In Celebration*, Jack and Harry of *Home*, and the patriarchal Slattery of *The Farm*. Having played mad Jack in *Home*, Richardson enthusiastically entered his next phase in Storey's saga, which hovered between exhibitionist paranoia and the *role* of one so afflicted. A trial to his daughter and her outwardly respectable husband, Kitchen is intermittently affectionate to his granddaughter Gloria.

It is Gloria's fiancé Steven who is the artist of *Early Days*. Like Arthur of *The Farm*, Steven is a poet, and the one lyric we hear—on the Biblical Samson—recalls Arthur's verse in its free meter, run-on lines, and reaches toward a metaphysical statement. Like Arthur, Steven is planning to marry although he cannot support a wife. And like Arthur, too, Steven is assailed by a pragmatic patriarchal figure: "No artist in this world can afford to be married. Marriage is a commitment to life. Art is a commitment to self-aggrandizement" (36). Apparently rambling, Kitchen declares climactically: "Beating and hardship will rid this young man of his poetical aspiration" (37). He may be right, but Steven was born into a class that has suffered no hardship and will suffer no beating. He functions in the plot by finding the old man when he eludes his caretaker. Unable to recite his own poems, Steven laughs at Kitchen's spontaneous risqué quatrains. In their brief conversation Steven insists that "people's lives can be changed to the good" (45), but Kitchen is obdurately pessimistic. In this character sketch of a once-active old man who rages against his dying, the idealistic young poet is a momentary intrusion.

In Storey's *The March on Russia* (1989), a middle-aged man becomes a writer almost by accident. As all reviewers noted, *The March* is a celebration twenty years later. The North Country parents, in their late eighties, are celebrating their sixtieth wedding anniversary, but unlike the planned festivity in the earlier play, this occasion is improvised. The retired coal-miner and his wife, their friends long dead, pass their days between television and crossword puzzles. Colin, their university lecturer son, has driven up from London but has not announced his presence to his two sisters, who arrive separately, also without informing one another. As in the earlier play, there is greeting and bickering, complaint and nostalgia, but tea has displaced alcohol as the beverage of predilection. Most importantly, this old couple resembles its predecessor in educating their children: "We gave you all an education. The best there was to have" (46). Yet no one sleeps well in this seaside bungalow, purchased for the old couple by Colin, who has accrued a tidy sum from his book *The Last Evangelist.*

As in the earlier play, the children divide on the parental desire to thrust them into the middle class. This time it is the sisters who differ, and Colin questions the sexist code whereby boys languish uncuddled in their infancy. One sister seems happy with her teacher husband and their two children, whereas the other, in the throes of a divorce, has a career as a town councillor. Colin has been prey to unexplained terrors—"gripped by a dementia which even now I couldn't describe" (30). Unlike his predecessor Steven of *In Celebration*, however, Colin has been able to write a book, in spite of neurosis.

For those familiar with *In Celebration*, the recognizable echoes are at once reassuring and deceptive—reassuring that Storey remains true to his subject matter, and that he can provide scope for the exhilarating skills of Constance Chapman and Bill Owen, again undertaking the parental roles (as well as for the scrupulous director-designer team of Lindsay Anderson and Jocelyn Herbert). But although *The March on Russia* inevitably recalls *In Celebration*, the two plays are quite different in tone; the vengeful lacerations of the one modulate to an elegiac compassion within the family. Although there are traumas in the later play as in the earlier, accusations are muted.

In *The March on Russia* Colin cannot control his occasional dementia, and his father cannot control his occasional kleptomania. Storey does not offer any simple cause-and-effect psychiatric diagnosis for either affliction, but the dramatic fact stares us in the face. Colin—wholly dissimilar from the bearer of that name in the earlier play—does not link his malady with his book, *The Last Evangelist.* A specialist in seventeenth-century English history, Colin has written a biography of nineteenth-century Jonathan Wroe. Born into the same working-class background as Colin, but one hundred twenty years earlier, Wroe had foreseen "the despoilation, [sic] the conformity, the dilution of feeling" of the Industrial Revolution, and he had waged a violent vendetta against it, "blowing up bridges, setting fire to mills, de-railing trains." Wroe and his mother were finally hanged "a few feet apart, and face to face" (21).

Colin never refers to his biography of The Last Evangelist with the word "art," but the passion he invests and the enthusiastic response he arouses are not unrelated to art. Finally, however, *The March on Russia* is not about Colin but his parents. His art is incidental to Storey's drama about an old couple shuffling toward death, mixing memory with confusion in a foreign world. Storey's play closes on a question posed by a Russian nobleman, who was perhaps encountered, perhaps imagined by Colin's father, the now childlike North Country patriarch. The question is relevant to Storey's art and his artists: "Oh where are we going to, my love?"

Notes

1. My discussion is confined to published Storey plays. Page numbers refer to their Penguin editions, with the exception of *The March on Russia*, London: French, 1989. References to *A Temporary Life* cite the Jonathan Cape edition.

2. I share Hutchings's belief that Storey committed his own aesthetic preoccupations to *Life Class*, but I take a far less sympathetic view of Allott, who seems to me both arrogant and self-contradictory.

3. Hutchings quotes Storey himself on Middleton: "He's restored to a very conventional bourgeois life, and that's really awful, a sort of living death" (55).

4. In the unpublished *Phoenix* (1985) Alan Ashcroft is the artistic director of a theater. See Hutchings 182–83 for details.

Works Cited

Ansorge, Peter. "The Theatre of Life." *Plays and Players* 20 (September 1973).

Cave, Richard Allen. *New British Drama in Performance on the London Stage, 1970–1985*. Gerrards Cross: Colin Smythe, 1987.

Hutchings, William. *The Plays of David Storey: A Thematic Study*. Carbondale: Southern Illinois University Press, 1988.

A PORTRAIT OF THE ARTIST AS CHARACTER IN THE PLAYS OF DAVID STOREY

Susan Rusinko

A painter, novelist, playwright, with a working-class background that includes professional rugby, Storey draws on his experience to dramatize the situation of the artist vis-à-vis his origins. His concerns range from the incipient (more accurately, stillborn) longings on the part of a schoolteacher who finds himself trapped in a stifling middle-class situation that goes nowhere (*The Restoration of Arnold Middleton*) to the naturalistic lyricism of footballers (*The Changing Room*) and of workers erecting a tent for a wedding party (*The Contractor*), or the disconnected dialogue of elderly residents at a mental hospital (*Home*), and the fragmented wanderings of a senile, once successful politician (*Early Days*). Although in only one drama (*Life Class*) does Storey attempt art and artists as his main subject, he has a progression of characters in a number of plays who in varying degrees illustrate his ongoing concern with the problems of the artist as he emerges from a working-class background. His emergence follows a pattern which begins with a desire on the part of parents for a better life than their own for their children and with education as a means to that improved life. The pattern continues with middle-class professional success and eventual alienation from both working-class and middle-class pretensions. Arnie Middleton, the first of Storey's potential artists, has stopped with the first two stages: education and a profession as

89

teacher. Now trapped by his circumstances, he can only remember
having wanted all of his life to be a writer. In succeeding plays, Storey
follows Arnie with Steven and Andrew Shaw in *In Celebration*; Allott
and his art students in *Life Class*; Arthur Slattery in *The Farm*; and,
finally, Steven in *Early Days*. Progressively, the artist-characters
represent stages in the development of the artist from his working-class
roots.

In an interview with *Plays and Players* magazine, Storey
described his art in terms of "three broad categories of plays" which he
writes: "One is what you might call poetic naturalism along the lines of
The Contractor and *The Changing Room*." Another is "the kind of very
traditional literary play like *In Celebration* and *The Farm*." The third is
the "more overtly stylistic play like *Home* and *Cromwell*." Central to
his plays, Storey asserts, is "the kind of activity [which] unifies people
in a way that perhaps they don't get unified anywhere else."[1]

The family is one of the "unifying activities" Storey uses in his
plays; there is also the rugby team, the construction gang, the art class,
or the mental institution. The most recurrent of these social units is the
family, and the central players in the family are sons and daughters
(especially the former) whose emotional injuries caused by breaks with
their roots have left them scarred or in conflict with themselves or each
other. Although successful in business, in a profession, or in the arts,
they may find the past has already taken its toll, as in the case of Arnie
in *The Restoration of Arnold Middleton*. Or, as with Steven in *Early
Days*, the past is no longer a concern. Between these two extremes can
be found the sons in *In Celebration* and *The Farm* and the student-
artists in *Life Class* who are caught in the process of change.

It is mostly in what Storey regards as his "traditional literary
plays" that the artist—as writer or painter—appears as a character.
Usually the growth of the artist is stunted early on or is at least
temporarily arrested by emotional or intellectual conflicts generated by
his alienation from the unifying sensibility of his roots and by a
subsequent inability to find a substitute for that loss. In whatever roles
they assume or however minimal those roles, Storey's artists are shaped
by the same conflicts and frustrations that accompany the aspirations of
the non-artist community. These aspirations begin with the parental

desire to improve the life of a son or daughter by means of higher education. The alienation from their roots caused by that education creates deep divisions within families, among friends, and, perhaps most importantly, within the characters themselves.

The treatment of the artist in Storey's plays has a beginning of sorts in Arnie Middleton (in *The Restoration of Arnold Middleton*) who is not an artist nor whose restoration, despite the ironic title of the play, is assured or, perhaps, even suggested. Yet the imaginative forms that his rebellion takes suggest those of a thwarted artist. A history schoolteacher, he derives small satisfactions from pampering by the many women who have shaped his life, from the staging of school plays, and from his obsessive collection of historical mementoes with which he clutters both classroom and home. The most recent of these, a suit of medieval armour, is delivered to his home one day, much to the consternation of his wife who keeps a spotless, dust-free home. This latest addition proves an embarrassment to his school principal, when Arnie unwittingly drags it in behind the principal who is conducting a school assembly.

Over time, Arnie's small satisfactions have developed into escapes that take the form of traditional English language games by means of which he lashes out at those closest to him. Arnie's games are a time-honored English schoolboy tradition (e.g., Tom Stoppard's *Dogg's Hamlet/Cahoot's Macbeth*), often not shed in adulthood. In a manner reminiscent of John Osborne's Jimmy Porter and Simon Gray's Butley, Arnie denounces a fellow teacher as a pompous boor whose "otiose circumlocutions no longer [are] sufficient to conceal the cringing, shivering coward within. . . ."[2] He uses limericks in mockery of himself: "There are things in your life/Not even your wife/Would think could pass through your brain./But give me a light/And I'll show you a sight/That would turn even Satan insane." (RAM, 31) Arnie's verbal abuse sometimes takes on Ionesco-like overtones: "If your Bob doesn't pay our Bob that bob that your Bob owes our Bob, our Bob will give your Bob a bob on the nose." (RAM, 37) He parodies Blake: "Tiger, tiger, burning bright, /In the forests of the night, /If you see a five pound note/Then take my tip and cut your throat." (RAM, 37) In a climactic scene, all control deserts him at a party at which he becomes drunk and verges on the edge of a nervous collapse. His mother-in-law, who lives with them and has been engaged in Lawrentian competition with her daughter, emerges from his bedroom dressed in his pajamas.

The next morning, reminiscing, he mentions his always wanting to be a writer, "fairly rhetorical in manner." (RAM, 82) The moment to do something, he feels has arrived, "yet it refuses to emanate." (RAM, 87) He looks for fissures that might let in some warmth and light. Sadly examining the suit of armour and choosing a patch on the wall to rub, he addresses that patch with a poetic reminiscence of his youth. The story, a negative tribute to his mother and his aunts, is one that recurs in other Storey plays:

> When I was young, my mother said to me:
> Never drown but in the sea—
> Rivers, streams and other dilatory courses
> Are not contingent with the elemental forces
> Which govern you and me—and occasionally your father—
> So remember, even if the means are insufficient, rather
> Than die in pieces, subside by preference as a whole,
> For disintegration is inimical to the soul
> Which seeks the opportunity or the chances
> To die in the circumstances
> Of a prince, a saviour, or a messiah—
> Or something, perhaps, even a little higher—
> You and me and several of your aunties,
> On my side, though working-class, have destinies
> Scarcely commensurate with our upbringing;
> I hope in you we are instilling
> This sense of secret dignities and rights
> —Not like your father's side, the lights
> Of which I hope we'll never see again,
> Who have, I'm afraid, wet blotting-paper for a brain.
>   (Pause.)
> 'Please, please my son,
> Don't fail me like your father done.' (RAM, 87)

Arnie's brief autobiography contains several recurrent themes in Storey's plays: the alienated son, the sense of disintegration, and the Lawrentian female as the cause of both. In a life shaped early by mothers and aunts, the latest females in his life are his wife, Joan, and his mother-in-law who lives with the couple. A combination of dependence on and escape from them causes Arnie's disintegration. In the play, Joan, doting wife and obsessive housewife, has been getting the house in order for a visit from Arnie's parents, a visit canceled at the last minute. A party is held despite the aborted visit, after which Joan ejects her mother from their home.

The final scene of the play is reminiscent of Harold Pinter's *The Birthday Party*, in which Stanley, the pianist, is carted away, a sterilized version of himself. Joan has removed Arnie's artifacts, leaving Arnie, in keeping with the obsessively neat living room as the end of the play, cleared of the clutter of his life. Only the sword from the suit of armor remains, and he tells Joan that his sentence is very heavy. Bereft of his escapes into schoolboy games, he now faces "Rest. Recuperation . . . Work." (RAM, 102) His "restoration" seems complete.

In the tradition of post-World War II stage anti-heroes such as Jimmy Porter and Butley, Arnie seems to be a victim of his own progress. Whatever talent he may have possessed remains stillborn. There is only his statement that all his life he has desired to be a writer. He is, perhaps, Storey's strongest illustration of a description by Andrew Shaw (in *In Celebration*) of the individual (or artist): "Dead, Zombies. Killed by good intentions, administered by the ones above . . . Corpses."[3]

It is a large step from Arnie to the characters of Steven and Andrew Shaw in *In Celebration*. Unlike Arnie Middleton, the major characters—three sons—have carved out for themselves successful careers, according to parental expectations. The play's events grow from a return to their provincial home to celebrate their parents' fortieth wedding anniversary. The occasion provides Storey with an opportunity to develop in greater detail than in *The Restoration of Arnold Middleton* the shaping influence of the family on the artist. The women in Arnie's early life—his mother and aunts—do not appear in the play. In *In Celebration*, however, parents are characters and, although spared the embarrassment of a face-to-face confrontation, the mother becomes the center of the emotional storm that swirls in the Shaw household. Omitting the central event, dinner at a local hotel,

Storey stages his celebration-turned-exorcism in the family home
before and after the dinner, introducing a style that he polishes to a
near-brilliance in later plays, *The Contractor* and *The Changing Room*.

Steven—the youngest of the three sons and a teacher, father of
four children, and a writer—has seemingly fulfilled the expectations of
his parents. As a young boy, he had been the favorite of his parents
because he was the brightest. Yet he appears troubled, reluctant to say
much, in contrast with Colin and Andrew. Much of the early conversation revolves around his book, about whose subject and state of
completion there is much curiosity. Steven uncomfortably evades direct
answers to questions, only to admit, when pressed, that he has "packed
it in." (IC, 33) His frustrations do not, like Arnie's, take overt form.
When his father expresses a standard working-class wish to get half "of
what you get . . . and for doing twice as much, " Steven merely
responds with a bland comment, "It's got its drawbacks." (IC, 13) His
internalized pain, however, manifests itself in nightmares that cause
him to cry out in his sleep.

In a painful verbal battle among the males, after Mrs. Shaw has
gone to bed, accumulated hostilities erupt as Andrew, the eldest, spares
neither himself nor his parents in his bitter recriminations. He reveals
that when Steven was born, his mother had kept Colin with her, but had
farmed out himself (Andrew) to a neighbor. When most in need of his
mother, he was denied her love, that denial only one of an accumulation
of repressed antagonisms that have taken their toll on him.

Thus, it is Andrew whose alienation from his roots has most
affected his life. A successful lawyer, he has given up law in order to
become an abstract painter. Married and the father of children nearing
university age, he even has serious doubts about the merits of providing
them with higher education. He is bitter about

> labouring to atone for . . . what? The texts I've had to study.
> The exams I've had to . . . with that vision held perpetually
> before me; a home, a car, a wife . . . a child . . . a rug that
> didn't have holes in, a pocket that never leaked . . . I even
> married a Rector's daughter! (IC, 83)

Andrew's revenge on his past is to abandon law and become an
abstract painter in outright defiance of the parental values. In a form of

contempt that is reminiscent of Arnie Middleton's, the defiance is expressed in cruel mockery of his mother's and his wife's expectations regarding the subject of his painting: " . . . young ladies with no clothes on. . . ." (IC, 25) Instead, he remarks, " . . . lo and behold. Triangles. . . . Abstract. . . . Not a sign of human life." (IC, 26) Although by his own admission not a very good painter, he has progressed beyond Arnie and Steven in breaking both working-class (parental) and middle-class (wifely) expectations. He deals especially harshly with his mother's middle-class pretensions, calling attention to her pig-breeding origins. In Lawrentian fashion, he attacks the hypocrisy of his mother even as he identifies with the honesty of his miner-father.

In varying degrees, all three sons have difficulty in reconciling past and present. Colin, still finding satisfaction in his work, seems to have retained the closest ties to parents' ambitions for their sons' career successes. Even he, however, has difficulty in speaking about personal matters. Steven, like Arnie Middleton a teacher, has nightmares and has "packed in" his unfinished book. It is Andrew who has travelled the greatest distance in severing ties with the better life envisioned by his parents. But he carries scars and seems to be motivated more by bitterness than by artistic inspiration. He shares with James Joyce's Stephen Dedalus an identity as mocker and sneerer in his attempts to be free of all nets that would bind him.

The growth of the artist in Storey's plays seems, at best, only begun, as in *Life Class*, Storey's only play primarily about art and artists. Distinctive as Storey's dialectic on modern art, *Life Class* lacks the usual conflicts generated by family ties. Instructor, students, and administrators in an art school—soon, it is rumored, to be turned into an engineering school—indulge their varying theories of art in a situation that Storey has drawn from his own experience at the Slade School of Art in London. Through Allott, the instructor, Storey updates the trends in art, moving beyond the abstract art of Andrew Shaw to the latest fad, the happening. In allowing the total removal of distinctions between art and life, Allott, in effect, replaces art with life. He lectures: "No one of any consequence paints the human figure, for instance, any more . . . it's not even a discipline because, if you presented me with a straight line and told me that's what you saw—under the absurd license of modern illusionism—I'd have to accept it." Artists may be among the world's exploited, "but between us, we convene . . . celebrate, evoke, a work, which, whether we are aware of it or not, is taking place around us . . . ."[4]

In illustration of his theory, Allott allows the line between life and art to disappear, as a student and the model engage in sex. Later the act is disclosed to be a hoax, although at the time the reality was so strong that the consequence for Allott is dismissal from the school. Allott's immediate reaction to the episode is his admission that presenting his own experience—his impending divorce—"isn't all that repellent to me." ". . . it would no longer be, as it were, a work of art . . . merely . . . another aspect of a human being." (LC, 227) When the class returns to normality, he to instructing and the students to being instructed, Allott draws together the theories of art discussed up to this point in his comment that "no work of art is complete without a personal statement." Traditionally, the artist synthesizes "natural elements convened by man . . . whereas we, elements as it were of a work ourselves, partake of existence . . . simply by being what we are . . . expressions of a certain time and place, and class . . . defying . . . hope . . . defying anguish . . . defying, even, definition . . . ." We are "figures in a landscape . . . . Singing to no one's tune at all." (LC, 228)

Allott's theory regarding the public act as art follows much sniggering by the students at the teacher's lectures. They mock his remarks regarding the importance of proportion, his trite comments on the unconscious nature of artistic creation, or his idea that "what we sing is wholly without meaning . . . it exists, merely, because it is . . . The one significant distinction between the artist and the scientist, indeed, between him and all his fellow men . . . What the artist does is purposeless. That's its dignity . . . its beauty." (LC, 177)

Throughout the class, the students indulge in lewd comments about the model and become involved in amorous postures with each other or with the model. At one point a debate ensues about why women are so frequently the models and so infrequently the artists, the topic reminding the reader that Storey's artist-characters are predominantly male. Questions by students and replies by Allott are the means by which theories and immediate personal experiences intertwine in a travesty of the very basis of the artistic process. It is inevitable that the convincingly real sexual act, later proved to be a hoax, occurs.

In the absence of any unifying principle, even though there are the ties that could bind students in an art class, instructor, students, and staff seem separated from each other. Their common pursuit seems lacking in artistic ideals or principles. Individually and collectively, they converse and behave in ways reminiscent of Arnie Middleton's schoolboyish games. With the firing of Allott and the loose rumors regarding future directions of the school, Storey provides no integrating or renewing idea or event to fill the vacuum that has been created. At one point, one student even questions why Allott teaches art. Others enjoy insider jokes at his expense for his spending so much time in the "bog" (the lavatory) writing poems. In fact, Allott informs the students that he neither paints nor sculpts, being of the opinion that traditional art has had its day and that "the artist has been driven back . . . to creating his works, as it were, in public." (LC, 188) With his farewell handshakes, Allott issues a valedictory comment on the necessity by the artist of " . . . violation . . . disruption of prevailing values . . . re-integration in another form entirely." (LC, 235) Yet, the necessary reintegration has not begun to occur, and the reader/audience is left with the shards both of Allott's life as art teacher and of the various art theories encountered in the play.

Storey continues his progression of the artist in *The Farm*, in the character of Arthur Slattery, a young poet who returns unannounced to a home that is dominated by an educated mother and his three educated sisters. It is also a home in which Arthur's poetic aspirations, when he had lived there, had been encouraged by the women but sneered at by his father. Here three educated daughters have chosen to remain at home, and the mother follows her own upwardly mobile inclinations, rather than foisting them on her children. The daughters—Wendy, Jennifer, and Brenda, in order of age—have chosen to remain at home, even as each has followed her private ambitions. The two eldest are schoolteachers, and Brenda, an idealist, works in various unspecified causes. She occasionally entertains her working-class boy friend,

Albert, who, intimidated by the educated women, sneaks into the living room through a window after the others have retired for the night. Brenda, like Steven in the earlier play, has been writing a book for years. She is a free spirit in a family whose members are intensely involved in their respective interests and professions.

Mrs. Slattery occupies her time with classes in psychology and sociology, acknowledging her husband (to whom, like Mr. and Mrs. Shaw in *In Celebration*, she has been married forty years) mostly in the matter of sexual companionship. Only Mr. Slattery remains a farmer at the farm, and he seems to have accepted, although with gusty protestations, the self-determined ways of the women in his life. If Mr. Middleton is not a character in *The Restoration of Arnold Middleton* (nor is he important in Arnie's life) and if Mr. Shaw in *In Celebration* is a man of few words, Mr. Slattery more than makes up for them in the full characterization accorded him in *The Farm*.

In his battle to hold on to the little dignity left him, Slattery constantly bemoans the loss of working class virtues. In Lawrentian fashion, he has been left with only his drink and his proud insistence on the traditions that have disappeared from his farm. With uncommon eloquence, he vents his sense of betrayal on hearing of his son's impending marriage to an older woman. He refers to the pounding of his blood "Fit to bloody burst . . . Feel that . . . Go on. Like a bloody engine . . . Get to bloody work . . . Hand to the plough: never look back."[5] Yet he realizes, as do the women, that his denunciations are the last empty gestures of a defeated man. In the underlying realization of his defeat, he evokes sympathy and even acquires a small measure of tragic heroism in his lament for lost values.

When Arthur comes home, entering by the same means as does Albert—through a window—he announces to Wendy that he (twenty-one or two) is going to marry a woman over forty "with two kiddies." Intimidated, like Albert, by the reception he thinks his announcement would have, he has booked his fiancee into the local hotel until the next day when, having given advance notice, he would present her to the family. The presentation does not occur as, for reasons left unexplained, she suddenly leaves. Thus the action in the play consists of Arthur's uncomfortable reunion with the rest of the family members and their preparations for his fiancee's welcome.

Although the women have accommodated the occasional drunken verbal eruptions of Slattery, it is obvious that Arthur is embarrassed in the presence of his father, especially on the matter of his fiancee. Unlike Slattery, the women react positively to Arthur's independence in forging a life for himself away from the family. In particular, Jenny remembers him as the "quite vulnerable" member of the family about whose literary gifts they had often spoken glowingly. She remembers "typing out his poems and sending them to some magazine . . . who sent them back and said most of them were a parody of Yeats." (TF, 70)

Not having brought a copy of his only published poem (in a magazine whose subscribers number only two or three hundred), Arthur at one point acquiesces to his mother's request and recites a poem entitled "Evening." But the *tour de force* in the play is provided by an untitled poem which his mother finds in his room and which he reads to her just before his departure:

> What will be left? . . . A line of bone
> and of the brain
> little else but dust and stone . . .
> the frame
> of one thought leading to another . . .
> And of all the things he played—
> a father, and the game of lover . . .
> nothing; except the spot where one limb has stayed
> the dust, held back a space
> and in the earth a gesture
> maybe measures out the trace
> of flesh, of blood—a creature
> still to those who can
> recognize in this the emblem of a man. (TF, 90–91)

The effect of the poem—a paradoxical tribute to his father and an elegy to the eventual disintegration of all that his father's life represents—is that Arthur is able through his poetry to do that which he is unable to do in a face-to-face encounter with his unsympathetic father. Unable to respond to Slattery's bluster as do the women, Arthur does sense in his father the use of rage as his only defense against the assault of the modern world on the past. For Slattery is, much like the males in O'Casey's plays, a hero by default. He enjoys, for example, a certain vindication in railing against Mrs. Slattery for having excused Arthur's failing of school examinations as the natural condition of a "bloody genius." While he slaved his "bloody gut out . . . there he [Arthur] was, twiddling his bloody thumbs and rhyming bloody moon with June." (TF, 64) Unlike his educated mother and sisters who are able to hold their own with Slattery, Arthur is reduced to silence or only a few words by his father's majestic display of discontent. Of all the artists in Storey's plays, Arthur is in a de-ritualizing stage, perhaps a healthy beginning of his future as a poet. The aborted reunion with his family is a progress of sorts from Arnold Middleton who was unable to harness his desire to be a writer, Andrew Shaw whose mediocrity as an abstract artist may be partly the result of his bitterness, and Allott and students who are unable to reintegrate the broken shards of traditional art theories. Although Arthur has published only one poem, he is still working his way to a detachment from working-class roots and is finding a unifying sensibility in his poetry. Also, the family females have encouraged rather than stunted his progress.

Yet another poet, Steven, appears in Storey's 1980 play, *Early Days*. The future husband of the main character's granddaughter, he has published a slim volume of verse, from which he reads a poem entitled "Samson." The poem ends with the line, "Where do one's debris start?"[6] The line becomes a fitting metaphor for the life of Sir Richard Kitchen, born the son of a grocer and now a senile, retired Minister of Health. Around Kitchen Storey builds a drama about three generations who have realized the success that working-class parents have wished for their children.

Like Krapp of Samuel Beckett's play, Sir Richard in his final days erratically recalls the most enjoyable moments of a long life. These include a cottage at the end of a wood, trees, gypsies, free people, and, finally, Ellen his wife. As the debris from Sir Richard's life falls away, important joys stand out, even as he recognizes that all that remains is his return to "a handful of dust; a handful of chemicals with which I began, in a backstreet shop, in an industrial town. . . ."

(ED, 52) The poetry of young Steven and the Beckettian wanderings of the old man become one. Steven's poem is like Arthur Slattery's in its celebration of man despite all the accumulated debris of a lifetime.

In Steven's poem, Samson (betrayed by the Philistine, Delilah) is Storey's metaphor for the necessary disintegration that is the life process. (It is interesting to note here that the original title of *The Restoration of Arnold Middleton* was *To Die with the Philistines*.) Philistinism characterizes the aspirations of working-class mothers for their sons and, as well, of the rituals of middle-class achievers such as the teacher, lawyer, social worker, etc. It is the cause of the constant breaking down of personal relationships, especially in families and in the kind of community experienced briefly by an athletic team or a construction unit. It is demonstrated not only by the sons as they painfully break away, but by the fathers as well. Old Shaw, for example, remains for the most part silent in his pain, even as he begins to understand. Old Slattery, however, roars his protests to the family, even as he realizes the futility of his protestations. Allott, a surrogate father-figure to a new breed of artists is mocked by his students and fired by his employer. Finally, there is old Kitchen, son of a grocer and no longer working-class, whose poetic sense of life blends with young Steven's. His hair, like Samson's, has been shorn by the seductress, life, and by the success he has enjoyed.

For the disunifying process, work provides a temporary solution, or at least some "reassurance to life which it otherwise would not possess."[7] The time spent in playing contains that reassurance for a footballer. "It's when you are unable to play anymore that things become desperate."[8] Arnie Middleton, whose playing has been only an escape (not the reassuring work) and whose escape has been cut off by the Philistines, seems desperate. The post-Middleton characters-as-artists, however, insist on detachment, not merely escape, to realize a degree of their own kind of success. As Andrew Shaw tells his brother, Steven, "The kind of detachment —or even the kind of involvement— you're telling me about: very soon . . . is going to rip you wide apart. You can't be for this crummy world and at the same time be for your own psychic . . . spiritual . . . moral autonomy. . . . It is now the season of the locusts, and if you have anything to save then save it now. Grab it in both hands and run." (IC, 52)

Storey's recommendation to the artist involved in the process of disunity or deritualization is the "impersonal contribution" of work. He insists that all other solutions, including "political action or social commitment, " or highbrow ideas like those in the plays of "the new Cambridge group of playwrights such as Howard Brenton and David Hare, are ideas that "never become real."[9] Storey's sense of reality embraces the disunifying nature of life. His insistence on the necessity for a reassurance that the impersonal contribution of work provides— for footballers or artists—is comparable to that of Chekhov, whose characters, convening to sell a cherry orchard or living dull lives that are brightened briefly by the arrival of military officers and by longings for Moscow, must eventually settle down to work. The arrivals and departures that constitute the substance and style of a Chekhov play are not unlike Storey's theme of unity and dispersal or unlike his style (*In Celebration, The Changing Room, The Contractor*) of deemphasizing the main event in favor of the more complex inner situations surrounding that main event.

In addition to his naturalistic plays, Storey is an artist of what he has dubbed his overtly stylistic plays. *Early Days* and *Home*, in this tradition, are minimalist plays (like Harold Pinter's), in which an old man and four asylum mates, respectively, indulge in randomly associated words and fragmented silences, as they see their once active lives dwindle to primary essence. Both kinds of plays, however—the poetically naturalistic and the overtly stylistic—are beyond the bounds of this discussion and, therefore, are only alluded to. It is in Storey's third kind, the traditional literary play, that one can trace however tentatively, a progress of sorts from Arnie Middleton to the suffering Steven Shaw, the detached Andrew Shaw, the cynical Allott and students, the poetically articulate Arthur Slattery, and the published Steven of *Early Days*. All derive from Storey's own varied experiences as son, teacher, footballer, artist, and, finally, writer. Their conflicts and as yet unrealized aspirations may be seen as part of Storey's own development into the successful novelist and dramatist that he has become. There is, finally, Storey himself as artist of the stage. In his naturalistically poetic plays like *The Contractor* and *The Changing Room*, there is the poetry of life as lived by workers or footballers who unconsciously participate in the rhythms of language and action in a communal activity, the kind of activity from which the conscious artists detach themselves. Without aspiring to become artists, members of a construction crew or rugby team illustrate Allott's theory of convening, celebrating, and evoking an event in which "whether . . . [they] are aware of it or not, is taking place around . . . [them]." They are "figures in a landscape . . . hurtling through time . . . Singing to no one's tune at all." (LC, 228) They may be Storey's ultimate artist-heroes, even though they do not appear as artist-characters, as they sing effortlessly in their words and actions.

Notes

1.   Peter Ansorge, "The Theatre of Life," *Plays and Players* 20:12 (September 1973), 32.

2.   David Storey, *The Restoration of Arnold Middleton* (London: Jonathan Cape Ltd., 1967), 73. Subsequent quotations to be noted in text as RAM.

3.   David Storey, *In Celebration* (London: Jonathan Cape Ltd., 1969), 46. Subsequent quotations to be noted in text as IC.

4.   David Storey, *Life Class*, in *Early Days, Sisters and Life Class* (Harmondsworth: Penguin Books Ltd., 1980), 192-193. Subsequent quotations to be noted in text as LC.

5.   David Storey, *The Farm* (London: Jonathan Cape Ltd., 1973), 65-66. Subsequent quotations to be noted in text as TF.

6.   David Storey, *Early Days*, in *Early Days, Sisters and Life Class* (Harmondsworth: Penquin Books Ltd., 1980), 41. Subsequent quotations to be noted in text as ED.

7.   Ansorge, 35.

8.   Ansorge, 35.

9.   Ansorge, 32.

Works Cited

Ansorge, Peter. "The Theatre of Life, " *Plays and Players* 20:12 (September 1973): 32–36.

Storey, David. *Early Days, Sisters and Life Class*. Harmondsworth: Penguin Books, 1980.

———. *The Farm.* London: Jonathan Cape Ltd., 1980.

———. *In Celebration.* London: Jonathan Cape Ltd., 1969.

———. *Life Class.* In *Early Days, Sisters and Life Class*. Harmondsworth: Penguin, 1980.

———. *The Restoration of Arnold Middleton.* London: Jonathan Cape Ltd., 1967.

DAVID STOREY'S AESTHETIC OF "INVISIBLE EVENTS"

William Hutchings

Although David Storey is among the most acclaimed and innovative playwrights of his generation, and although his plays have on the whole received quite favorable reviews, a common reservation recurs in a number of them. It is typified by the comments of an American reviewer of *The Farm*, who remarked that

> although you discover certain things about these characters that you didn't know at the outset, you also discover that nothing has happened. . . . And in the theatre, something *ought* to happen. That . . . is what theatre *means*. But if [the play in question] isn't theatre exactly, it's an interesting something-or-other.[1]

Yet, however frequently such objections are voiced and however widely they are held, they are based on a conception of theatre that is not only restrictively narrow but also a century out-of-date—the equivalent of a belief that all contemporary poetry should rhyme and contain regular metrics, that all novels should contain a cleverly constructed and intricate intrigue, or that all music should have a hummable tune. By focusing the audience's attention on unique and autonomous images rather than on traditional machinations of a plot, Storey's plays demand new standards that are comparable to those that seemed so revolutionary in the other arts nearly a century ago, when narrative verse, representational painting and sculpture, and intricately plotted fiction were the conventional order of the day—and the modernist movement was soon to be born. In each of Storey's best-known and most theatrically innovative plays (i.e., *The Changing Room*, *The Contractor*, and *Home*), the play's central action is what Storey calls an "invisible event," the formation and dissolution of a collective bond as his characters are united—though *only temporarily*—through a common purpose and a shared endeavor.

A proper critical assessment of such "plotless" plays, therefore, must be based on a judgment of the effectiveness and eloquence of the theatrical image rather than on traditional considerations of conflict, action, contrivance, and character development. Several of Storey's plays, for example, lack major incidents of a traditional plot: in *The Contractor*, the central action is the constructing and dismantling of a tent in which a wedding reception is held; in *The Changing Room*, members of a rugby team come together, prepare for the game, win their match, change from their uniforms back to their regular clothes, and leave. As they subordinate self-interest to the collective effort, the workmen and rugby players find a satisfaction and mutuality that their lives in the outside world do not afford. This, then, is the truly significant "change" in *The Changing Room*: as the players change their clothes, they cast aside their various differences and the preoccupations of the outside world and assume their responsibilities and interdependencies as members of a team. In effect, as the players put on their uniforms, they *become* uniform, putting aside individual differences as they remove the street clothes which reflect the personal tastes, individuality, class, income, and occupations that must be subordinated to the team effort during the game. Similarly, the workers in *The Contractor* must subordinate their personal differences to the collective enterprise, for which the constructed tent is not only the eventual product but the central theatrical image. Depicting seemingly ordinary events in a style that he terms "poetic naturalism," Storey's plays virtually abolish conventional plot in order to focus the audience's attention on the naturalistic depiction of the play's "invisible event."

Whereas the "invisible events" of *The Contractor* and *The Changing Room* are embodied in physical actions that take place on stage, no such activities occur in *Home*; instead, its central image is portrayed through a series of events that are almost as "uneventful" as those in *Waiting for Godot*, and the audience's *perception* of that image undergoes a radical change as the nature of the "home" in which the characters live is gradually revealed. As they pass their time idly in mundane but seemingly ordinary conversation, they are first perceived to be "ordinary people, really," as Storey himself has remarked, insisting that they are not "afflicted in any way more than anybody else is afflicted" (Lanouette, 1970, 20). Gradually, however, it becomes clear that they have been institutionalized—abandoned by their families, confined in an asylum, and forsaken, left to their own meager resources, passing their time idly as they await death, resisting only feebly a capitulation to despair. Having no "home" in which they can find the support and refuge that the family traditionally provides, they have been placed in an institutional "home," an impersonal agency of a bureaucratic society, the welfare state's *ultimate* "place where, when you go there, they have to take you in." Yet by disclosing the nature of the "home" in their reviews, critics tainted the audience's experience of the play as surely as if they had revealed the solution to a mystery, as Storey remarked in a conversation with Ronald Hayman:

> The reviews did a disservice to the play in saying that it was about a nuthouse. In fact it's not the material of the play itself and to say it's a mental home . . . sets you away from the emotion, from the suffering. . . . To stress the metaphor of the mental home rather distorts the play. . . . Any of the characters . . . could quite as easily have been outside as inside, I feel. . . . There is a sort of disclaimer really when it becomes firmly a play about a mental home.[2]

Such objections reveal the need for new standards in the assessment of allegedly plotless plays: in the absence of an easily summarizable, conventional plot, an excessive critical disclosure of the play's complex and symbolic central image can reduce it to an unambiguous, literal fact—and can thereby diminish the audience's own experience of it in the theatre.

In an interview with Brendan Hennessy that was published in 1969, shortly before the works for which he would become most renowned were produced, Storey remarked that

> I don't mind a play where there's nothing said at all, as
> long as it's right. I feel that progressive theatre is basically
> as didactic as Pre-Raphaelite painting. It is distorting reality
> in much the same way.[3]

The Contractor, *The Changing Room*, and *Home* could equally well be termed plays "where there's nothing said at all," since they are, as he remarked elsewhere, "plays of understatement in a way, and if you don't get what they're understating, then you've really had it, because there's nothing great going on on the surface."[4] It was not until *Life Class* was produced in 1975 that Storey offered a more overtly "didactic" play—set, appropriately, in a classroom where, before an onstage "audience" of students, the protagonist expounds his theories of life, art, and what he terms "invisible events." *Life Class* is not only Storey's most complex play but one of the most original and unusual works of metatheatre in contemporary drama, offering his most detailed discussion (and justification) of his unique dramatic theory of "invisible events" that is best embodied in *The Changing Room* and *The Contractor*.

Surprisingly, however, Storey's exposition of these aesthetic principles occurs in the context of a play that is ostensibly "about" avant-garde art and makes no direct reference to the theatre at all. The central character is a beleaguered art instructor in a run-down provincial school, where he expounds his theory of "invisible events" to an uncomprehending "audience" of students in the shabby classroom, where they meet to draw the nude human form. The model's act of posing is inherently a *theatrical* event as well as an "artistic" one, however, for reasons that Peter Brook explained in *The Empty Space* (1969):

> I can take any empty space and call it a bare stage. A man
> walks across the empty space whilst someone else is
> watching him, and this is all that is needed for an act of
> theatre to be engaged.[5]

In *Life Class*, however, each watcher's gaze is directed toward a nude woman rather than Brook's hypothesized man, and she stands motionlessly in the "empty space" for extended periods of time rather than walking across it; still, her activity is no less inherently "theatrical" than the example that Brook proposes. Accordingly, an early stage direction specifies that the play's protagonist, who is identified only by his surname Allott, "circles the platform, chin in hand, contemplating the empty space" before he "sets the pose" of the model for the students.[6] In so doing, he is, in effect, the deviser, the director, and the designer of the theatrical event occurring before the on-stage audience of students as well as the audience in the theatre.

The selection of the graphic arts as a metaphor for his activity in the theatre seems particularly appropriate for Storey, who, earlier in his career, studied at the Slade School of Art in London and subsequently worked as both an artist and a teacher in a particularly rough school in London's East End.[7] Allott is said to have been "one of the leading exponents of representational art in his youth" and was (according to his colleague Philips) comparable to Michelangelo. More recently, however, he has become "an impresario . . . purveyor of the invisible event . . . so far ahead of its time you never see it" (70). Explaining why he no longer paints or sculpts, Allott tells one of his students, Catherine, that he believes in a more "public" art (i.e., one more like the theatre), which can nevertheless be understood within the artistic tradition:

ALLOTT: It's my opinion that painting and sculpture, and all the traditional forms of expression in the plastic arts, have had their day, Catherine . . . It's my opinion that the artist has been driven back—or driven on, to look at it in a positive way—to creating his works, as it were, in public.

CATHERINE: In public, sir?

ALLOTT: Just as Courbet or Modigliani, or the great Dutch Masters . . . created their work out of everyday things, so the contemporary artist creates his work out of the experience—the events as

> well as the objects—with which he's
> surrounded in his day to day
> existence . . . for instance, our meeting
> here today. (42)

These rituals—the class meetings and the posing—constitute the on-stage "invisible events" that are discussed at length throughout the play, though Allott alone recognizes their value.

The "event" taking place in the classroom—and by extension in the theatre—subsumes the "realities" of the mundane world outside, where, as Allott remarks,

> We all sail, to some extent, under false colours. . . . I mean,
> you may not see yourself as an artist . . . I may not see
> myself as a teacher. . . . Stella [the model] earns her living;
> I earn my living . . . you earn your living . . . but between
> us, we convene . . . celebrate . . . initiate . . . an event,
> which, for me, is the very antithesis of what *you* term
> reality . . . namely, we embody, synthesize, evoke, a work,
> which, whether we are aware of it or not, is taking place
> around us . . . all the time. (46)

The essential function of this "invisible event" is, the teacher points out, "to incorporate everything that is happening out there into a single homogenous whole" (38), which is also, of course, a functional definition of the Aristotelian "unity of action" in the theatre. Alllott's audience of students fails to grasp his meaning, however—and one of them voices exactly the complaint that is often lodged against Storey's plays:

> CATHERINE: (*gazing at* STELLA). There's nothing
>   happening, sir.
> ALLOTT: There's a great deal happening . . . Not in
>   any obvious way . . . nevertheless sev-
>   eral momentous events are actually
>   taking place out there . . . subtly, quiet-
>   ly, not overtly . . . but in the way artistic
>   events *do* take place . . . in the great
>   reaches of the mind . . . (38–39)

Despite the shortcomings of his students, Allott reminds them of the importance of the purpose for which, in theory if not in fact, they have convened—a purpose transcending the present moment and subsuming the cares of the workaday world: "Art is above sex," Allott insists, finding there a refuge from the failure of his marriage, ". . . and it's above politics, too. That's to say, it absorbs sex, and it absorbs politics" (33). Like the event taking place in the theatre, the art class itself is in fact a ritual—a patterned (regularly scheduled) event, the purpose of which Allott eloquently summarizes as "to pursue a beautiful and seemingly mysterious object, and to set it down—curiously—as objectively as we can" (33).

This wonder-filled "perusal"—an appreciation of the complexity and beauty of the "life" before them—is more important than the actual lines that the students commit haltingly and tentatively to paper. Accordingly, art has become—for Allott, if not for his students—the surrogate religion of a desacralized world, and the classroom is the "sanctified space" (exactly as the earliest theatres were in the ancient world) in which the celebrants convene for an exalted purpose that is inherently related to the concept of *performance*: "The lesson that we've been convened, as it were, to celebrate . . . [is] that we are life's musicians . . . its singers, and that what we sing is wholly without meaning . . . it exists, merely, because it is" (30).

The model herself is thus the central symbol of the play— occupying center stage for much of the time, embodying the "impersonal" and idealized state for which Allott yearns, but disrespected and defiled by those who fail to realize the symbolism, the transcendence, and the ritual that she represents. Thus, in addition to his aforementioned roles as a director, deviser, and impresario of inherently theatrical "invisible events," Allott, as the teacher, is also a virtual priest of art, extolling its virtues and presiding over the novices' performance of a ritual that surpasses the temporal reality. Unfortunately, however, Allott's particular novices neither appreciate their teacher's beliefs, nor understand his values, nor share his priorities; the students demonstrate neither particular aptitudes for art nor a serious interest in it, and they maintain a recurrent—almost constant—chorus of crude remarks, sexual innuendos, double-

entendres, and coarse references to the model who poses before them
and to each other as well. Nevertheless, as Allott himself observes
while consoling the model in her remorse over being no longer
"youthful young," the students are "myopic . . . disingenuous . . .
uninspired—. . . pubescent excrescences on the cheeks of time" (15–
16). Without particular concern, he points out that their priorities (in
obvious contrast to his own) place "mass before beauty, excrescence
before edification . . . [and] salaciousness before refinement" (40).

Such a view is not far removed from Storey's own view of the
theatre-going audience, as he remarked to me during an interview in his
home in 1985:

> When we opened *The Contractor* in the West End, we were
> in competition with a play called *No Sex Please, We're
> British*. We were in competition because we both went to
> the same theatre [the Strand], and in the end our
> management panicked and went to a much smaller one
> around the corner, the Fortune. . . . We opened within a
> week [of each other], and that play got absolutely diabolical
> reviews. . . . They said it was absolute unmitigated rubbish
> and insulted the intelligence of the audience. It's been
> running ever since . . . a roaring success! We in *The
> Contractor* ran absolutely ecstatic reviews from all the
> critics, popular and highbrow, and it survived—but just—
> for about a year, and it came off.

The almost unrelievedly vulgar banter and crude antics of Allott's
students suggest that their teacher's characterization of them is both
accurate and insightful, but in some ways it exceedingly objectifies the
problem and neglects both the cruelty and the dehumanization that are
implicit in their classroom behavior, which culminates when two of the
students, Mathews and his friend Warren, enact an appallingly brutal
rape of the nude model who poses defenselessly before the class—an
act which Allott, with characteristic detachment and indifference, does
nothing to prevent.

Symbolically, the rape is the ultimate, destructive assertion of
the most crude physical and temporal reality over the transcendent,
ethereal, and spiritual one—a vile and violent disruption of art by the
most brutish form of life; certainly, no one can possibly object that

"nothing happened" in *this* Storey play. Yet, virtually before the stunned audience on stage—or its counterpart in the theatre—has had time to recover from the shock of the event that has just been observed, an equally surprising fact is suddenly revealed: amid raucous laughter and gibes at their fellow students, the perpetrators of the rape reveal that it was in fact a *simulation*—a calculated hoax, a convincingly realistic deception, an "imitation" of "life," a work of artifice if not of art, and (the ultimate irony of the play) an "act of theatre" performed before the shocked onstage "classroom" audience; it is, in effect, Storey's play-within-the-play. The extent of Stella's complicity in the hoax remains unclear, though the fact that she does resume posing shortly after the incident implies that she too was aware of the students' ploy.

Simulated though it turns out to have been, the rape of the model remains, obviously, the ultimate assertion of unrestrained "natural impulses" as the most "ungovernable" and primal of urges "creates its own form" before the shocked members of the class (44). Allott's "spiritual" reality of transcendent art and invisible events is violated by the intrusion of its "antithesis" (46), the most base and sordid of worldly "realities." As Saunders (another of Allott's students) remarks while Mathews removes some of his clothing prior to the rape, "It's the dividing line, you see, between life and art . . . Stella represents it in its impersonal condition . . . Mathews represents its . . . " (77–78). Saunders's ethereal reflections are interrupted by Warren's shouts of the coarsest and crudest possible form of encouragement for Mathews: "Get your prick out. . . ! Here . . . here, then! Go on. Grab her!" (77–78). As such, it is also the ultimate profanation of Allott's "temple," an outrage revealing the unworthiness of the priest as well as the novices—and causes the former to lose his job. Ironically, Allott is dismissed because of an event that never *actually* occurred. Yet, with typical cynicism and detachment, he accommodates even the act of violation itself within his theory, as he lamely tries to explain to Stella, the victim: "Violation, they tell me, is a prerequisite of art . . . disruption of prevailing values . . . re-integration in another form entirely. What you see and feel becomes eternal" (89). After this final (and unsuccessful) attempt to account for the "ungovernable" in his

Allott is conscious that he is a better
artist and a more intelligent person than his
students

theory, Allott's comments degenerate into nebulous (and rather trite)
musings on the growth of flowers and the passage of time.

As Allott expounds the value of "the experience—the events as
well as the objects—with which he's surrounded in his day to day
existence . . . for instance, our meeting here today," his point is equally
applicable to the theatre itself:

> ALLOTT: . . . the feelings and intuitions expressed by
>   all of us inside this room . . . are in
>   effect the creation—the re-creation—of
>   the artist . . . to the extent that they are
>   controlled, manipulated, postulated,
>   processed, defined, sifted, *re*fined . . .
> CATHERINE: Who by, sir?
> ALLOTT: Well, for want of a better word—by me. (42)

Implicitly, this speech affirms the presence of the author's controlling
consciousness in selecting and portraying the episodes of the play
itself—although, ironically, the fact that Allott does *not* "control" the
events taking place in the classroom is clearly demonstrated during the
rape scene. The ultimate "purveyor of the invisible event" (70) is thus
David Storey himself, and much of *Life Class* seems to offer a defense
and explanation of his dramatic technique—particularly in his allegedly
plotless plays.

The action of *Life Class*—and by extension the "invisible
events" that constitute *The Contractor* and *The Changing Room*—are
not merely random "slices of life" or the theatrical counterpart of
cinéma-vérité. Their action—a detailed and naturalistic "imitation of
life"—has been "controlled, manipulated, postulated, processed,
defined, sifted, [and] refined" toward the expostulation of the Storey's
recurrent thematic concerns. Clearly, too, the playwright wishes to
differentiate himself from those whom Allott describes as "the
manufacturer of events who . . . sees art as something accessible to all
and therefore the prerogative not of the artist—but of anybody who
cares to pick up a brush, a bag of cement, an acetylene
welder . . . anyone, in fact, who can persuade other people that what he
is doing is creative" (30). Unlike various types of undisciplined and
free-form "happenings" (to which Allott's "invisible events" have

sometimes mistakenly been compared), Storey's "plotless" plays are deceptively simple, enabling both theatregoers and critics to overlook the significance of the actions taking place on stage.

Allott's lecture to his snickering students on the appreciation of the complexity of the human form is equally applicable to the understanding of any work of art, whether on canvas or on the stage:

> It's merely a question . . . of seeing each detail in relation to all the rest . . . the proportion—the width as well as the height . . . the whole contained, as it were . . . within a single image. Unless you are constantly relating the specific to the whole . . . a work of art can never exist . . . It's not merely a conscious effort; it is, if one is an artist and not a technician—someone disguised, that is, as an artist, going through all the motions and creating all the effects—an instinctive process (29–30).

Accordingly, both *The Changing Room* and *The Contractor* present "a single image" (i.e., an "invisible event") within which "the whole" of the play is contained.

Surprisingly, many of the most abstract thematic statements in *Life Class* are given to Saunders—the student who reports the rape incident and causes Allott to lose his job—but one who, according to his classmates, talks, looks, and smells like Allott. "*He is Allott!*," they exclaim (49), and, in terms of conveying many of Storey's principal themes, he clearly fulfills the same function as his teacher:

> SAUNDERS: The human condition . . . is made up of many ambivalent conditions . . . that's one thing I've discovered . . . love, hatred . . . despair, hope . . . exhilaration, anguish . . . and it's not these conditions themselves that are of any significance, but the fact that, as human beings, we oscillate between them . . . It's the oscillation between hope and despair that's the great feature of our existence, not the hope, or the despair, in themselves.
>
> (*Pause.*)

STELLA: It's a wonderful observation . . .

(*Pause.* SAUNDERS *settles himself: gets out his equipment.*)

I like people who think about life.

SAUNDERS: I don't think about life. I'm merely
            interested in recording it.

STELLA: I see. (74)

Similarly, Storey has also maintained his own preference for
"recording" rather than "thinking about" life, claiming that
"Intellectualism, it's the English disease . . . All these attitudes towards
experience . . . it's the English Tradition, isn't it? (laughter) . . . in the
end, there's no experience *there*."[8] Nevertheless, earlier in the play,
Saunders offers another observation on dispassionate realism (which is
surely an "attitude towards experience" itself) as a technique in art:

> There's something dispassionate in human nature . . . that's
> what I think . . . something really dispassionate that
> nothing—no amount of pernicious and cruel experience—
> can ever destroy. That's what I believe in . . . I think a time
> will come when people will be interested in what was
> dispassionate at a time like this . . . when everything was
> dictated to by so much fashion and techniques. (49)

Yet despite the meticulous detail and realistic portrayal of the subject,
as Allott points out, "The essence of any event . . . is that it should
be . . . indefinable. Such is the nature . . . the ambivalence . . . of all
human responses" (80–81). Similarly, in discussing his own works,
Storey maintains that "the best things I do, I don't know what they're
about when I've finished them. When I have the ideas first, they're
usually no good . . . At best, the illustration of a thesis, at worst
pretentious bullshit."[9]

Although the "thesis" is more explicit in *Life Class* than in *The
Changing Room*, *Home*, or *The Contractor*, the great majority of
thematic statements in *Life Class* concern *how* the play is to be
understood (a technique that is also applicable to his other plays) rather
than specifically *what* the action of the play means. "The artist sings his
song," Allott remarks, "but doesn't contemplate its beauty, doesn't
analyze, doesn't lay it all out in all its separate parts . . . that is the task

of the critic" (30)—a position that Storey has also maintained in his interviews. Nevertheless, with so much instruction being offered to the audience, it is appropriate that the setting for *Life Class* is a classroom—and the subtle irony of the title (that the play instructs the audience in understanding the author's other works) becomes clear.

Throughout its latter half, there are a number of indications that *Life Class* was intended to be a farewell to a certain *type* of theatre—if not, as was suspected by a number of reviewers at the time, a farewell to the theatre itself.[10] In a reference to his series of "invisible events" that seems equally appropriate to the author's series of naturalistic but allegedly plotless plays, Allott declares that his work to date has been "Ahead of its time . . . impossible to perceive . . . the pageant is at an end now. . . . The process, as you can see, is virtually complete" (88)—as if Storey felt a certain discouragement that his plays had been neither properly understood nor recognized for their innovativeness. Despite Allott's assertion that "I've achieved some of my best work, I think, in here" (90)—a statement that is equally true of Storey's relationship with the Royal Court, where *Life Class* and his other works had been produced—he (Allott) foresees no continuation of it in his career: "My next work may be something altogether less commendable . . . That's to say, more . . . substantial . . . if not altogether more extravagant than what I appeared to have achieved today . . . I shall have to see . . . sans means . . . sans wife . . . sans recognition who's to know what I . . . might rise to . . . " (88). There is also little hope that his works will be better understood in the future, as his conversation with his colleague Philips reveals:

> PHILIPS: Posterity, old son. If they don't see it now, they'll see it later. We're building up an enormous credit . . . (*Gestures aimlessly overhead.*) somewhere . . . You with your . . . events . . . me with my designs . . . book-jackets, posters . . . Letraset . . . singular embodiments of the age we live in.
>
> ALLOTT: Sold anything lately?
>
> PHILIPS: (*shakes his head*) . . . You?

ALLOTT: How do you sell an event that no one will
                admit is taking place? (55)

Whatever value might later be recognized in Philips's graphics, his
remarks are irrelevant to Allott's "invisible events," which leave no
artifacts for posterity to judge. Such is not entirely the case with
Storey's plays, of course, since a number of them have been recorded
on film and videotape, and the texts of all except *Phoenix* have been
published. The apparent implication that he has been unable to "sell"
his works could be easily refuted by citing the success of his
productions at the Royal Court and the lengthy list of favorable reviews
and awards that his plays have received (though relatively few have
been revived since their initial productions). Nevertheless, the analogy
between Allott's "invisible events" and the live performance of
Storey's plays in the theatre (as opposed to their filmed or videotaped
counterparts) remains clear.

   Like John Osborne and Edward Bond, Storey has expressed a
deep dissatisfaction with both critics and audiences who, he feels, have
neither understood nor recognized (i.e., have not "bought") the ideas
that his works embody. Even Katharine Worth's incisive *Revolutions in
Modern English Drama* (1973) discusses Storey's work only briefly
and in terms of the realism of the 1930s, noting that he "moves between
novel and drama with Maugham-like ease" rather than attributing to
him any innovations in form.[11] "How does one live as a revolutionary,"
Allott asks, "when no one admits there's a revolution there?" (56). Yet
whereas Osborne and Bond have repeatedly and contentiously
explained and defended their plays, proclaiming their social and
political beliefs at the same time, Storey seems relatively resigned to
the lack of comprehension that he detects. He has maintained a rather
taciturn endurance of what he perceives to be the state of affairs in
contemporary theatre, and he issues neither prefaces nor manifestoes to
explicate his plays. Even so, as he recalled his anger "at the reception—
or rather lack of reception—of [his] first two novels," he remarked
(during the interview with Victor Sage in 1976) that in the early stage
of his career he had not

> learnt that there's nobody out there . . . nobody knows what
> the hell you're doing. . . . It's no use telling everybody:
> "Look, this is what I'm doing." It's no use beating a fool
> about the head . . . you've got to find other, more subtle
> ways. . . . There's no audience, even at the Royal
> Court . . . every time you do a new play, you have to whip
> up an audience . . . they're all so bloody bourgeois . . . they
> sit there like this (laughter). . . . I can't go to the theatre
> myself, it's the audience, they put me off.[12]

Like Storey, Allott finds himself surrounded by those who do not
comprehend the meaning of his works: his students maintain that
"there's nothing happening" as he describes the "invisible events" that
are taking place before them, and when he quotes a Latin epigram
(which summarizes a major theme of both *The Changing Room* and
The Contractor) to encourage their efforts, his audience—predictably—
fails to understand:

ALLOTT: Good . . . good. That's the spirit . . . Labor
            Ipse Voluptas Est.
WARREN: Rest, sir?
ALLOTT: No, no . . . Just carry on.
            (*Fade.*) (57)

The students in Allott's classroom and the audiences for contemporary
plays are apparently quite similar, in Storey's view, in both their lack of
appreciation of art and their priorities, preferring "excrescence before
edification . . . salaciousness before refinement" (40), as the record-
breaking runs of such anodyne fare as *Oh! Calcutta!* and *No Sex
Please, We're British* reveal. Arguably, the rape in *Life Class* may even
provide a sole concession to those members of the audience who
complained that "nothing happened" in Storey's previous plays.

   Yet whether or not such speculation is warranted—and Storey
has given no indication that it is—a recognition of the analogy between
the students in the classroom and the audience in the theatre (both of
which are being instructed in the appreciation of "invisible events" at
the same time) counters the seemingly valid criticism of the students
that was noted by John Weightman in *Encounter*.

> There is never any indication that they are specifically art
> students, *i.e.* people who, in addition to their randiness and
> bowel-movements, are genuinely interested in the problems
> of art. They are all perfectly philistine. . . . In the most
> benighted educational institutions—and I have seen a
> few—there are always one or two teachers and pupils who
> save the honour of the place.[13]

Ironically, insofar as anyone "saves the honour of the place," it is
Saunders, who reports the rape incident, "taking the part of public
decency and order in this matter" as Allott himself remarks (84).[14]
However, the most significant reason why the students "are all perfectly
philistine" seems to be the suggestion that they are, in Storey's view,
exactly like the audience for his own *theatrical* "invisible events":
"there's nobody out there . . . [who] knows what the hell [he's] doing."

In fact, then, Storey has included within *Life Class* a summation
of his views of life and art—a statement surpassing the discussion of
impersonal methodologies and the technique of avant-garde "invisible
events." The most poetic of these summary statements occurs near the
end of the play, as Allott muses that art traditionally

> leaves objects—certain elements of its activity—behind . . .
> stone, paint, canvas . . . bronze . . . paper . . . carbon . . . a
> synthesis of natural elements convened by man . . . whereas
> we, elements as it were of a work ourselves, partake of
> existence . . . simply by being what we are . . . expressions
> of a certain time and place, and class . . . defying hope . . .
> defying anguish . . . defying, even, definition . . . more
> substantial than reality . . . stranger than a dream . . . figures
> in a landscape . . . scratching . . . scraping . . . rubbing . . .
> All around us . . . our rocky ball . . . hurtling through
> time . . . singing . . . to no one's tune at all. (82)

Allott recognizes the value of the traditional heritage, even as he seeks
to explore beyond it and to open new frontiers. Accordingly, Storey's
ostensibly "valedictory" play is best regarded as the culmination of a
series of particularly innovative if seemingly "uneventful" plays, during
the course of which a new dramatic form—the theatrical "invisible
event"—was developed, refined, and ultimately defended in a uniquely
provocative way.

Notes

1. Clifford A. Ridley, "Oops—the British are Coming," *The National Observer*, 2 November 1974, 23.

2. Ronald Hayman, "Conversation with David Storey," *Drama* 99 (Winter 1970), 49, 52.

3. "David Storey in Interview with Brendan Hennessy," *Transatlantic Review* 33–34 (1969), 10.

4. Hayman, 49.

5. Peter Brook, *The Empty Space* (1968; New York: Avon, 1969), 9.

6. David Storey, *Life Class* (London: Jonathan Cape, 1975), 17, 19. All subsequent references cite this edition and have been inserted parenthetically into the text.

7. For Storey's most detailed account of his career as a teacher, including his account of his involvement in a rooftop brawl with some of his more thuggish students, see Guy Flatley, "'I Never Saw a Pinter Play," *New York Times*, 29 November 1970, sec. 2: 1, 5.

8. Victor Sage, "David Storey in Conversation with Victor Sage," *New Review*, October 1976, 64.

9. Sage, 63.

10. See, for example, W. Stephen Gilbert, "Life Class," *Plays and Players*, May 1974, 26.

11. Katharine Worth, *Revolutions in Modern English Drama* (London: G. Bell and Sons, 1973), 26.

12. Sage, 63, 65.

13. John Weightman, "Art Versus Life," *Encounter,* September 1974: 57–58.

14. Despite the obvious difference in gender, the relationship between Allott and Saunders is remarkably similar to that between Miss Jean Brodie and Sandy in Muriel Spark's *The Prime of Miss Jean Brodie* (1961), which was dramatized by Jay Presson Allen and later made into a much-acclaimed film (1969). Like Allott, Spark's central character is an eccentric and controversial but quite dedicated schoolteacher whose outspoken views and avant-garde attitudes are "out of place" in the conservative Marcia Blaine School for Girls in Edinburgh during the late 1930s; furthermore, she loses her job after being

betrayed by her most promising student, who has been a model for (and later the mistress of) a married art teacher, Teddy Lloyd, a would-be lover of Miss Brodie's as well. (He, obviously, is the counterpart of Stella as the object of the "gaze" of both teacher and student, though there is no indication that Allott takes any sexual interest in her; his "gaze" is, in fact, wholly aesthetic and as "impersonal" as he contends art must be.) Beset with problems and frustrations in her personal life, Miss Brodie loses her job after an incident for which she bears at best only indirect responsibility (the death of one of her young charges, who, inspired by Brodie-instilled heroic visions, went to Spain to join her brother on the battlefront of the Spanish Civil War), just as Allott is made to bear indirect responsibility for the ostensible rape of the model. The future remains similarly uncertain for both protagonists when their respective works end.

MADNESS AND THE FAMILY
IN DAVID STOREY'S PLAYS

Laura H. Weaver

In David Storey's works the family is both life-enhancing and life-denying: it supports its members emotionally but also denies their individuality. Some of his works (for example, *In Celebration* and *Saville*) depict both features of the family; others demonstrate primarily its destructive qualities. Life-denying families generate these responses from protagonists: "Families kill me" (Arthur Machin in *This Sporting Life* 186); "Families ... are just like vicious animals, radiant with solicitude, [sic] and affection until you touch them. Then they rear up like crazed beasts" (Howarth in *Flight into Camden* 68–69); "I dread families" (Catherine in *Present Times* 252); and "Families are an illusion ... You have to destroy them to stay alive" (Adrienne in *Sisters* 147).

In some of Storey's works family-induced problems lead to emotional illness. Family members experience mental breakdowns (Arnold Middleton in *The Restoration of Arnold Middleton*), fear madness (Allott in *Life Class*), or are hospitalized for mental illness (Yvonne in *A Temporary Life*, the characters in *Home*, Adrienne in *Sisters*, and Sheila in *Present Times*). Sometimes madness is produced by the family's inculcating allegiance to its (and society's) version of reality. However, that version, not the individual's only option, is one of two kinds of reality, juxtaposed revealingly in Storey's "Blake," an early unpublished poem printed on the program of *The Restoration of Arnold Middleton* (Royal Court Theatre, 1967). In that poem the

speaker laments the damaging influence of a teacher, who, calling
Blake's vision of angels "a total abberation [sic]," tries to teach his
students

> His particular hallucination
> That reality is something
> Which,
> Communally, can be registered outside. (n.p.)

When the deviant family member acts according to another version of
reality, the family, like the teacher, labels him insane. The supposedly
insane person may, however, be saner than the rest of the family.[1]

This vision of the family as a contributor to mental illness
resembles R.D. Laing's theories, an affinity recognized by Storey in the
unedited (unbroadcast) version of Bernard Bergonzi's 1968 BBC
interview of him.[2] Although denying his having been influenced by
Laing (Bergonzi 3–4; Hutchings 80), in the Bergonzi interview Storey
explained that Laing and he "reached the same point" by different
means, Laing through "intellectual methods" and he through
"experience and intuition"; Laing "suddenly made things very clear, the
sort of things I was intuitively aware of." Summarizing Laing's
theories, Storey said, "Every group . . . seizes upon one member . . . to
become a focus of their own disabilities, and . . . in a schizoid family,
the schizophrenic in fact becomes the insane element of that family."
As evidence of their similar views, Storey referred to his novel
Radcliffe: ". . . I . . . only got to know about him [Laing] after I'd
written *Radcliffe* [published in 1963]. . . . I think *Radcliffe* is a kind of
working demonstration of that thesis which I write [sic]
intuitively. . . . Radcliffe [the protagonist] is schizoid precisely that
way. He lives in an untenable situation, and becomes, as it were, a
function of other people's disabilities" (Bergonzi 4–5). In describing
another of his works, *The Restoration of Arnold Middleton*, Storey uses
similar language: that play is "a reflection on the same process of a
man . . . who is a function of his environment disabilities. . . . he
[Arnold] . . . becomes completely buried by his past and his
environment" (Bergonzi 8). Storey's recognition of these parallels with

Laing's theories[3] illuminates not only the works he specifically mentioned but also other works, especially *Home*.

According to this vision, the family, often violating its members' autonomy, cultivates the formation of a false self, which usually involves "an excess of being 'good,' never doing anything other than what one is told, never being 'a trouble,' never asserting or even betraying any counter-will of one's own." This "good" behavior, often exhibited by the model child, husband, or clerk, reflects not the individual's real desires but a "negative conformity to a standard that is the other's standard . . . and is prompted by the dread of what might happen if one were to be oneself in actuality" (Laing 98–99).

Such characters appear in Storey's works. For example, Colin Pasmore (the protagonist of the novel *Pasmore*)—a faithful husband, teacher, and son—tries to please "tribes of people back home" (18). Similarly, the familial home of Yvonne Freestone (in the novel *A Temporary Life*) stresses common sense and compliance; causing "no trouble" (180–81) is a priority. Yvonne's mother, Mrs. Sherman, resembles Julie's mother in Laing's *The Divided Self*: Mrs. X, who had "given her life" for her daughter, valued Julie's being "never 'a trouble,'" always doing "what she was told." And the Sherman family, as a unit, resembles the X family, in which "expressions of an inner deadness" constituted "expressions of the utmost goodness, health, normality" (Laing 183–84). Likewise, in Yvonne's marital home, her husband Colin, while sometimes sensitive, often does not encourage her development. Like Dr. Lennox at the hospital, Colin finds her interest in causes too abstracted, and he tries to impose on her his own standard of toughness (Guiton, "Comments" 26). On one occasion, during her weekend visit from the mental hospital, he expects her to accept as a home the flat he has just rented (ATL 171).[4]

Members of these families need to escape from, not return to, their homes. What Storey said elsewhere about Pasmore might apply also to Yvonne and to other characters in Storey's works: Pasmore "gives up in his attempt to escape, and goes weakly back to the situation he needed so desperately to leave" (Taylor, *David Storey* 13); his homecoming to the family he had left means "accepting the very thing that's going to shackle him for the rest of his life" (Sage 64).

One form of the individual's escape from a family is to go to another home—the mental hospital, both an institution and an alternative home. Since the family may have directly or indirectly caused psychological problems, the mental hospital may not be as undesirable as it at first seems and may even be preferable to the family home. In *Home*, Marjorie says of the mental hospital, "One thing you can say about this place—. . . . S'not like home"; and Kathleen replies, "Thank Gawd" (137). Some individuals may need, then, a place "not like home."

In the mental hospital the individual may achieve reassurance or unity. According to Storey, insanity is like work and sports, which give "a structure and a dignity to life"; in the mental hospital, Storey says, a person can unify his/her "particular condition . . . and become one with other people" (Ansorge 35). Although the mental hospital may possess some of the negative features of family homes, it may also provide escape and, possibly, in the shared experience of madness, a haven.

Two plays in particular, *The Restoration of Arnold Middleton* (1967) and *Home* (1970), dramatize the contrast between the homes provided by the family and the mental hospital; and *Mother's Day* provides a farcical angle from which to view this contrast. In *The Restoration of Arnold Middleton*, protagonist Arnold Middleton, a history teacher, has an emotional breakdown. Although containing some references to the school where Arnold teaches history, this play, set in the Middleton home, focuses on the two families (his parents and his wife Joan) who have contributed to his difficulties. *Home*, the second play, takes place entirely in a mental hospital[5] and consists of conversations among five patients whose family homes were no less "madhouse[s]" than Arnold's (RAM 22). In this play familial conflict is shown not in the present but in the past.

The Restoration of Arnold Middleton depicts Arnold's actions (labeled madness by his wife Joan and his friends) as originating, paradoxically, in both his superior insight and an illness from which the family should rescue him. Arnold engages in activities that shock other people: pretending to be a child reading a comic book, barking like a dog, and acting out scenes from the school play, "Robin Hood and His Merry Men." Arnold's most recent offenses against propriety have been his purchase of a suit of armor and his relationship with Mrs. Ellis, his mother-in-law. These actions provoke questions about Arnold's sanity: Joan and the Middletons' friends wonder what has gotten "into" him (53, 61).

The play offers both positive and negative interpretations of the behavior that Arnold's family and friends judge unconventional. Arnold, marching to a different drummer, lives according to the visionary's version of reality described in "Blake," a world not understood by his friends and by Joan, who laments that Arnold is "always inventing things when he thinks it suits him" (41). Unlike many adults, Arnold has retained the ability to play and to fantasize. But Arnold may also be hiding behind his unusual actions. His "charade," Storey said elsewhere (Hayman 53), is "the battle of a man to protect his own insecurities" (Cox 50). Perhaps not only in his playing but also in his living in the world of Robin Hood (with whom he identifies as "a refugee . . . from the proper world" [95]), Arnold tries to protect himself.

Whatever the motivation for Arnold's actions, he clearly experiences familial conflict, generated by Joan's expectations and his attachment to his mother. Although some of the blame for Arnold's predicament lies in events "long before conception" (86), the immediate cause appears to be the family. With his wife and his mother, he finds not the "decent home" he wishes for (21) but sterility, possessiveness, hollowness, and confusion.

The sterility in Arnold and Joan's relationship is already evident in the setting described in the stage directions. The "scrupulously clean" house contains various objects that "suggest the rudiments of a museum, but bereft of any specific human connotation": among them, a stuffed eagle, a sword, a model airplane, and a full-size suit of armor dominating the room (11). While Arnold must assume responsibility for the objects, Joan creates the atmosphere of excessive orderliness. A compulsive cleaner like Mrs. Shaw in *In Celebration*, Joan constantly tidies and "re-tidies" the house (58) so successfully that "there's not a mark nor a sign of life anywhere" (68).

Arnold's mother, who does not actually appear in the play, is another earlier source of his problems. To call attention to her

possessiveness, Storey included in the program for the Royal Court
Theatre's production of this play a quotation from Jessie Chambers's
D. H. Lawrence: A Personal Record [by E. T.]:

> I wanted to make the effect of his mother's attitude clear to
> him . . . our long conflict had dated from the time
> when . . . he . . . told me that 'he had looked into his heart
> and could not find that he loved me as a husband should
> love his wife.'" (n.p.)

While not explicitly defining the attachment between Arnold and his
mother, this play does, in several episodes, emphasize its importance.
In his mother's absence Arnold has found surrogate mothers in Mrs.
Ellis and Joan. He wants Mrs. Ellis, who has grown fond of him, to stay
with them. Even Joan, having been told earlier by Arnold's mother to
"look after my only son" (58), acts as a replacement for her. Now
Arnold's parents' cancellation of their visit because of his mother's
illness precipitates a crisis for him—possibly despair at her absence but
more likely triumph at his release from her control.

Arnold's relationship with his mother also has social
implications. Instilling in him an obligation to attain goals ("destinies /
Scarcely commensurate with our upbringing") not reached by her
husband, his mother had encouraged Arnold to rise above his working-
class background and even to fantasize about kingship and godhood.
An important speech in Act III-Scene I recapitulates the conflict
between Arnold's father and mother and his mother's use of that
difference to manipulate her son. Arnold, addressing a spot on the wall,
reenacts his mother's imploring, "'Please, please my son, / Don't fail
me like your father done.'" After recalling that guilt-inducing plea,
Arnold stands tensed, then relaxes, and responds, "When I was young,
when I was young,/ There were so many things I should have done"
(87–88). As his monologue indicates, Arnold has become aware of his
mother's control. Perhaps now, by this reenactment, he can begin to
unfetter himself.

Home for Arnold has meant not only sterility in his life with
Joan and domination by his mother but also a series of hollow
relationships, suggested by the suit of armor (bought, Arnold says, as a

gift for his parents) and madhouse confusion. Observing the lack of "decent conversation" in his house, he cries out, "I teach in a madhouse all day, then come home to another at night" (22). Perhaps not the unconventional Arnold but the conventional home is mad. As Storey said in his summary of Laing's theories, the individual thought to be schizophrenic actually behaves rationally in a family built on irrational premises (Bergonzi 5).

   The Restoration of Arnold Middleton portrays Arnold, isolated from the family, as the possessor of both special wisdom and an illness. In some respects madness brings Arnold insight similar to that of *Radcliffe* protagonist Leonard, whose extraordinary operations of his mind constitute "not so much a disorder as a heightening of his perceptiveness" (R 59). Arnold himself (using imagery reminiscent of Laing's description of the schizophrenic's "cracked mind" which "may let in light" denied to "intact minds of many sane people whose minds are closed" [27]) refers to "the insights that irrationality brings . . . Cracks . . . Openings. Some little aperture of warmth and light" (87). Indeed, the play as a whole may show Arnold's developing perceptiveness about his home (discussed earlier) and about fellow teacher Hanson; his courageous confrontation of an undefined terror; and his attainment of the reassurance that Storey associates with insanity.

   One of the first things Arnold learns during this period is to drop pretenses. During one of Hanson's visits to the Middleton home, Arnold unmasks Hanson's boorishness and cowardice (73) and later freely discusses his friend's uneasiness at this crisis. And Arnold can now face desolation. He apparently sees what other people do not, "a sight / That would turn even Satan insane" (31); but he somehow survives the terror. Out of his pain have come compensating insights and courage for the unknown. While his terror does not disappear, he may find in insanity a unity like that in work and sports. He himself may experience the "reassurance" he envied in Mrs. Ellis, who was "broken in two" (85).[6]

   But while this play suggests that Arnold gains illumination from madness, it also presents his situation as an abnormality from which he should be saved. Accordingly, his restoration involves an expulsion of

objects and persons from the house and a confrontation with Joan. By
the beginning of Act III-Scene 2 the Middleton living room has, at
Joan's insistence, "been cleared of all Arnie's possessions" (given to
the refuse-man to crush up in his lorry [88–93]), and his mother-in-law
has been asked to leave. Then in the last scene of the play occurs
Arnold's outburst. Confirming the other characters' earlier impressions
that something has gotten into him, he speaks of its "coming out."
Complaining of something "hard," he clasps his head and screams. A
little later Arnold asks Joan, "Have I finished?" When she says, "Yes,"
he thanks God (103–104).

The clearing away of possessions and the encounter between
Arnold and Joan seem, on one level, to be signs of recovery for Arnold.
But the conclusion also implies a defeat for him. Giving his objects to
the refuse-man, for example, destroys the museum-like quality of the
Middleton home (14) or reinforces its sterility. After the removal the
room is immaculate—but here, as in the beginning of the play, tidiness
suggests the absence of life.

Similarly, Arnold's confrontation with Joan is ambiguous. The
screaming may be an "exorcis[m] . . . of the demon from the brain"
(Peel 24), the expulsion, begun in the earlier monologue, of his
mother's control—accompanied by Arnold's restoration to his position
as Joan's husband. If so, "I've finished?" (104) constitutes an
affirmation. Storey himself, on one occasion, offered that interpretation:
when Arnold's mother-in-law leaves, he "has to confront his wife and
under this pressure a sort of birth takes place. . . ." (Cox 50). Several
critics have also convincingly presented positive interpretations of
either this scene or the play as a whole. This scene dramatizes Arnold's
"pass[ing] . . . his crisis and begin[ning] . . . his restoration" (Taylor,
"David Storey" 147); contains "a sharp physical climax when Arnold's
recovery of sanity is represented as a 'happening'" (Worth 38). Or, as
Kalson suggests, "the entire play is his 'restoration'—his growth
toward awareness, understanding and acceptance" ("Insanity" 128).
Hutchings analyzes the importance of the sword as "a religious
symbol" in Arnold's "personal reintegration": Arnold "has found a
more sustaining and transcendent 'emblem' of truth in the sword, even

though the specific discovery (like the outcome of Pasmore's journey) 'was hard to describe'" (51, 57).

But the last scene also suggests a psychological lobotomy (Peel 24) for Arnold, his ultimate surrender to others' control. Instead of being able "to leuchotomize" his wife, as he had planned (102), Arnold submits to his wife's lobotomy of him. Since, in his mind, his substitute mothers Mrs. Ellis and Joan merge with his real mother (30), the conclusion signifies his continued domination by women: "finished" thus means the end of his tentative self-assertion. This lobotomy episode is foreshadowed by a castration one in Act I—Scene 2: Mrs. Ellis cuts Arnold's hair while Joan holds him and cries out, "Go on Mam. Give him a cut." After they are finished, Mrs. Ellis delights in Arnold's reduction to young manhood or boyhood: "He looks younger already!" (35–36). The cutting imagery used in that earlier scene and suggested now by a lobotomy vividly dramatizes Arnold's emasculation. Just as his possessions are destroyed by the lorry blade, he himself is vulnerable to destructive women.

The Restoration of Arnold Middleton ends with a highly ambiguous recovery for Arnold. This crisis may have completed (or at least begun) his emancipation from his mother, but problems with his wife continue. Madness has brought him insights, but eventually he accepts the reality of the family and society. Arnold's restoration to a sanity of conformity, similar to that of Margaret and Howarth in *Flight into Camden*, re-establishes family unity according to its version of reality. Consequently, although this play closes with his "restoration" rather than his literal suicide (as in an earlier unproduced version, *To Die with the Philistines* [Taylor, "British" 22]), it also suggests psychological suicide. The restored protagonist still needs deliverance from home—the home that is "not a home [but] . . . an institution" (14).

Unlike *The Restoration of Arnold Middleton*, *Home* focuses on people no longer in conventional family homes but, instead, in a mental hospital/home. Covering one day in the lives of five patients, this play ends as it begins—with the patients remaining in the mental hospital. In the absence of characters representing communally-defined sanity, we see and hear, firsthand, the people considered deviant: Harry, Jack, Kathleen, Marjorie, and Alfred. Although *Home*, unlike *T h e*

Restoration of Arnold Middleton, contains no scenes actually showing the intricacies of the patients' relationships with their families, it does report some details. Although two of the patients, Harry and Jack, still have "great faith in the institution of marriage" (98), the conversations taking place in this group reveal negative features of their family homes: estrangement of husbands and wives, parents' lack of fulfillment in child-rearing, and the threat of violence.

Even the marriages of idealistic Harry and Jack have been inadequate: Harry and his wife have separated, and Jack confesses the failure of his marriage to be what "it should be" (112). And the women, Kathleen and Marjorie, are openly skeptical about men and marriage. Kathleen reminisces pessimistically about quarrels with her husband and, in fact, opposes conventional marriage; the ideal, she thinks, would be for couples not to live together all the time but to meet once in two weeks. If husbands and wives do not bring fulfillment, neither do children, who instead bring physical and emotional suffering. Marjorie reports that the birth of her daughter harmed her physically (all her teeth "went rotten" [109]) and that now her daughter, as an adult, neglects her. Kathleen's and Marjorie's disillusionment about children is shared by Jack, who laments the responsibility of parenthood and questions its worth.

In their family homes these patients had also encountered verbal and physical violence. Kathleen recalls her husband's declaration that she should be fumigated and that the operator should then "forget to switch it orf" (126). Marjorie asks Jack a revealing question about the force used by the family home: "Wife put you away?" (132). Apparently, family members may solve conflicts by putting the offending member in a mental hospital, as they do, or threaten to do, in other Storey plays (to Adrienne in *Sisters* [139] and to Kitchen in *Early Days* [43]).

The hospital, this second home to which the patients have been sent, is both like and unlike their family homes. It has its own unpleasantness: regimentation and violence. Here are perhaps one or two thousand people (114, 142). Meals are, of course, served according to schedule, with certain foods on certain days of the week, in a group dining room where the patients have to queue. The mental hospital also has a prescribed time for remedials: Alfred, for example, makes baskets. To enforce order, the hospital uses not only regimentation but also the violence of a lobotomy, as in Alfred's case (134, 138), or the "padded whatsit" (132). For these people, the hospital has the potential of being, as for Yvonne, a "hell-place" (ATL 34) or, for Adrienne, "worse than hell: it's all fastened up" (S 140).

However, despite the negative aspects of institutionalism, the mental hospital, not a home, may also be more than a home in the compensations it furnishes: the assembly and temporary union of dissimilar people who share the hospital routines and the usual human physical and spiritual concerns. The hospital brings together into one place very diverse people. Harry and Jack, gentlemen in appearance, reminisce about boarding school, travel, and military service, but remain decorously reserved about their private lives. Unlike the men, the informally-dressed lower-class women, with the uninhibited vitality characterizing workmen in *The Contractor* and rugby players in *The Changing Room*, talk about sex, crying spells, and family difficulties. The fifth character, Alfred, a lobotomized wrestler, says little except "yeh" and "no" but performs feats of unusual physical strength, like lifting a table above his head.

Incompatible as they may appear, the patients share daily activities in the hospital. They read the newspaper and go to meals. They wonder whether they will have sausage or corned beef hash for lunch, stress the need to take walks and do exercises, and complain about bladder trouble and aching feet. Aware of other people's needs, they give physical help, like supporting a limping patient or holding a chair. While these patients, especially the women, sometimes ridicule each other (for example, about sex), they still seem genuinely interested in others.

Naturally anxious about physical realities, the patients also agonize about spiritual matters: self-identity, communication, and the meaning of life. Throughout the play the patients talk about their identities and ponder the relationship between fact and fiction. The information they give about the past and the present is elusive and contradictory but not necessarily untrue. Jack presents several versions of his jobs and family, and Harry defends fantasy (123). Kathleen's question concerning Jack, "He really what he says he is?" (123), could be asked about all of them.

Regardless of who the patients are or have been, they wrestle with the need for communication. Often failing to communicate, they speak in elliptical phrases or lapse into Pinteresque silences. At other times they do communicate or at least recognize their inability to do so. Jack, for example, distinguishes between seeing people and talking meaningfully with them: "One meets people. But very little communication actually takes place" (97).

During this representative day in the mental hospital, the patients share another universal preoccupation: as they talk about the past and the present, they try to determine the significance of their lives. With very human mixtures of optimism and pessimism, insight and rationalization, they alternate between despair and resignation, and both affirm and deny struggle. Sometimes they reveal to each other their wishes for death; Kathleen confesses, "Shoot my brains out if I had a chance" (128). Or they can weep together, as do Jack and Harry at the end of the play. In less gloomy moments the patients take misfortunes for granted; knowing that failures are universal, they have compassion for themselves and for others ("our little foibles, our little failings" [117]).

With insight not always achieved by the conventionally sane, one patient, Kathleen, perceptively notes the paradoxical value and irrelevancy of struggle. Near the end of the play, just after the weeping Harry declines to hold Kathleen's offered hand, Marjorie suggests that they leave:

> MARJORIE: "Try and make something. What you get for
> it?"
> KATHLEEN: "Get nothing if you don't try, girl."
> MARJORIE: "No."
> KATHLEEN: "Get nothing if you do, either." (139)

Whether Kathleen is referring to the attempt and failure to get the men's attention or to all of life, she effectively compresses life's contradictions.

Despite its limitations, then, the hospital creates a setting where routine activities and feelings about life and death can be shared. Like the tent-erecting group in *The Contractor* and the rugby game in *The Changing Room*, the mental hospital brings together previously unrelated people. Making no distinctions among social classes and temperaments, madness unites, even if only temporarily, all the patients in several common interests. An institution like this one may have the qualities that Jack attributes, whether idealistically or realistically, to the military service and the airfield, "one great big family" (104).

Like a tent-erecting group or a rugby team in still another way, the hospital may accomplish for patients what erection of the tent and completion of the rugby game do for workers and players. Insanity, as Storey said in the Ansorge interview already cited, gives reassurance, just as sports and work do. Here in the mental hospital the patients can gain rest from their previous homes and the world. From the outside the patients hear of "damn bad news" (88)—possibilities of bombs, floods, or nameless catastrophes (102). Life there, Kathleen and Marjorie report, was like being with "a steam engine" or "a boa constrictor." But here, in the clean, well-lighted place of the mental hospital, "you get a good night's sleep" (109–110).

Admittedly, sleep has ominous implications, especially in the conclusion, with the shadows suggesting both the literal end of day (143) and the end of life after experiences on "a long road" (128). When Alfred asks Harry and Jack, "You finished?" (143–144), he ostensibly means the chairs, but "finished" may be as complex here as in *The Restoration of Arnold Middleton*. Finished with another day and perhaps with life, these patients, at rest, at home, ambivalently look forward to and fear another home. But despite these melancholy overtones of death, the patients redeem their stay in the hospital. As they share experiences, help each other, and resiliently try to communicate, they transcend the institutional origins of this home and develop community—Storey's reassurance. This diverse group in an isolated place poignantly exhibits in microcosm the ability of people to create and endure—accepting its contradictions of prison and haven—a temporary home.

Home constitutes a natural development from *The Restoration of Arnold Middleton*. The earlier play shows the family's contribution to Arnold Middleton's difficulties. Only partially successful in asserting his autonomy, he remains in his home—possibly forced into a psychological lobotomy. In *Home* the patients from deficient family homes, now in a second home which also sometimes utilizes force (whether through involuntary incarceration or restrictive schedules), are not necessarily in worse surroundings than before. They are perhaps in better surroundings—in the fellowship created among them and in their freedom from communally-defined reality. Behavior considered strange in families (Arnold's, for example) is more acceptable in mental hospitals. Though carrying a social stigma, the label of insanity gives plausibility to unusual conduct. In a setting like *Home* the abnormal becomes normal.

Depiction of the abnormal as normal achieves its culmination in *Mother's Day* (1976), a madness-and-the-family farce which provides another perspective from which to examine *The Restoration of Arnold Middleton* and *Home*. This play, called a parody of Storey's earlier works "revealing the family group as exploiters of themselves and others" (Kalson, "Mother's" 261) and "a nightmare version of your average Storey family" (Brown 36), presents madness as normality. Thematically, this play is clearly related to Storey's other works, as he explained to Hutchings: ". . . everything in *Mother's Day* was supposed to be a family where every traditional value was carefully inverted and the obverse was true of everyday reality. . . . Everything which was against the rule and totally unacceptable in family life was the norm in this family" (115). The effectiveness of this inversion is demonstrated by the ease with which lines from this play apply to other families in Storey's plays. The family in this house, in which "There isn't one person . . . who isn't crazy" (MD 216), "needs looking into" (190). Similarly applicable are Farrer's question, "What sort of house have you landed us in?" (212); Mrs. Johnson's exclamation, "Oh. What it is to have a family" (252); and Mrs. Johnson's assessment: "Oh, we're just an ordinary family. . . . No better, I can assure you, and certainly no worse than most" (259). Furthermore, although many characters in this play are called or call themselves "mad" and "insane," one member (in this case, Lily) is specifically designated as "a raving lunatic" (201) and "brainless" (253). Again, as in other Storey plays, this character "is not quite as mad as she seems; she is often the one to draw attention to what is really happening" (Kerensky 13).

Mother's Day, then, expands the vision of family madness; paradoxically, it contains bizarre inversions of and consistencies with family reality. Among the Johnsons (as in *Home, The Restoration of Arnold Middleton*, and *A Temporary Life*, for example), "home" possesses multiple meanings: "It changes, you see, quite often," Judy says (MD 181). Finally, the label "our little nest" (MD 255) is no more inappropriate for the Johnson family than the label "home" for some conventional families in Storey's plays.

Given the alternative of the conventional family home, the patients in the mental hospital might agree with Storey, who once said of *Home*: "The longer you stay bonkers the safer you are" (Ansorge 35). Although conceivably the mental hospital may impose on the patients a peace consisting of drugged stupor, insanity levels social classes, provides a perspective denied to outsiders; and creates a feeling of unity and security. The patients "are all at home here" (Rosen 138). Both *Home* and *The Restoration of Arnold Middleton*, containing themes resonating throughout Storey's works, "expose [as Anita Guiton says of *Home*] an ambivalence in our expectations of 'ordinary' and 'family' life, showing how subtly yet inexorably this can lead to the asylum" ("David Storey" 73). In a universe offering no adequate homes, the mental hospital may be at least an approximation. Arnold Middleton's home may be an institution, but the institution, the mental hospital, may be a home.

Notes

1. However, madness is not always allied with the family in Storey's works. Instead, in *Cromwell*, for example, madness is allied with various forms of ideology: "One madness exits but to greet the next," and ". . . a madman clears the field apace; where thistles, grass and nettle grew a second madman

plants the weeds anew," declare Logan and O'Halloran, respectively (C, 54, 56). In that play, "Regardless of the nature of the commitment—whether secular or sacred, traditional or anarchic, altruistic or pragmatic, institutional or merely self-interested—the presence of an ideology gives each person a semblance of madness in the estimation of those who do not share his views" (Hutchings 39).

2. Bernard Bergonzi, "Novelists of the Sixties" [interview with David Storey], Programme 1, BBC; unedited (unbroadcast) version provided by Bernard Bergonzi and used by permission of Bergonzi, David Storey, and the BBC. The references to Laing did not appear in the edited [broadcast] version, 20 February 1968, also used by permission of Bergonzi, Storey, and the BBC. In the original version all page numbers are preceded by the designation 2/ (e.g., 2/3, 2/4); for purposes of clarity I have omitted the use of 2/ in citations in this text.

3. Storey's articulation of the parallels with Laing's theories occurred around the time (1964–1966) that *The Restoration of Arnold Middleton* was revised from the earlier version, *To Die with the Philistines*, and that other plays—*In Celebration*, and *Home*—were composed (1967). (See Hutchings's chronology of composition and production of the plays [10–11].) *To Die with the Philistines* was first written around 1959 (Hutchings 9; Taylor, "British" 22), the year in which Laing's *The Divided Self* was published.

4. In parenthetical citations, Storey's works will be identified by their acronyms.

5. At first, Storey explained in an interview, he thought these characters were in a hotel, but then he began to realize that "they were bonkers." But he objected to an exclusive identification of the setting as a mental hospital: ". . . the characters . . . are what you might meet in the street any day." Instead of thinking, "These people are mad and we're not mad," spectators should feel at one with them (Hayman 49, 52).

6. Kalson suggests, "For some . . . [of Storey's characters], to lose the mind is to gain the self" ("Insanity" 111). This seems true of Arnold.

Works Cited

Ansorge, Peter. "The Theatre of Life: David Storey in Interview with Peter Ansorge." *Plays and Players* September 1973: 32–36.

Bergonzi, Bernard. "Novelists of the Sixties" [interview with David Storey]. Programme 1, BBC, broadcast 20 February 1968. (Both the unedited [unbroadcast] version [provided by Bernard Bergonzi] and the edited [broadcast] version [provided by the BBC] are used by permission of Bergonzi, David Storey, and the BBC.)

Brown, Geoff. *"Mother's Day." Plays and Players* December 1976: 35–36.

Cox, Frank. "Writing for the Stage: Keith Dewhurst, Peter Nichols and David Storey Talking to Frank Cox." *Plays and Players* September 1967: 40–42, 50.

Guiton, Anita. "Comments on David Storey's 'Pasmore' and 'A Temporary Life.'" *Delta* 53 (1975): 20–28.

———. "David Storey: From Saville to A Prodigal Child." *The Cambridge Quarterly* 13 (1984): 71–90.

Hayman, Ronald. "Conversation with David Storey." *Drama* 99 (Winter 1970); 47–53. Reprint. Ronald Hayman. *Playback*. London: Davis-Poynter, 1973. 7–20.

Hutchings, William. *The Plays of David Storey: A Thematic Study*. Carbondale: Southern Illinois University Press, 1988.

Kalson, Albert E. "Insanity and the Rational Man in the Plays of David Storey." *Modern Drama* 19.2 (June 1976): 111–28.

———. *"Mother's Day." Educational Theatre Journal* 29 (May 1977): 260–61.

Kerensky, Oleg. "David Storey." *The New British Drama: Fourteen Playwrights since Osborne and Pinter*. London: Hamish Hamilton, 1977. 3–17.

Laing, R. D. *The Divided Self: An Existential Study in Sanity and Madness*. London: Tavistock Publications, 1959. Reprint. Baltimore: Penguin, 1965.

Peel, Marie. "David Storey: Demon and Lazarus." *Books and Bookmen* 17 (March 1972): 20–24.

Rosen, Carol. *"Home." Plays of Impasse: Contemporary Drama Set in Confining Institutions*. Princeton: Princeton University Press, 1983. 128–46.

Sage, Victor. "David Storey in Conversation." *New Review* 3.31 (1976): 63–65.

Storey, David. "Blake" [poem]. *Program of The Restoration of Arnold Middleton.* Royal Court Theatre, London, 4 July 1967. Provided by Anne Jenkins (Royal Court Theatre) and used by permission of David Storey.

——. *Cromwell.* London: Jonathan Cape, 1973.

——. *Early Days.* In *Early Days, Sisters and Life Class.* London: Jonathan Cape, 1975. Reprint. in this collection, Harmondsworth: Penguin, 1980.

——. *Flight into Camden.* London: Longman, 1960. Reprint. Harmondsworth: Penguin, 1976.

——. *Home.* In *The Changing Room, Home, The Contractor.* London: Jonathan Cape, 1970; London: Jonathan Cape, 1972. Reprint. New York: Bard-Avon, 1975.

——. *Mother's Day.* In *Home, The Changing Room, Mother's Day.* London: Jonathan Cape, 1970; London: Jonathan Cape, 1972. Reprint. in this collection, Harmondsworth: Penguin, 1978.

——. *Pasmore.* London: Longman, 1972. Reprint. New York: Avon, 1975.

——. *Present Times.* London: Jonathan Cape, 1984.

——. *Radcliffe.* London: Longman, 1963. Reprint. New York: Avon, 1975.

——. *The Restoration of Arnold Middleton.* London: Jonathan Cape, 1967.

——. *Sisters.* In *Early Days, Sisters and Life Class.* London: Jonathan Cape, 1975. Reprint. in this collection, Harmondsworth: Penguin, 1980.

——. *A Temporary Life.* London: Allen Lane, 1973.

——. *This Sporting Life.* London: Longman, 1960. Reprint. New York: Avon, 1975.

Taylor, John Russell. "British Dramatists: The New Arrivals No. 3: David Storey: Novelist into Dramatist." *Plays and Players* June 1970: 22–24.

——. "David Storey." *The Second Wave: British Drama for the Seventies.* New York: Hill and Wang, 1971. 141–54.

——. "David Storey." Writers and Their Work 239. Ed. Ian Scott-Kilvert. London: Longman, 1974.

Worth, Katharine J. *Revolutions in Modern English Drama.* London: G. Bell, 1973. 26–30, 38–40.

"WHAT IT IS TO BE A WOMAN" IN THE PLAYS OF DAVID STOREY

Lois More Overbeck

Overtly naturalistic in their detail, from the sweat and liniment of *The Changing Room* to the raising of an actual tent in *The Contractor*, Storey's dramas are noted as well for their Pinteresque tendency to slice a cross-section of the psyche. Embedded in irony, the dramatic action sets a scene to spoil it, establishes a social tie that binds (or at least locates the characters as a group) only to unsettle it. The seismic tremor that shakes the status quo is often generated by an "outsider" whose presence provokes secrets otherwise repressed by the dominant narrative.[1] The "difference" of the "outsider" challenges the terms by which identity, value, or relationship has been maintained. However, when the decentering crisis passes, the social interaction seems to retreat to those patterns established in the opening scene.

Does this apparent retreat and closure suggest that complacency or resignation is a sufficient response to conflict? By the end of the plays the "outsider" is either removed or subsumed into the group, a pattern fairly typical of comedy. Austin Quigley suggests that when relationships have "run up against their limits," when the "disparity between the world [sought] . . . and the world that actually surrounds. . . ." has been exposed, there may be a more "authentic, more subtle" bond.[2] If the bond is more authentic, as in *Mother's Day* or *The Farm*, perhaps it is because everyone's vulnerabilities have been exposed. Despite their return-to-"near"-normalcy, Storey's plays actually suggest a range of responses to the difference between expectation/desire and reality: the roles and pretenses that covered up conflicts may be affirmed in order to comfort the pain of vulnerability (e.g. *Home*, *The Farm*, *In Celebration*) or modulated to accommodate new circumstances (*Mother's Day*, *The Changing Room*), or displaced (*Sisters*, *The Restoration of Arnold Middleton*), but they are not simply reinscribed. Although the surface of the characters' lives appears little changed, audiences (particularly those who are discomforted that unresolved tensions can ease back into normalcy) may resist. In that resistance, the "invisible event" of the play has its effect.[3]

Much discussion of Storey's plays has emphasized the identity that individuals find as part of a group related by action (e.g. rugby, tent raising, alliance against the enemy, life art class, sexual license or familial convention), that they find integration into "a significant unity that transcends the self" and a sense of "place" within a hierarchy.[4] However another characteristic of Storey's groups is that their bond/sameness is affirmed by their *difference from* a figure outside of the group. The son and son-in-law are "insiders" in the social world where money and education count, but outsiders to the skills and ethos of the work crew in *The Contractor*; familial bonding is limited by the differences of values between father and children, indeed to any values derived from the temporary. In *The Changing Room*, Kendal is considered a wimp by the group because of his difference from the men of the team (his tools are associated with his wife's domestic demands, his injuries take him out of the game); his difference threatens their identity which depends on separation from weakness and, hence, sexual dominance over women. Adrienne, the estranged prodigal in *Sisters*, is at first naive about the arrangements that seem to make strangers into intimates in Carol's house; but, when Adrienne catches on and becomes the life of the party, thereby threatening to intrude on both the profits and the illusion that the house of prostitution is a home, she is taken away.

Most of Storey's central characters are male. Women in his plays tend to be identified mainly by their roles in relationship to men (as mothers, wives, girlfriends) in which they are more played off against than playing (*The Restoration of Arnold Middleton*, *The Farm*, *Life Class*, *The Contractor*, *In Celebration*, *Home*). The plays present women in conventional and often denigrating stereotypes (as victim of rape or prostitute or sex object, as a manipulative and controlling angel of the house). This should not surprise, for the socialized roles with which Storey's characters identify themselves and others are established and perpetrated through difference. The measure of self cannot be taken except by measuring from a point outside: usually this point is a woman.

Yet, identity that is defined through difference (of gender, between group/outsider) is only real-for-the-moment, never permanent. When such identity is challenged or threatened or thrown over, "awareness of the disparity" or the interiorizing of difference constitutes an uneasy truce.[5] In plays where the pattern of conflict has been described as "a desire to expose" in tension with "the desire to keep things as they are," acceptance of such disparity does not construe resignation or resolution.[6] Upheaval or crisis challenges the defining terms of the arrangement, so characters and audience have to come to terms with or acknowledge difference; they can no longer just keep it outside. Even the outsider who leaves the scene also leaves a mark. The point outside is interiorized; difference becomes inherent.

Woman as Accessory

Women are a point outside in many of Storey's plays, an object of difference from which men take their bearings and over whom men need control. As sexual objects, women are clearly outside the world of *The Changing Room*.[7] Walsh twits Trevor with innuendoes about the girls he teaches: "Old Trevor: guides them over the road, you know . . . by hand" (98); maths is one of his subjects, "T'other's the bloody lasses" (150). Walsh, just come from his brother's wedding, takes pity on the bride ("poor lass"). To fit into the locker room group, Walsh calls the opposing team a "Load o' bloody pansies. Tell it at a glance. . ." (99) and continues to bash Trevor, who is married, by bragging about "some skirt at that bloody wedding, Jagger . . . (To Trevor) Steam thy bloody glasses up, old lad" (99). Trevor is married to a woman who has a university degree, which marks her as different from most of the team, although the only difference the men are willing to acknowledge is sexual. Because she does not come to see Trevor play, the boys suggest that she employs this time in other ways (with other men). The fraternity of male pride draws the line, however, when Walsh insinuates that Sandy has been "having it off with Trevor's wife" (106).

Kendal is set apart as they look over his parcel, impugning his manhood and his domestication in one slighting glance: "Bought her a do-it-yourself kit have you?" Women are domesticating; their refinement imposes confining limits on men. Patsy has a woman waiting for him after the game, a teacher in Trevor's school; Jagger and Fenchurch ridicule his submissiveness, telling him to mind his language or his girlfriend would take offense and make him write a thousand times: "I must not bloody swear, you cunt" (153). Having a permanent relationship with a woman is just a joke: "Gi'e her a big kiss, then, Patsy, lad" and "for me, an all," followed by a chorus of "for me's." Real men are in control of their relationship with women; they have tarts and go to "Nude-arama" (100).

This is locker room talk, and the locker room is the middle ground between the outside world and the playing field. In the game, these men are players, a team victorious in contest with rivals. But the game ends: Kendal's injury leads others to say that he is too old to continue, and Owens admits—"One more season, I think: I'm finished" (168). The male bonding of *The Changing Room* depends on the teamwork on the field, but participation in the game is only temporary. In the locker room, the team is broken down; the competition is man to man. Here the score in the game of manhood is measured by sexual control over women. Will this game suffice outside of the changing room, in the world of men and women?

In *The Contractor*, Ewbank confronts the temporary nature of the work that has defined his life.[8] In this play, the women characters are mother, wife, daughter; the occasion is a wedding that bonds men and women in family ties. Nonetheless, women, particularly the daughter whose wedding is being celebrated, are barely a presence in the play, and the marriage occurs between the acts. The customized tent that Ewbank created especially for his daughter is left in shambles after the wedding. Furthermore, Ewbank's pride and function is challenged:

a tent raising typically makes him part of a team (as artisan not worker), but when it is for his daughter's wedding on his front lawn with his family watching, his role becomes ambivalent. He is both consumer and provider of services ("It's the first time I've hired a bit of my own tenting. . . . Pay meself with one hand what I tek out with the other"), which distances him from his role (139). He takes an artisan's pride in his craft, but the marriage of his daughter to a man of a different class displaces him and the values on which he has built his life.

To extend his own male identity, he cuts Paul off from participation in his world, and yet is shattered that he has educated a wanderer (cf. Slattery to his son in *The Farm*). To reclaim his authority with the foreman, Ewbank ridicules his son's efforts to lend a hand: "I'd forgotten you'd hands on inside them pockets" (118); later, when Paul offers to hold down the ropes, Ewbank dismisses him to deal with the flowers (177). On the other hand, although differences between the workers are acute, they "do not disparage one another in the presence of outsiders."[9] Even if in the end, father and son are "reconciled to their differences" as Hutchings suggests,[10] the disparity of values distresses them both.

Daughter Claire rates wolf whistles from the crew; when Glendenning admits his attraction for her, the men make a vulgar rhyme about her physical prowess: "She was only a tentman's daughter/ But she knew how to pull on a guy" (132). Although Ewbank has made a "bloody thunderclap" out of the wedding, he also resents her superior difference from him, underscored by her marriage to a doctor: he is one with his men in saying, "they're [women are] only good for one damn thing. And for that you don't have to read a book" (139).

Ewbank's grand house (built with the money he didn't pay his workers) and his concern that the lawn and his family remain untarnished by their work, make the crew testy. As Katharine Worth points out, the context of the men at work (swearing, fights, broad humor, animal behavior) contrasts with the "lovely . . . marquee," the flowers, the "air of elegance."[11] Glendenning, the stuttering simpleton, is made to tiptoe over Ewbank's lawn by the men, who resent Ewbank's order that no holes be made in the grass. Glendenning's obvious question turns out to be central to the play: "How're you going to k . . . kkkk . . . keep it up?" (125).

By the end of the play, not only is the tent down, but the progenitor has been left without an heir to his craft or a validation of his worth. The values for which he has lived seem to be, like the tent, temporary structures. The canvas has been specially made and even has Ewbank's name on it (140), the stitching is beautiful (127), and Mrs. Ewbank admires the work ("It's not often I see one of your father's tents go up" [152]), but the wedding rabble mocks his care. "I came out here, you know, this morning. . . . Saw it all. . . . Damn near broke my bloody heart . . ." (218).

The day after is marked by leavings and of reckonings: "You could put us all into a string bag, you know, and chuck us all away, and none'd be the wiser" (219). When Mrs. Ewbank joins her husband, she offers nothing more than an ear to his musings, judging rather than understanding why he gave the crew a nip. She is only a point outside of his experience. Ewbank does not "keep it up": "You think you'd have something to show for it. . . . What's to become of us, you reckon?" (222–223). To be sure, as he walks to the house with his wife, to see "the old uns off," normalcy is apparently restored, but the perception of value and relationship is radically altered: "the stage stands empty" (223).

In *Home*, the empty words and banal banter of Harry and Jack might be taken as the coded conversation between two familiars sitting in the smoking room of a stuffy club, and not the evasion "duologues" of asylum inmates.[12] The ambiguity is probably intentional, since they "reiterate the historical, geographical and cultural co-ordinates of the England they admire"[13] Women are a part of their chat, as well as their lives, but only in a passing way: a mother with seven children whose husband was emotional but dominated, an aunt with arthritis, sisters who died, a wife who is delicate. Neither man is particularly successful in marriage: "One endeavours . . . but it is in the nature of things, I believe, that, on the whole, one fails" (44). Both men are prone to weeping.

Kathleen and Marjorie are women of a different cut; their clothing, dialect, and open reference to sexuality and the asylum

("Don't want me to escape") counterpoint comically with the self-sustaining if evasive dignity of the two men. Kathleen's major contribution to conversation is a swooning "Oooh!" to all of Marjorie's sexual allusions: "know what he'd spend it [the whole of one's life] inside if he had half a chance" (50).

When they are together, in the foursome or as a pair, the women bring out a little more in the men than they are comfortable discussing. When Kathleen and Harry are alone after lunch, she tries to get Harry to reveal why Jack is in the "home": "Your friend come in for following little girls?" Harry, who never finishes a sentence, is always circumspect: "certain proclivities," "certain pressures," "encouraged to come here for a little er" (59). As Kathleen supplies the narrative, he merely assents or defers "Well, I . . . ," "Oh yes" (62). Kathleen, who has tried to kill herself and others, declares that she "wouldn't be a woman. Not again . . . " (63). Yet according to Marjorie, she is forever a woman and one who "Can't keep away from men" (66). And Kathleen can reach out a hand to comfort Harry, "who is able to take it because she makes it possible for the chivalry to be his."[14]

When Jack and Marjorie join them, the men retreat to general chatter, withdrawing from the innuendoes of the ladies: "with frequent recourse to the impersonal 'one' construction . . . and statements repeatedly prefaced with a defensive 'oh' . . . " [15] Jack is forever changing the subject and Harry is always affirming or adding to Jack's comments. As Kathleen leads Harry off for a stroll, Marjorie tells all about Kathleen's troubles, but Jack responds only with assent or non sequitur. Having found little action for their trouble, the women leave; the men return to banal noncommunication, both coming to tears in the end.

Among other things, the suggestion of the play's structure and its canters is that Jack and Harry are in the home because they cannot "connect" in a normative way with women or with their lives. They certainly veer from the sexual axis that Kathleen and Marjorie would be happy to supply. Although dramatically they are contrasted to the specimen physicality of Alfred, who has had a lobotomy to control his strength and feelings, Harry and Jack have chosen to disconnect from those situations that cause them pain. They fall back "on the shared little-Englander attitudes and assumptions that lie behind their symbiosis, taking comfort from them after the disruptions caused by the women."[16] The schematics of dramaturgy resemble the geometry of a figure defined in relationship to the point outside. All of these characters are abandoned, and their home, the asylum, confirms the isolation that they cannot confront. So they live with reference to the society that is outside and prefer to keep it there:

JACK:	Heart-break.
HARRY:	Oh, yes.
JACK:	Same mistake . . . Won't make it twice.
HARRY:	Oh, no.
JACK:	Once over. Never again. (82)

Although in *Life Class* Storey's characters discuss the sexism implied by having only female models ("It's different for a girl"), the fact remains that the nude model for the *Life Class* is both a subject for art and a sex object for the class.[17] Despite Allott's insistence that true art is impersonal and that art is "above sex . . . absorbs sex" (179), the students debate: is the female an object because the greatest artists have been male?; is woman an object because men like "contemplating their slaves" (180)?; are no women artists because in women talent is "made to seem unnatural" (181)? Although Allott does not take sides ("I'm accepting that anything is possible" [182]), he is aware of the puerile licentiousness of students in the presence of Stella's nude body, particularly the exhibitionist tendencies of Mathews. Having caught Mathews prancing around on the model's platform wearing Catherine's hat, Allott positions Mathews as if a model, invites him to lower his trousers, and lets the class laugh at him; Mathews later disrupts with laxative jokes (the "raspberry" is his characteristic sound effect), sexual overtures to and finally the simulated rape of Stella. Mathews explains himself: "You act up to what people expect of you" (214).

Absent at the beginning and toward the end of the "rest" period, Allott is "disinterested" (absent-though-present) in the pretended rape of Stella that dismantles his professional role as well as the class. To Allott, art is "merely a question . . . of seeing each detail in relation to all the rest" (176). He has given up conventional media for the event—

trying to find a relation to "all the rest." By the end of the *Life Class*, Allott himself is the point outside. His objectification of the rape scene and all of the sexual harassment that precedes it "neglects both the cruelty and dehumanization" implicit in the student's behavior.[18] Allott's events are invisible (210); as with his drawing of Mathews (who had posed for over a half an hour), it is symptomatic of Allott's art that "There's nothing there . . ." (216).

"How do you sell an event that no one will admit is taking place?" (202). Allott offers to become model for the *"Life Class"* and stimulates an "event." Mathews immediately jumps to the platform and, spurred on by the other males in the class, appears to rape Stella. To others in the class, and especially to the women students, the simulation seems real. If art as a process "enables the transcendence of space and time," then symbolically the rape intrudes "the most base and sordid of worldly 'realities'" over the transcendent.[19] With practically no overt reaction, Allott invites Stella to resume her pose. The relationship between Allott, the students, and the model constitute an event—both in the sense of a staged play and in Allott's understanding of an invisible event which is at the heart of Storey's plays—a kind of synergism of characters, audience, and society. It is, as Allott says, indefinable; it is more real than reality. If it appears value neutral, it seldom remains so for its audience.

"No work of art is complete without a personal statement" (228), says Allott as he sets the students back to the task of the life class. The "event" of Mathews's simulated rape of Stella has been felt as embodiment of an attitude about women as less valued, able to be used by the desire of men, about a society which limits and punishes, which makes the victims guilty for being the victims. If Allott did not make the event happen, he let it happen.

In a sense Allott's voice may be one with the sensibility that has shaped these plays: "I've gazed over the edge, Philips, long enough . . . it's the staying there that worries me . . . I'm beginning to think I'll never get back . . ." (203). Except for *Life Class*, all of these plays do drift back into the normalcy defined in the opening scene. And even the life class will be given again tomorrow, with a new teacher.

But the audience has also gazed over the edge, and while they may not stay there, the invisible event will no doubt stay with them.

Woman as Axis

When women are central figures in Storey's dramas, they provide an axis for a "family" that is often a perverse inversion of conventional and sentimentalized values (e.g. *Mother's Day, Sisters, The Restoration of Arnold Middleton*).

Though one never knows whether Arnie Middleton is joking or taking a jest too far, when he says "All my life I've looked for some positive reaction in people," it rings true.[20] Nonetheless (like the character of Robin Hood in the play that he is directing for the school), he is a usurper, an outlaw, "always on the outside of things." Arnie asserts that kingship is something he has studied all his life; for him, kings are "a sort of receptacle, if you like. Into which flow all the goodness and intentions of mankind: and out of which in turn flow benevolence—and decisions. Authority. Rule" (96). Like the archaic values represented by the suit of armour, kingship represents Middleton's "longing for the security" of spiritual hierarchy.[21] At one point in their drunkenness, Joan even explains to the incredulous Maureen that Arnie is God.

Having tested the waters of madness, having spun out of emotional control, Arnie becomes willing to consider "alternatives. . . . To Kingship"(98).

> Everything has to be defined. Yet how can you define
> anything except by its limitations? Why!—my limitations
> are limitless (99).

Joan does provide Arnie with a defining axis. Arnie wants to be drawn into her center, yet he pulls away and flies off at tangents to the curved path of their marriage (routine and relationship). As he careens through scene after scene of drunken free-for-alls and mad revelry, Arnie spins out of himself, canceling expectations and relationships. If at all, the very brief glimpse into the "restoration" of Arnie Middleton comes at the end when, exhausted, he submits to Joan's directives.

Having "taken refuge in insanity," Arnie returns to the driving axis of Joan's domesticity (87). If this is "restoration," it is along the lines of a "psychological lobotomy," suggests Laura Weaver.[22]

Joan Middleton's middle-class drawing room competes with Arnold Middleton's "rudiments of a museum" (11). While the first scene displays Joan as the driving force of the household, Arnold's resistance constitutes the play's action as he projects himself through obsessively gathering artifacts (interesting things), acting out before the student body, playing with the fawning attentions of a student Sheila, apparently seducing his mother-in-law, and finally adopting madness. Joan is a point outside, from which Arnold measures his mark. Her reaction defines the effect of his actions, which are, at the same time, calculated to separate himself from her. His faculty colleagues introduce a wider form of social propriety from which Arnold Middleton can deviate.

Even before Arnie enters, Joan rants about him, irritated by a full suit of armour he has ordered; she sees it first as a "joke" (11), then as an insult (12), and finally with paranoia ("They're like spies" [13]). His "interesting" things intrude on her control over house and home and also displace her as object of Arnie's attention. Raging that she will not be among Arnold's trophies, Joan leaves by the back door as he enters through the front. However, her studied indifference is lost on Arnold and denied by the stage business of the first scene, which has been her bustling preparation of his afternoon tea. Joan appears to be a weakened variant of "wife-as-mother."

Arnie plays with women as he plays with life. He greets his mother-in-law as "Loved one" and, to her appreciative encouragement, whips his coat about as if a master lion tamer of students (17), crawls to her feet and explains her "shoes are full of hope" (18). Clearly he is not. Though he playfully sweet-talks her, as Mrs. Ellis talks about household tensions and reminds that his parents are expected, his histrionics settle into the mundane (cup and pipe), and Arnold appears to be hemmed in, caught in the quarrel of his wife and her mother, equally disinclined to accept the attentions of wife or the doggedly admiring female student who follows him down the lane, of whom he says, "I never know whether she's keeping me in, or keeping the others out" (56). Hanson says of Arnie, "He's a lie himself. If you measured him by any reality he'd be invisible" (71). This is Arnie's problem: he needs to measure himself from a point outside, yet he refuses to let others (women) define him by their needs. He would be king, but he cannot find a self.

Joan's paranoia seems real to her; her tactics are manipulative; her respect for Arnold nil. Although his intentionality is harder to assess, his jokester tactic is to unsettle; he never delivers what is expected. In Act I, Joan plots a confrontation over his armour which she has hidden in the closet, so he puffs on his pipe with nonchalance and foils her hostility with sweet reasonableness: "You're very aggressive, Joan. Has it assaulted you . . . ?" (26). Then he fans her ultimatum by swashbuckling about the room with the sword snatched from the cupboard.

Arnold acts as re-action. Between acts there has been a drunken carouse, and so the ménage-à-trois enters having had a "good time" only to dissipate into old quarrels and mother/daughter jealousy over Arnold, a leg-judging contest, and a mock Samson and Delilah scene in which mother abets daughter in cutting off Arnold's hair. In vengeance, Arnie chooses Edie's legs as best; he meets Joan's flashpoint with school yard verses that trivialize her anger, finally walking away from both women. By playing one off against the other, Arnie keeps both outside his realm.

Arnold's defensive and diversionary by-play has escalated by Act II. In pompous verbosity, colleague Hanson outlines his view of the woman issue and indirectly underscores Arnie's insecurities. Hanson observes that women are "gradually acquiring a physical superiority to men." Arnie responds to his concern with a joke, but Hanson continues "whereas we are always under this obligation to them [for birth], they are never under a reciprocal obligation to us? They, as it were, divulge us: whereas we—we are simply exposed" (46–47).

Arnold is exposed, but he also displays himself at every turn. Joan says, "You show nothing but a parody of yourself" (49). Mocking her, he pretends to be child victim of Ladybug's neglect, calling "Help! Help! . . . HELP!" His bluff seems called by Joan: "It's not a game, is it?" (50). She calmly studies his face. She holds him in her gaze. He has lost control. Although she leaves Arnie sitting impassively at the table, her question hangs over the stage image like a caption: "What are you frightened of?" (50).

When Joan reenters, she fixes him in her gaze momentarily, and then brusquely begins to settle the issues: they will clean house of his collections ("I suggest we get rid of all these" and "while we're clearing everything away there's one other thing. It's time my mother left . . ." [52]). Arnie's embedded attachment to mother-wife and objects suggest psychological dependence and insecurity. In doggerel he claims, "When I was young, my mother said to me/. . . . 'Please, please my son,/ Don't fail me like your father done'" (88). Another root of his insecurity is suggested as Joan tells of the time when Arnold's mother told her to "look after my only son" and Arnold quickly inverted: "Your only sin, Mother (58–59)." Whether atonement is for the mother's guilt and/or the father's inadequacy (cf. *In Celebration, Mother's Day*) or displacement of the father by the son (cf. *The Farm*), it does indicate that Arnie's problems run deep, and are symptomatic of a "more fundamental and profound spiritual . . . inadequacy."[23]

Despite his acting out, his refusal to be governed by Joan's axis, his claim in verse that ". . . the only women I ever see/ Are the ones that need hanging from the nearest tree" (30), Arnie's threnody stresses interdependence: "You can't turn people out like that. . . . Not when they rely on you" (54). Joan has rid the house of her mother and his collections, yet Arnie cannot separate from Joan's axis, not when he relies on her. Of the "restoration" in this play, Storey said, "He's restored to a very conventional bourgeois life, and that's really awful, a sort of living death, yet the ambiguity comes in— . . ."[24] Indeed, Arnold has kept his sword: "The King, though broken by his plight,/ Shall rise again to set things right!" (91).

In *The Farm*, the patriarchal identity of Mr. Slattery is both the family's centripetal force and its crisis.[25] Jenny describes the family as "one, huge, corporeal mass . . . a sort of animal with seven heads . . ." (44).

Having "no great opinion of women" (62) but surrounded by them, Slattery consoles himself with drink. Although Wendy, Jenny and Brenda are differentiated as female types, to Slattery they are, collectively, "unmarried daughters." Brenda says, "Your trouble is . . . You see me . . . and Jenny. And our Wendy . . . Like some sort of primeval cattle. Cows" (18). Slattery says, "If a woman can't have babbies when she's young, I don't know what else she can have" (15), and so he claims that his daughters are "going to rot" (14). Blind to anything but what he wishes to see (cf. 76), Slattery takes his daughters' rejection of "family" values as mockery of himself. Though overstated, his fear of role inversion shows how stripped of identity he would be without his place as father and provider (cf. 75). Wendy comments perceptively: "all idealism, at some point, presupposes a certain degree of paranoia" (68). To put women and his son in their places salvages his own, at their expense.

The three daughters, all choosing to live at home past the time of their youth, present aberrant variations on the female role. Wendy, who reads only books written by women authors, has married, then abandoned marriage and moved back home. According to Jenny, she has "Been battling with her femininity all these years . . ." (72), or as Wendy says of herself, "I battle with my sense of inferiority in being a woman" (73). On the other hand, Jenny bounces from man to man and bed to bed. Brenda calls her a whore (11); Wendy says she "battles with . . . lasciviousness" (73), but is "incapable of . . . committing [her]self to anything" (69). Jenny only laughs and says, "Child of nature: what I am" (70).

As much as she declares difference from her father, Brenda is most like him. Battling "with her social ideals" (73), Brenda has made placards and intervention in labor disputes her forte; a "real subversionist is Brenda" (67). Even Slattery notices that she "Tell'd me last night I was nothing but a sot . . . Comes up with a tumblerful [of whiskey] this morning" (52). As the youngest, she is most judgmental and blunt, having come early to the "perverse vicissitudes of life" (12). Albert, the village lad, is intimidated by her, "You're always laughing. . . . scoffing" (24). Like Slattery, he cannot understand their choices; "Why don't you women ever get married?" (25). But as Brenda says later to Wendy, "I feel at times we already are [married]" (31).

In their differences from Slattery's idea of female adequacy, each woman serves as counterpoint to their father's idea of his familial role, and his demands overdetermine the way they have defined their own sexual identity. Slattery needs "family" as a validation of his role. Though he milks it for self-pity ("Meks no difference to me. Gone their own bloody ways . . . Gi'en no bloody attention to me" [54]), the refusal of all the children to fashion themselves in his way challenges his life pattern. Similarly he decries encroaching automation, because it saves the labor that has been the measure of his worth.[26]

> I've worked like an animal all my life. . . . Lived like a bloody animal, an' all. . . . Like a dung-heap is this house . . . grow cows and bullocks and geese and hens . . . Be-asts . . . be-asts . . . be-asts for meat, and milk . . . and bread . . . (87).

Brenda said to her father, "You're nothing but an animal yourself . . . All these years . . . We've tried to think of you as something else" (18).

So has Mrs. Slattery, who is protective of and sometimes subservient to her husband, despite the apparent independence of her outside interests. His identity is their problem, too. From her attempt to ration Slattery's liquor to fussing about his breakfast, his health, and his mood, she placates him to keep the peace. In return, Slattery attacks her where she is most vulnerable: that Arthur would choose to replace her attentions by marrying an older woman, that she is the one that ruined him ("Bloody immortalised that lad afore he was even born" [63]). Slattery expects the attentions of his wife (21), and she has felt desired ("He was very much the sort of man, you know, who, if he saw a thing, went out and got it" [22]), but he resents her difference from him, epitomized by her study of psychology and sociology, and her encouragement of Arthur's writing. "I know my bloody place," he says, to put Mrs. Slattery into hers (19).

Arthur has never measured up. Having displaced him in Mrs. Slattery's attentions and disappointed him in choosing words over work, Arthur is doomed to lose in his father's estimation. His return home is furtive; word of his engagement is dropped clue by clue, as he tests the familial waters to see how his choice will be received before he brings her home. Aged twenty-two, he proposes to marry an actress, over forty, who is divorced with two children: "a father quicker than you thought" (36). Arthur seems his father's opposite; in every way, he is evasive rather than direct.

His return drives all the old grudges into the open: "Don't know what he bloody well has come home for. . . . Never done a day's bloody work. Not all his life" (59). Slattery irritates festering quarrels, attacks his wife for taking evening classes, blames her for spoiling Arthur. Arthur's news is demeaned and mocked, "not drawing her old age pension yet?" (65). When Slattery learns that the intended is divorced and has two children, he works himself into apoplexy: "Have I ever done ought to deserve a family . . . the likes of the bloody one I've got? Have I transgressed?" This is the "last of the bloody line" as far as he is concerned (65).

Although for only a fleeting moment, Arthur's "invisible event" does turn them out as a family group. "It's astonishing what Arthur's done for us. I can feel the vibrancy running through the building . . ." (71), Wendy says wryly. Even she has had what she calls a "bloody-minded reversion" and put on lipstick; Slattery pours out appreciation for Brenda ("Look like a bloody lass, at last. Almost given up bloody hope" [74]) and even his wife ("Look at your mother: couldn't look lovelier than that" [74]). When the prodigal arrives without the bride, Slattery berates him: "We're all bloody well waiting . . . we're all collected . . . we're all on bloody tenterhooks" (81). Slattery feels he's been made a fool, that the others knew secrets that have been kept from him: Arthur is pushing him into his grave.

Caught between desire and reality, Slattery spins out of control. Led to bed, he soon is up again, crashing down the stairs to announce "Apologies." Plying him with drink, the daughters manage to get him back to bed. The disparity of the scene is emblematic of the disparity of the life. Arthur's poem, read aloud at his Mother's request when they are alone, underscores the pathos of misperception:

> 'And of all the things he played—
> a father, and the game of lover . . .
> nothing; except the spot where one limb has stayed

the dust, held back a space
and in the earth a gesture
maybe measures out the trace of flesh, of blood—a creature
still to those who can
recognize in this the emblem of a man.' (90–91)

By morning Arthur is gone, his going made a commonplace by
Slattery ("A journey before midday, tha knows, is best" [93]). Apparent
calm is restored, and Slattery enters the family scene as "maister of the
house." Exaggeratedly polite, he will not sit until Mrs. Slattery does,
and even holds her chair. "I'll not bloody start, tha knows, till thy starts,
love" (94). With full irony against the scene played out with Arthur,
Slattery welcomes Albert to the table—the son rejected, a stranger is
greeted with familial warmth. Back in control, as if the disturbance has
never happened, Slatterly has the illusion of his role; the group defines
him, but those who play out their roles with him know that "remorse
eats him out" (88).

Throughout *In Celebration*, remorse eats away at the Shaw
family as well.[27] Mrs. Shaw is "one woman in a house of men" (55),
and she is kept one dimensional by her family. Each of the men
expresses repressed feelings when mother is offstage (upstairs dressing,
upstairs sleeping); her feelings are never represented but are only
discussed by them.

Like the glassed-in seventeenth floor restaurant of the Excelsior
Hotel, the event of celebration marks both a new perspective and the
differences between the self-perceptions of the couple. Whereas Mr.
Shaw describes the view, "From the muck-heap at one end to the muck-
heap at the other," Mrs. Shaw sees beauty and order: the light of the
sunset "glinting on a stream . . . miles away" and "Lines of lights . . . .
And a train. Just like a snake . . . winding in and out." She is amazed,
"We've lived here all our lives and I've never seen it like that" (64). It
is an evening of new ways of seeing, or at least expression of long-
repressed ones.

What begins as a celebration of the parents' fortieth anniversary,
ends with the deep scars of psychological fissure being exposed and a
dispersal of the family. Andrew's analysis of Steven ("You're like a
man with one foot on either side of an ever-widening chasm") is true of

each of them; the gap between what is and what appears to be threatens to "rip [them] wide apart" (54).

Shaw openly speaks of his disappointments in life. He says of his time in the mines: "You get a view of life you don't get anywhere else" (69). Two hundred yards under the Rawcliffe seam, with thirteen inches for his body and the "centre of the earth beneath," a man is "nothing but a piece of stone" (69). Despite the danger, the black lung, his constant sense of impending mortality, he will not retire. He cannot relinquish the pride that his work gives him: "You can't just come out and leave it. What's it all add up to?" (69). This question, asked as well by Ewbank, Slattery, and Pasmore (*The March on Russia*), is the remainder of all of Storey's plays.

But the woman's voice is neither expressed nor heard; its influence is felt only as it has an effect on others. What has been kept nearly invisible is Mrs. Shaw's depression following Jamey's death; she tried to kill herself ("She was already six months gone with Steve . . . sitting here . . . on the floor . . . hugging a knife" [51]). Its consequences unravel now in the lives of the sons, but not in hers. Snaking through her life, the pain and guilt of the death of a son conceived illegitimately has marked her landscape no less than the river has the valley. Yet, the gestures and relationships that characterize her all gloss this repressed pain.

"A family like this, That's all that counts" (76); Shaw's words seem ironic by the time Andrew has finished with his truth telling in the night. Mrs. Shaw's father raised pigs—"Not dirty animals at all, unless their environment was allowed to become polluted" (101); she continued the habit. The high school award for hygiene was the ethos of her being, yet was compromised by her life:

> raised up by a petty farmer to higher things . . . ends up
> being laid—in a farm field—by a bloody collier . . .
> hygiene . . . never forgiven him, she hasn't. . . . Dig coal he
> will till kingdom come. Never dig enough. . . . Retribution
> (49).

According to Andrew, their lives have been an atonement: her sexuality and his blackness from the mines have been scrubbed and tidied

("Cleaned your shoes? Washed your faces? Ties straight? Got your handkerchief?. . . got your coats?" [56]). Mrs. Shaw's obsession with coats might be explained by Jamey's sudden death from pneumonia at the age of seven; but according to Andrew, he also died of perfection: "Guilt. Subsequent moral rectitude. They fashioned Jamey—as a consequence—in the image of Jesus Christ" (49). Shaw dotes on his wife, but Andrew says to him, "You've enshrined that woman in so much adoration that she's well-nigh invisible to you as well as to everyone else" (84).

Steven, remote and withdrawn, has stopped his writing, fathered a multitude of children, and has waking nightmares that cause him to sob in the night. His father recounts taking him out as a young child to see the bombs falling, saying he "took it to heart" (71). Always the brightest, Steven's passivity and withdrawal worry his parents and annoy Andrew.

Andrew seeks revenge for having been sent to stay with Reardon until after Steven was born and for his memory of standing at the door crying to be let in and having his plea rejected by the overwrought mother ("I've never been in" [84]). He will not let Steven have everyone's pity: "His affliction, I can assure him, is not endemic to his solemn, silent nature, atrophied while inside my mother's remorseful tum" (52). Andrew wants vengeance for her exacted atonement ("When I think of all the facts I've had to learn. . . . The exams. . . . I even married a Rector's daughter! . . . The edifice of my life—of his life— built up on that" [86]). He wants to be released from being a "semblance . . . a pathetic vision of a better life" (87); he wants to wrest control from his mother, "that goddess" (83), the "Godhead" (86).

Andrew keeps Colin in line by innuendoes of homosexuality, he challenges Steven to confront the cause of his depression, he readies his disparagement for final delivery to the parents. But Steven pulls back, refuses to confront: "I don't want you doing any harm" (101). Andrew holds everyone's attention, looks each of them full in the eye, and then his uncomprehending mother, appears to retreat himself: "No harm . . . no harm" (101), yet then nurses his psychic wound: "I am bad. I am. . . . I used to cry outside that door . . . Why wasn't it ever opened" (102). He shouts it at Steven three times, fixing him in his gaze. Jamey died, Steven was born, both displaced Andrew, who was a "bad boy" for trying to get into his mother's affections; Andrew places blame on Steven and recycles the family affliction, recrimination. Andrew turns to his mother and asks her to dance. Unaware of his exorcism, she fails to understand that what they are coming to, in Andrew's terms, is "Salvation."

If sons Andrew, Colin and Steven are "the Revenger, the Crippled, the Crucified," then the only woman in the house, Mrs. Shaw, is the axis on which all the men's lives have turned.[28] Her overcompensation for a lost self, a lost son has perverted the lives that have been defined by her. As affectionately as she is held by Shaw, her life of devotion has "extracted its toll."[29] They feel that her difference judges them, separates them from self-regard and dignity and worth. None of the sons have work that satisfies—even Colin, whose negotiating power puts him between others rather than in charge of himself. Andrew would be like his father (not a lawyer, nor an artist) except for his fear of being a bad boy, disappointing the middle-class pretensions that have been imposed by his mother's expectations.

Although Mrs. Shaw's resignation apparently prevails ("these things somehow work out" [92]), the recriminations are so enormous that it is obvious that they will never be worked out. Like Colin the negotiator and Reardon, the neighbor who has lived through "two world wars and several minor ones" by avoiding conflict, the Shaws have made the best of it. When the boys take their leave, Shaw helps his wife straighten the house, so her haven from the tempest, normalcy, is apparently restored. Even if Mrs. Shaw is uncomprehending of the narrative told of her by her sons, the scene Andrew caused in the kitchen has left "The others . . . somewhat overwhelmed. Events have caught up with them so to speak" (103).

Nearly ten years later, Storey's farce, *Mother's Day*, reshapes the situation; this mother is well off the pedestal, but still the axis for what is here a perversion of family values.[30] The putative "Mother," Mrs. Johnson denigrates husband and all her children, save for lecherous Gordon, her youngest. This is a home where the tea kettle is hidden, and everything else is out in the open. Storey intended it to be "mind-boggling," an inversion of family values.[31]

a sort of
Strindbergin effu

Out of a circumstance that is not unlike the repressed secret that undermines the family ties in *In Celebration*, Mrs. Johnson claims that her seduction at the age of sixteen by a house painter caused her to be disowned by her wealthy titled parents; as a result of her misalliance with Mr. Johnson come several unwanted children. "What it is to have a family. What it is to be a woman: what it is to be a mother. What it is to have no redress," says Mrs. Johnson (252). All of the women in *Mother's Day* are sexual ciphers.

Mrs. Johnson comes from a long line of Storey's women who were ashamed of the men that they married. She blames the quality of her life on Mr. Johnson, who, she says,

> was an inexperienced and vulgar man when he deflowered me, and vulgarity has been a plant that has flourished, vigorously, in the manure of his existence. (198)

Whatever the cause, Mrs. Johnson encourages Gordon to repeat the masculine prerogative with the boarder, Judith ("Go up and comfort her, Gordon . . . that's what she needs, a man's affection" [201]), and she applauds son Harold's choice of his sister as a bride, encouraging him in his determination to buy himself out of the service with Her Majesty's Royal Air Force to marry her.

Gordon, who has "been preoccupied nearly all his life with sex," has a track record of rape that began at the age of thirteen when he assaulted his teacher and was excused by the judge "because they couldn't prove she hadn't provoked him" (212). Perversion of values is a matter of course: innocent Lily lives in a cupboard, is not permitted to eat, is abused by her mother as a liar and a "brainless, simply horrible venomous child" (253); Mr. Johnson is restricted from having food or access to his room unless his wife permits it; Harold claims that he is charged "very little" for his brief stays at home: "I take up space. I breathe the air. I sometimes feel the fire when they have it lit" (213). Gordon has threatened to kill Mr. Johnson, but he takes it as a normal pattern (the fisher king legend), as he explains to Harold who has come home to rescue him:

> MR. JOHNSON: A son has to kill his father, son. It's what
> life is all about.

| HAROLD: | I don't want to kill you. |
| MR. JOHNSON: | You've sublimated it all in gliding. That, of course, and the R.A.F. A man who serves the Queen can't possibly desire to ravish his mother. (218) |

Sex and money are the ties that bind. The sub-plot consists of several variations of the "robbers robbed" in a chase routine that veers into sexual violation. The middle-class value that reigns is profit. To the public eye, propriety is preserved: to Mr. Peters, the investigator who seeks one Judith Waterton who has been seduced by a married man and brought to the Johnson household, Mrs. Johnson says,

> I don't wish to look at the photographs of young girls. If you're trying to make indecent proposals I better warn you that my husband is upstairs in bed. (223)

For purposes of self-promotion, Mrs. Johnson claims to be a family woman to Mr. Waterton, yet when Harold announces he is going to leave home and the R.A.F. to marry his sister, Edna, Mrs. Johnson says, "You don't have to leave home to fuck your sister" (243). By the end of the play, she has defrauded Mr. Peters of his reward, Mr. Waterton of daughter, wife and their money, and made Judith over to Gordon and Mr. Johnson for their pleasure: "Seducing's natural" (238).

Although Hutchings suggests that the highly vaunted sexual exploits and exploitation that occur off-stage may not occur at all, Storey's use of farce exposes conventional familial values as masks for repressed sexual aggression.[32] While most of the characters may emerge unscathed, the play did not. As Storey said, "The critics all reacted like members of a normal family would . . . with these people as next door neighbors." Naturalistic treatment of even perverted values makes their claim on social propriety and pretensions. Storey said, "'Everybody involved in it is screwing everybody else, which is a reflection of the world we live in.'"[33]

If the Johnsons have found their "true vocation," the return to normalcy at the end of *Mother's Day* raises more than eyebrows. She greets Mr. Johnson's announcement that Gordon is "seducing the eyeballs out of Judith," with a family platitude: "we've got one another . . . A fine, young family above our heads" (269). To slightly rephrase Mrs. Johnson's words (252): What is it to have a family? What is it to be a woman? What is it to be a mother? What is it to have no redress? Enacting social circumstances even intensified and possibly challenged through farcical extremity nonetheless reinscribes woman in cultural history; it poses the question, but it does not presume an answer.

In *Sisters*, women take the center stage, but the roles that they choose for themselves are defined and dominated by men: by a father who was "dreamer," by husbands and/or lovers (real and imagined) who demand loyalty but fail to treat them with regard.[34] Secrets drive the narrative. The first act is an attempt to keep Adrienne from noticing the real nature of the arrangements of the household. Adrienne evades her circumstances by projecting a husband who has left her, a child who was never born. Although she claims that she hated her father's failures, particularly as he measured "his dreams in my mother's eyes" by trying to make "her feel grand: he wanted her to feel he'd really succeeded" (103), she has done the same by imagining what she cannot make real: she left home fantasizing about a future life of greatness yet refused to return home for either parent's funeral because she had nothing "to show." As Terry says, "everything that happens now is a consequence of things that happened before . . ." (90–91).

Adrienne has arrived on Carol's scene a "day early," and one by one the other characters ask when she might be leaving. She has intruded on a domestic situation where strangers seem intimate, or "living in one another's pocket": Beryl and Terry offer Adrienne a drink and Crawford expects her to serve him one; Jo cannot find her eyelashes in the bathroom, Terry knows that cigarettes are kept in the kitchen, and the neighbor, Mrs. Donaldson, introduces herself as Carol's mother. Carol explains that the house keeps "irregular hours" (69), "friends are coming round in a while" (75), Tom "works at home" (75), people are "booked in" (78); Jo describes herself as an "intermittent paying guest" (83). Carol says "One day: well, we won't have to live like this" (79).

For Carol, Adrienne is that point outside—"you're like an eagle: you've flown to the top of the mountain and seen what lies the other side.... It's the thought of you being up there that keeps me going ... " (80). It only gradually dawns on Adrienne exactly what Carol does to keep going. Ironically, policeman Crawford, who has a highly refined sense for public vs. private morality, says "If she's living in a knocking-shop, I think somebody ought to tell her" (105). By the time she joins the party to celebrate her "homecoming," Adrienne has a good idea. Resolved to forget the past and the future, she becomes the life of this party.

By Act Three, the "outsider" is trying to be taken in—propositioning Tom to become a partner in the business.[35] Tom's career as a star footballer "got screwed up with my wife fornicating with another man" (127). Twice cheated, he is possessive of all he has: the house, the business, and Carol. Now Adrienne threatens to move in on his territory. Suddenly her demeanor is lively, confident; none of Tom's intimidations ("People pay for the things they use round here" [123]) faze her. Tom exerts demands and control: "I call the tune" (123). But Adrienne has a hold over him, because he does not expect her to ask if he is a pimp. "No one talks to me like that. No one. No man. No woman" (124). Especially no woman.

ADRIENNE:	How would you describe yourself in that case, then?
TOM:	I'm in business.
ADRIENNE:	What business?
TOM:	I sell pleasure. I hire pleasure out.
ADRIENNE:	Do you hire my sister out? (124)

She meets his gaze. When she challenges his strength by calling him "insecure," he threatens to punch her. The more he throws his weight around, the more Adrienne shows him up by ignoring his bluster. She draws him into conversation by talking over how he makes the business work: "the sort of people who come here are a guarantee of immunity from this country's present hypocritical judicial system . . ." (126); and so it is that his house specializes in maintaining its facade out of self-interest of its patrons: housewives meet respectable professionals. When Adrienne admires Tom, he betrays his fears as a man: "[Carol] puts one foot out of line, she knows precisely where she stands" (128).

Off-stage, Tom abuses Carol. His behavior is explained: he cannot tolerate being seen through. Adrienne's gaze met his, and he lost his control. Carol feels that she knows him and herself well enough to change him ("You have to change: and by you changing they change also" [137]). Terry analyzes Tom's motives for Adrienne: "It's his first wife he's beating when he starts to hit Carol. He lived in a man's world that came apart. . . . but [the wife] refused to idolize him"; Tom's preconceptions ("Men should be men and women should submit") require that women be the object of his gaze (133). When he beats Carol, he goes "for the eyes" (134). Being a brothel keeper is "his vision of a world where women are screwed and men enjoy themselves" (134).

Although doubly a victim, Carol chooses the possibility of changing Tom in the future over the bond with her sister that had sustained her past ("I don't live in fantasies" [137]). Perhaps she acts in order to hold on to Tom and her dream of a better life; perhaps it is for Adrienne's own benefit. First she exposes Adrienne's tales as lies, then she comforts her ("We're sisters"). Made vulnerable, "Aid" says that Tom came to her in the night, that Crawford made advances to her, that she cannot stand to be betrayed. Carol refuses to rejoin Adrienne's life and take care of her. Instead, Carol (perhaps with Tom's encouragement) has arranged for Adrienne to be returned to the mental hospital. Ironically, for all of her begging for a place in Carol's life, Adrienne's last words to her sister are "Families are an illusion, Carol. You have to destroy them to stay alive" (147).

Victorious, Tom toasts the return of reality. Carol is silent, hands on her stomach. Pregnant with a child that will be born into anger, retribution, use and abuse, hers is not a return to status quo. The disparity exposed will not leave the future alone.

Storey's latest play, *The March on Russia,* rehearses themes seen before in the family plays, but here they are presented in a new tonality.[37] As in *In Celebration*, family members reunite at home on the occasion of their parents' anniversary: "Sixty years of penal servitude," says Pasmore (16); "Cant. Sixty years as a collier's wife. It sums it up exactly," says she (18). The adult children have had an education and have made life-choices quite different from or unavailable to their working-class parents, whose life-long financial uncertainty has been assuaged in retirement through the generosity of a prosperous son. And yet, the patterns of family life are embedded in the adult choices; for example, in sibling rivalry for a mother's love and a father's pride, the divisions follow gender. Wendy says to her father,

> Digging out a spadeful for a daughter didn't carry the same weight as it did for a son. Nevertheless, I made it count. I made it count. (46)

Wendy's need for recognition is expressed in political life. Though successful, Colin is drawn to a story of son and mother joined in tragedy, perhaps an extension of a need unfilled in childhood. He asks his mother to account for maternal affection she withheld from him. Although it was shown to or demanded by the daughters, Mrs. Pasmore says, "I always thought if you [Colin] had too much cuddling you'd grow up soft. . . . As a boy. I used to let him lie" (47). The children have given thought to an offhand remark made during their childhood: "Remember the occasion when father said we'd have been much better if we'd reversed the sexes?" (29). Though skeptical that "Colin was cut out to be a woman," Eileen insists that Wendy was "cut out to be a man" and so was she, a comment on how unlike their mother they are and yet how little they had set that as their course (29). Although far less stridently than Slattery's judgments about his children's choices (*The Farm*), the Pasmores do find it puzzling and disappointing that their children do not repeat their life patterns—that marriages and children and work are not sufficient values, not for any of them.

Although this husband and wife bicker ("In principle I'm allus wrong" [28]), it is in modulated tones compared to the noisy conflicts of *Sisters, Mother's Day* or *The Farm.* A lifetime of work, though tedious and exhausting for both husband and wife, allowed them to eke out an existence with great effort. Even now, in the village house provided by their son, the rooms enclose the characterizing habits that remain from the patterns of a lifetime together. For Pasmore, labor is the male prerogative: "All I do is bloody work. She has the ideas. A woman's world. It allus was" (19). The ritual of bringing in the coal ("Concessionary coal. . . . Comes half price" [53]) and arranging the fire are the remnants from a lifetime of digging in the mines; he takes pride in this: "A house wi'out a fire is like a home wi'out a woman" (36). For Mrs. Pasmore, the labor of laundry (boiling of copper pots to wash, hanging wet laundry before the fire when it rained (cf. 35) and making ends meet has its residual in tidy housekeeping and the exacting pleasure of the crossword puzzle. She takes umbrage that her husband would use a kitchen towel, her towel, to polish his shoes: "I keep the house clean. All he does is dirty it up" (37).

Structurally *The March on Russia* is a well-made play, with extended exposition bringing the backgrounds into focus (dialogues between parent and child, daughters and mother, children alone). The twilight of lives in relationship is painted in soft tints of blue and gray (cf. Jocelyn Herbert's set for the production at the National Theatre).[38] The play's crisis turns on the second-hand ring given by Pasmore to his wife. Mrs. Pasmore rejects it: "It's made to fit a giant" (39); "It's like someone else's clothes" (40). In doing so she rejects him, until— prodded by the children—she sees the harm done and says, "I appreciate the thought. I mean that" (40). Of course, the occasion demands more than second-hand feelings, but Pasmore could make the same claim about her response. As Wendy remonstrates, Mrs. Pasmore could have bought a gift as well: "You don't have to sit there and let it all come to you" (43). Edgy unease gives way to revelation of Pasmore's kleptomania, recriminations about his life of nearly fruitless labor, a jibe about his foolishness over the back fence with a twenty-five-year-old neighbor.

The story Pasmore narrates as the play opens and is prodded to recite for comfort as the play ends, the march on Russia, is the one experience that has distinguished his life. By helping him retell it in the final scene, his wife helps him recover the shambles made of his integrity ("He puts things in his pocket. A life of honesty thrown away" [48]). Of all the gestures and platitudes of love expressed because of the occasion (and most have been qualified by either action or extension of thought), this is the gesture of a life lived together: "We accepted each other for what we were" (16).

There is little question that the adult children's ideas of relationship and responsibility are more modern, and that they are able to see and challenge those cultural patterns that enforced difference and thus limited the lives of men and women and their relationships. Colin's scholarship took passion when he read *The Prophecies of Jonathan Wroe,* which projected the de-spiritualization and dystopia of modern life (cf. 21); despite his success as a writer and his intellectual grasp of despair, Colin's own terrors paralyze him. Wendy, an independent politician, accepted her husband's infidelity and their childlessness and claims to look forward to life on her own. When Mrs. Pasmore comments, "It seems to me, my dear, you are full of despair," Wendy responds, "So are you. But mine, my dear, is on the move." Whether independence provides a better option than the patriarchal mold that shaped the older woman's life, is not the issue. What is more poignant is that despair prevails. Finally it is that tone that tempers sentimentality in the play. Despite the apparently easy acquiescence to role as Mrs. Pasmore gently urges her husband to narrate his tale, hers is a gesture in response to pain, not one that denies it. Both have had dreams that are presentiments of death. Out of need they reach to each other as "Hilda" and "Tommy"—as persons with common needs.

In many of Storey's plays, individuals are isolated; they lack the validity of group identity and meaningful action that is significant because it is shared. Like the work crew in *The Contractor,* they are outlaws; like Arnold Middleton, they are mad Robin Hoods. Not surprisingly, for groups that define themselves through difference from a point outside, being "different" is a great fear. When the gap between inner and outer reality widens, and the illusion of the defining group (team, family, crew) breaks down, the differences are confronted as real but seldom embraced. As described by chaos theory, an aberration forces the normal loop more and more out of control, until the energy wanes, and the normal cycle returns. Much the same description could be applied to Storey's plays.

Women are a difference, a sexual cipher, a point outside, or an axis which men would like to escape. Until this difference is acknowledged as a part of the self and not a mark against which the male self is measured, the denial maintains the cultural determinism that makes women invisible as persons. Ironically, it is when the men of these plays come to a place where they reckon with their own invisibility that possibility opens: "Cracks. Fissures . . . some little aperture of warmth and light."[39]

Notes

1. Cf. William J. Free and Lynn Page Whittaker, "The Intrusion Plot in David Storey's Plays," *Papers on Language and Literature*, 18, no. 2 (Spring 1982): 151–165.

2. Austin Quigley, "The Emblematic Structure and Setting of Storey's Plays," *Modern Drama* 22, no. 3 (Sept 1979): 263, 265, 260.

3. Cf. William Hutchings, *The Plays of David Storey: A Thematic Study*, Carbondale: Southern Illinois University Press, 1988, 161.

4. Hutchings, 17, 20.

5. Quigley, 265.

6. Susan Shrapnel, "No Goodness and No Kings," *The Cambridge Quarterly* 5, no. 2 (Autumn 1970): 182.

7. David Storey, *The Changing Room*, in *Home, The Changing Room, and Mother's Day*, New York: Penguin, 1984. All subsequent references to this play will be to this edition; page references will be cited parenthetically in the text.

8. David Storey, *The Contractor*, in *In Celebration and The Contractor*, Harmondsworth, England: Penguin, 1977. All subsequent references to this play are to this edition; page references will be cited parenthetically in the text.

9. Hutchings, 176.

10. Hutchings, 168.

11. Katharine Worth, *Revolutions in Modern English Drama*, London: Bell & Sons, 1973, 28.

12. David Storey, *Home*, in *Home, The Changing Room, and Mother's Day*, Harmondsworth: Penguin, 1978. All subsequent references to this play are to this edition; page references will be cited parenthetically in the text.

13. Quigley, 266.

14. Shrapnel, 186.

15. Richard Dutton, *Modern Tragicomedy and the British Tradition: Beckett, Pinter, Stoppard, Albee and Storey*, Norman: University of Oklahoma Press, 1986, 157.

16. Dutton, 159.

17. David Storey, *Life Class*, in *Early Days, Sisters, and Life Class*, Harmondsworth: Penguin, 1980, 178. All subsequent references to this play are to this edition; page references will be cited parenthetically in the text.

18. Hutchings, 63.

19. Hutchings, 63, 68.

20. David Storey, *The Restoration of Arnold Middleton*, London: Jonathan Cape, 1967, 81. All subsequent references to this play are to this edition; page references will be cited parenthetically in the text.

21. Hutchings, 49.

22. Laura H. Weaver, "The City as Escape into Freedom: The Failure of a Dream in David Storey's Works," *West Virginia University Philological Papers* 28 (1983), 153.

23. Hutchings, 53.

24. Hutchings, 55.

25. David Storey, *The Farm*, London: Jonathan Cape, 1973. All subsequent references to this play are to this edition; page references will be cited parenthetically in the text.

26. Cf. Hutchings, 153.

27. David Storey, *In Celebration*, in *In Celebration and The Contractor*, London: Penguin, 1971. All subsequent references to this play are to this edition; page references will be cited parenthetically in the text.

28. John Holmstrom, "Keep it Mum," *Plays and Players* (June 1969): 9; quoted by Hutchings, 86.

29. Hutchings, 96.

30. David Storey, *Mother's Day*, in *Home, The Changing Room, and Mother's Day*, Harmondsworth: Penguin Books, 1984. All subsequent references to this play are to this edition; page references will be cited parenthetically in the text.

31. Cf. Hutchings, 115.

32. Hutchings, 110.

33. Hutchings, 115.

34. David Storey quoted in Oleg Kerensky, *The New British Drama: Fourteen Playwrights Since Osborne and Pinter*, London: Hamish Hamilton, 1977, 12.

35. David Storey, *Sisters*, in *Early Days, Sisters, and Life Class*, Harmondsworth: Penguin, 1980. All references to this play are to this edition; page references will be cited parenthetically in the text.

36. The resemblances between Adrienne's new role and Ruth's inversion of expectations in Harold Pinter's *The Homecoming* seem obvious, but Storey denies this influence; cf. Hutchings, 137.

37. David Storey, *The March on Russia*, London: Samuel French, 1989. All references to this play are to this edition; page references will be cited parenthetically in the text.

38. Jocelyn Herbert, designer for *The March on Russia*, Lyttelton Auditorium, The National Theatre, premiere 6 April 1989.

39. Storey, *The Restoration of Arnold Middleton*, 87.

"INSURING PEOPLE AGAINST DISASTER": THE USES OF COMEDY IN THE PLAYS OF DAVID STOREY

D.S. Lawson

Throughout a distinguished dramatic career now spanning over twenty years, British playwright David Storey has written a number of different types of plays. His work has ranged from historical drama (*Cromwell*), to absurdist plays (*Home*), through farce (*Mother's Day*). He is most commonly thought of, however, in terms of neo-naturalism, a "slice of life" theatre which presents realistic characters in relatively plotless plays in which routine (though sometimes violent and unexpected) events make up the action; this strain of his work is exemplified by *The Contractor, The Changing Room, Life Class*, and *In Celebration*. One might trace the roots of this theatrical sub-genre back to Chekhov's dramaturgical practice at the turn of the century, but Storey's plays bear his own theatrical sensibilities and are not derivative.

David Storey in England and Lanford Wilson in America both practice neo-naturalism at a very high level indeed and have therefore become the two playwrights whose names are most often mentioned in connection with it. Moreover, Storey's work has been popular on both sides of the Atlantic, having been successfully produced both in London's West End and on New York's Broadway. In the decade of the 1970s Storey was three times honored with the New York Drama Critic's Circle Award for Best Play of the Year and twice won the

Evening Standard Drama Award in London. In addition to reviews in the usual newspapers, magazines, and journals, a number of important scholarly articles as well have been devoted to Storey; chapters on his work have appeared in several books, and a book-length study of his plays appeared in 1988.

Most of the attention, however, has been given to the neo-naturalistic plays which make up the main body of his oeuvre. Indeed these plays may be termed his "most representative" work and have generally been the most successful and popular. I would like to examine a group of three plays outside this main contingent, however, and ask how Storey uses various comedic techniques in his work.

The comedy of Storey's plays arises mainly out of an element of parody. Word play, broad farce, satire, and wit also play important roles in Storey's work, but their function is relatively transparent and definitely subsidiary to the parodic. Much of Storey's comedy arises out of misunderstandings, sometimes deliberately caused. When the generations misunderstand one another (as in *In Celebration*), or when married couples fail to communicate (as in *The Restoration of Arnold Middleton*), or when a group of people sets out to deceive someone (as in *Mother's Day*), one result can be humor. However, a great deal of what is funny about Storey's work requires an awareness on the part of an audience or a reader that something (often something very specific) is being parodied. The laughter elicited by a David Storey play is often dependent upon an intertextual awareness of the sources for parodic elements he incorporates into his work. Any intertextual analysis presupposes that a given text is intelligible only in terms of reference to an already existing body of texts; as Julia Kristeva (who originated the term intertextuality) puts it, "every text takes shape as a mosaic of citations, every text is the absorption and transformation of other texts" (146).

Jonathan Culler expands this view, arguing that an intertextual reading allows a "dialectical opposition which the text presents [resulting] in a synthesis at a higher level where the grounds of intelligibility are different" (151). Owen Miller describes the specific usefulness of intertextuality, advancing the notion that it "comes into play when those approaches which insist on the text as a self-regulating unity and emphasize its functional independence are felt, for one reason or another, to be inadequate or untenable" (20). Miller also comments, "the identification of a specific intertext is not only admissible but an essential feature of intertextual identity. What signals the intertext, as well as specifying it, is the notion of a *trace* discernible in the focused text" (31).

Certainly many parallels between Storey's work and the work of others can be cited. William J. Free, for example, notes comparisons to Harold Pinter, John Osborne, Arnold Wesker, and John Arden (307), but proceeds in the main analysis of his article not to consider the important ramifications of these areas of overlap. Likewise, Richard Dutton claims that Storey's plays are clearly in a line of development from Beckett and Pinter despite important areas of difference between the playwrights (151). John J. Stinson again cites Pinter, but also stresses Storey's affinities to Chekhov (131) and discusses Storey's work vis-à-vis novelist D. H. Lawrence (132) and dramatist Peter Shaffer (138). An intertextual reading of three Storey plays and a number of other texts whose traces Storey's works bear may help deepen an apprehension of the materials with which Storey is working; while I do not always have a specific analysis of the importance or "meaning" of these parallels in mind, an awareness of their presence heightens an appreciation for Storey's plays themselves. Furthermore, by linking Storey's plays with their intertextual roots, a reader often can make more explicit the concerns of and questions raised by Storey's own works, thus enriching a reading of the plays at hand.

Obviously the notion of intertextuality is central in any examination of parody since the effect of parody is dependent on foregrounding the "traces" upon which the parody is based. Furthermore, critics who attempt to read Storey's comic plays in isolation from these sources (as if they were written in some sort of vacuum) will miss one very important element of their construction and effect. Moreover, traditional literary methodologies come up short when applied to Storey's funny plays, and only a reading which acknowledges and builds upon their intertextual nature will result in a full and satisfying engagement with these texts. Storey's first play *The Restoration of Arnold Middleton* is ripe with comedic, parodic

7 intertextual elements. It concerns a middle-aged academic who perhaps
is losing his grip on reality and seeks satisfaction, validation, and
meaning from unconventional sources. Specifically, he has purchased a
suit of armor and has it brought into his home, which is already filled
with various artifacts from history—mute testimony to his continuing
search for something from the past which could fill a void in his life.
Arguably he is mad and in the course of the play is forced to return to a
more conventional life, a more societally acceptable relation with the
world at large.

A variety of intertextual traces comes immediately to mind.
Middleton may be a sort of modern-day British Don Quixote, his head
so full of the history he teaches that he has mistaken it for the physical
reality of his existence. Indeed the quixotic nature of his life is obvious:
in a world he finds unsatisfying, Middleton has turned to relics of an
earlier (arguably simpler and more clear-cut) age for solace. If his
world is one in which he can no longer make sense of his place
(specifically in this play the gender roles assigned to him as a husband
and a son-in-law), he trades it (at least in part) for a chivalric world in
which the roles (again, particularly gender roles) were very specific and
clearly delineated. Hutchings frames this theme well:

> In the artifacts that he accumulates in both his home and his
> classroom, he seeks a means of personal contact with a
> more meaningful past, as if the objects themselves are
> tangible verifications of the pattern, purpose, and
> significance that once characterized individual and
> collective existences. (46–47)

Clearly this is the main theme of the play, and its quixotic nature is an
important element of that theme. The connections between this search
for "a more meaningful past" and the unsatisfactory gender roles which
are, for Arnold Middleton, one specific aspect of his inability to find
significance in his life are very important for any reading of the play.

Arnold and Joan could also be read as variations on George and
Martha from Edward Albee's *Who's Afraid of Virginia Woolf?* (1962).
Certainly a number of at least superficial resemblances can be traced—
an academic couple in some marital trouble whose illusions come to be
tested and found wanting.[1] Both plays end with a bleak but hopeful

note: George and Martha climb the stairs to their marital bed, honest and aboveboard with each other for the first time in years as the sun rises (that eternal symbol of optimism); likewise, Arnold and Joan make a "restoration" at the end of Storey's play as its title promises, as they apparently call a marital truce. The mother-in-law is to be expelled, Arnold mentions the possibility of throwing a party, the value of work is reasserted, and Joan reaches out her hand to him in a symbolic representation of a desire for reconciliation.[2]

Elements of Harold Pinter's *The Homecoming* (1965) come to mind as well. The parallels here involve a younger-generation figure who is an academic, and an inter-generational incestuous relationship. Although Storey's play—particularly toward the start, but arguably throughout—lacks the menace of Pinter's world, the echoes are strong.[3] One recurrent motif in Pinter is a younger man sleeping with an older woman (Bert with Rose in *The Room* and Stanley with Meg in *The Birthday Party*, for example), and Storey seems deliberately to be playing with this idea in his characterizations of Mrs. Ellis and her son-in-law, Arnold Middleton.[4]

The drunken scene at the end of Act One in which Mrs. Ellis and Joan cut off some of Middleton's hair is resonant with Biblical parallels to the Samson and Delilah story. Middleton's fierce attachment to relics of the past can be read as representative of a source of strength (as Samson's hair was). Joan's rejection of Middleton's relics (her indignation over the house being more a museum than a home, her downright anger and disbelief over the suit of armor) could be her attempt to drain the strength from her husband so that she can more easily dominate him. The cutting of his hair might be seen as linked to Joan's desire to wrest Middleton away from his collection of objects. After all, at the play's end the house has been cleared of all of Middleton's objects and the playing field is level for the start of a new game with new rules. Is history professor Middleton to be seen as a representative of culture and learning at the mercy of the Philistines? Probably the note of Biblical typology in *Middleton* is nothing more than just a hint, but that constitutes an important and suggestive trace nevertheless.[5]

These intertextual parallels do not amount to a systematic exploitation of source materials on the part of Storey; Storey clearly is not deliberately parodying *Don Quixote* or *The Homecoming* in the way that Henry Fielding parodied Samuel Richardson's *Pamela* in his own *Shamela*, for example. Rather, Storey evokes isolated characteristics or motifs from other works and combines them in new and illuminating ways to make a play which, while using parodic elements, speaks in his own voice. An awareness of the parallels (and the parodic treatment of them by Storey) heightens the reader's or the audience's perceptions of the play's depth and subtlety as a presentation of a world bereft of recognizable moral landmarks, a depiction of madness in the modern world, an examination of a very particular marital situation, etc. One aspect of what Storey accomplishes in this multi-faceted play is parody.

The presence of parody in *Middleton* surely is amusing to a reader aware of the parallels and it also allows questions such as the ones enumerated above to be asked of this play when otherwise they might not come to mind. One might well ask, What is funny about *Middleton*? Perhaps the scenes involving Mrs. Ellis, the mother-in-law, are the most overtly funny scenes. From the play's opening where Mrs. Ellis and Joan discover the recently delivered suit of armor for the first time, up through Arnold's flirtations and discussions with her, Mrs. Ellis is the center of the humor of the play. At the start of the play, she tries to drive a wedge between Middleton and Joan by her carefully chosen words and reactions to the armor. After saying deliberately provocative things, she reacts to Joan's angry response with, "Well. I'm sure I don't want to quarrel about it" (200). The incongruity between her actions and her stated intentions creates one of the play's first instances of verbal humor, though the actual discovery of the armor at the rise of the curtain could certainly be played broadly for laughs.

The most celebrated and studied of Storey's comedies is *Home*, a play which in some important ways straddles the line between comedy and the neo-naturalistic plays for which Storey is more famous. Certainly *Home* is a relatively plotless play peopled with fairly realistic characters. It is set in an insane asylum (though the reader or audience is unaware of this fact throughout a great deal of the play) and follows four characters on what might be a typical day at their "home."

Obviously *Home* is related in important ways to *The Restoration of Arnold Middleton*. Commenting on her husband's collection of artifacts in their house, Joan Middleton says, "It's not a home it's an institution" (202). This sentence might very well describe a reader's initial reaction to discovering the true nature of the "home" in *Home*. The potential madness in Arnold's and Joan's lives is the focus of *Home*—a play about people who have not been able to reconcile themselves to an unsatisfactory contemporary world, as Joan and Arnold apparently at least begin to do at the conclusion of their play.

The most obvious trace present in *Home* is Samuel Beckett's *Waiting for Godot* (1952). As in the absurdist masterpiece, *Home*'s characters are essentially waiting throughout the action of their static and plotless play. There is even a character who has recurrent problems with ill-fitting shoes. Clearly these characters are in the hands of (at the mercy of?) a greater power. Does the institution equal Godot? Can an insane asylum have the mythic, archetypal, and religious resonances commonly associated with Beckett's Godot? Perhaps the answer to these questions is No, but the point seems to be that the parody of *Waiting for Godot* allows the questions to be raised; the point does not necessarily have to be that the parallels are indeed vaild either in the real world or in the play itself.[6] Indeed, the purpose of these intertextual notes of parody in *Home* is quite probably to allow Storey to limn the depths of human experience so poignantly depicted in *Godot*. The allusions to *Godot* permit Storey to move beyond a superficial treatment of some sad and lonely characters into a portrayal of basic human needs and situations. Without these elements of parody, *Home* might well be nothing more than a trite, realistic melodrama about society's outcasts; even though the absurdist elements of *Home* are primary parodic, their mere presence connects Storey's play with the dominant trend of post-war drama.

Another play ultimately deriving intertextual resonance from *Godot* but perhaps also contributing to *Home* is Tom Stoppard's *Rosencrantz and Guildenstern Are Dead* (1967). Like the title characters of that play, Jack and Harry are people to whom life has happened, and decisions are made for them by a higher power (the institution), just as Rosencrantz and Guildenstern are manipulated by the plot of *Hamlet*. None of these characters has any real freedom, but all of them must pass the time of their lives in some way to help alleviate the boredom and disguise the awful, frightening truth about their condition.

Dutton notes important elements of overlap between *Home* and Pinter's *The Hothouse* and Ken Kesey's novel *One Flew Over the Cuckoo's Nest* (156), all works which take a mental institution as a primary setting. Carol Rosen notes parallels between *Home* and many other plays set in confining institutions, for example Peter Weiss's *Marat/Sade* and Durenmatt's *The Physicists* (128).

Again, we are left with the question of what is funny about *Home*. Certainly the dialogue finds Storey at his most absurdist; the constant reiterations of meaningless phrases (Harry and Jack's "Really" comes immediately to mind) or sounds (Kathleen's wordless and vaguely obscene "Ooooh!" which Marjorie even falls into on occasion) are stock in trade of absurdist drama, at least as practiced by Samuel Beckett. The various discussions of apparently innocuous subjects (a trip up the Amazon, for example) become funny when a layer of double entendre is superimposed upon them by the well-timed "Oooohs" uttered by one or the other of the two women. Read in this light, large sections of the play become salacious and terribly funny.[7] The audience's growing awareness that these characters exist in some indefinable world also makes *Home* funny. Have the two men known each other for years or have they only just met? Are they two well-to-do men having a chat or are they inmates of a looney bin? The strange but familiar flirtations and posings between the sexes is comic: by presenting us with two older (mid-forties to fifties) men as the focus of his play, Storey adds an element of satire to the depiction of "mating rituals" he stages in *Home*; these older, institutionalized men act surprisingly like younger, presumably sane men do when confronted with the opposite sex.

David Storey's most obviously funny play is his overtly farcical *Mother's Day*. All the word play, double entendre, bedroom hopping, and distortions of reality commonly associated with farce are present here. The intertextual parallels, particularly those relating to the work of that master of modern farce, Joe Orton, are especially important, however. The primary situation of a person seeking or inhabiting lodgings and the strange landlady is the center of Pinter's *The Birthday Party* (1958) and Orton's *The Ruffian on the Stair* (1964, revised 1966) and *Entertaining Mr. Sloane* (1964).[8]

The play's focus on sex is shared with many Pinter and Orton plays. Moreover, the ontological questions raised by *Mother's Day* are shared by Beckett, Pinter, and Orton in various ways and, arguably, are the one central, unifying theme of much of post-World War II British theatre: who *are* these characters, really, since their identities—at least as they announce them—can change so rapidly to suit their convenience? Hutchings frames this issue stating that, "More than any of Storey's other plays, *Mother's Day* sets forth the various means whereby language . . . defines and shapes each person's individuality" (114). Clearly these characters define themselves by what they have to say about their past and their personalities, just as Sloane does in Orton's play or as Stanley does in Pinter's *The Birthday Party*. Throughout the play, various characters shift identities merely by announcing that they are not who they have seemed to be: Farrer becomes Mrs. Johnson's niece's husband replete with an interest in equine pursuits, Gordon changes from being a dangerous sex offender to Judith Waterton's rescuer, Peters the detective disguises himself as Mrs. Waterton, and so on.

There are parallels as well with the other Storey plays under consideration here. Surely Gordon's sexual fixation constitutes a type of madness—he will do whatever it takes to acquire sexual partners—and Lily certainly exhibits signs of mental illness throughout the play. To the extent that Mrs. Johnson's residence is a boarding house, it too is a type of institution. A reader certainly wonders what kind of "home" this is, just as he does with the institution in *Home*.[9] Judy is manipulated by others just as Middleton is in his play. The appearance of a private investigator on the scene (hired by Judy Waterton's concerned parents) parallels this device as used by Orton, specifically in *Loot* (1966) and *What the Butler Saw* (1969), and by Tom Stoppard in *Jumpers* (1972). Although the comic nature of investigative and police work generally has been a staple of popular films, for example, at least as far back as the Keystone Kops and Charlie Chaplin's early

films, Storey's use of Peters here seems consciously to be modeled on
Orton and Stoppard.

On the whole, I would agree with Hutchings when he claims that
"the play suffers in comparison with almost any of Orton's farces"
(117). Storey's foray into farce is his clearest engagement with a set of
dramatic conventions and is his most direct connection with a
recognizable and definable literary tradition. If this is a mark of the
play's lack of originality, it must needs also be an indication of Storey's
participation in the literary canon—a paticipation with obvious
intertextual ramifications. In other words, just as Storey in *Mother's
Day* is clearly operating within a sub-genre of dramatic literature, he is,
in his other comedies as well, making use of existing motifs and
conventions—only in a parodic manner.

To what uses has David Storey put comedic elements in his
plays? Certainly, he uses comedy to entertain. The laughs elicited by
Mother's Day are its *raison d'être*; the humor of *Middleton* and *Home*
help to make more palatable the serious situations and themes dealt
with in these plays. In *Mother's Day*, Storey has Mrs. Johnson give a
slightly creative description of her son Gordon's job in an insurance
office: "Insuring people against disaster" (214). Perhaps those words
best describe Storey's uses of comedy in the plays discussed here: by
introducing comedic elements, Storey hopes to avert the kind of
disaster potentially present in plays which treat such subjects as
insanity, infidelity, institutionalization, and sexual exploitation with
utter seriousness. Also, one should not overlook the importance of
humor in the "art" of Storey's plays; surely the complexities of plot on
which the farce of *Mother's Day* is dependent are evidence of a
supreme artificer at work on the stage.

By creating dramatic situations in these three comedies which
echo other, well-known literary works, Storey is able to add a frame of
reference to what he has to say. Sometimes by exploiting dramatic
conventions or staples of dramatic literature, sometimes by parodying
specific texts, Storey uses comedy throughout these plays as a way of
placing his work and what it connotes to a sensitive reader familiar with
the canon within a recognizable discursive space. His variations on
traditional themes and motifs, his parodies of dramatic situations and

specific literary works, and his own original voice and methods all combine to create a rich and theatrically successful body of work which can be placed within that canon he so often evokes. He is also able to raise important questions from his plays by their allusions to these other works; after all, in a very fundamental way one is making a sweeping allusion whenever one parodies a literary text or convention.

Notes

1. William Hutchings has pointed out a number of important parallels to Albee's *A Delicate Balance* in *The Restoration of Arnold Middleton* (*The Plays of David Storey* 58–59).

2. This ending was not the original one for *Middleton*, however; Storey's first produced version had Arnold committing suicide at the end (Randall, "Division and Unity in David Storey" 261). Thus the intertextual echo I am arguing for here is part only of the later revision of the play.

3. Stinson claims that Storey's use of minimalism and silences and desultory conversation, while bearing a resemblance to Pinter's technique, evokes "not nameless menace, but a kind of saving grace unsuspectingly found abounding in the dreary world of everyday" (131). In interviews with Flatley and also with Hutchings (137), Storey himself explicitly denies having had any familiarity with Pinter's work when writing his plays.

4. Of course this motif is also to be found in Joe Orton's celebrated play, *Entertaining Mr. Sloane*. I would argue that Pinter is the common source for this, however, and would not find it fruitful to discuss Orton's impact on *The Restoration of Arnold Middleton*.

5. Storey uses the Samson motif in *Early Days* as well, cf. Scene 3 (41).

6. Hutchings points out that the characters of *Home* have a plight much like those of *Godot* while arguing that "the causes of their anguish are primarily social rather than cosmological—and its depiction is realistic rather than 'absurd'" (121). He proceeds convincingly to demonstrate a number of parallels between *Home* and other Beckett plays—*Endgame, Happy Days*, and *Krapp's Last Tape*.

7. Storey uses this strategy in other plays as well, particularly *The Contractor, The Changing Room,* and *Life Class.*

8. This is duly noted by Hutchings, who writes that *Mother's Day*, like *Entertaining Mr. Sloane*, "involves the attempted sexual exploitation of a lodger by various members of the landlord's family" (110).

9. Hutchings quotes Storey as saying that "*Mother's Day* was supposed to be a family where every traditional value was carefully inverted and the obverse was true of everyday reality. The family lived out a life which was the reverse of every traditional practice. Everything which was against the rule and totally unacceptable in family life was the norm in this family" (115).

Works Cited

Culler, Jonathan. *Structuralist Poetics: Structuralism, Linguistics, and the Study of Literature.* Ithaca: Cornell University Press, 1975.

Dutton, Richard. *Modern Tragicomedy and the British Tradition: Beckett, Pinter, Stoppard, Albee and Storey.* Norman: University of Oklahoma Press, 1986.

Flatley, Guy. "I Never Saw a Pinter Play." *New York Times,* 29 November 1970, sec. 2: 1, 5.

Free, William J. "The Ironic Anger of David Storey." *Modern Drama* 16.3,4 (December 1973): 307–316.

Hutchings, William. *The Plays of David Storey: A Thematic Study.* Carbondale: Southern Illinois University Press, 1988.

Kristeva, Julia. *Semotike.* Paris: Seuil, 1969.

Miller, Owen. "Intertextual Identity." *Identity of the Literary Text.* Ed. Mario J. Valdes and Owen Miller. Toronto: University of Toronto Press, 1985. 19–40.

Randall, Phyllis R. "Division and Unity in David Storey." *Essays on Contemporary British Drama.* Ed. Hedwig Bock and Albert Wertheim. Munich: Hueber, 1981. 253–265.

Rosen, Carol. *Plays of Impasse: Contemporary Drama Set in Confining Institutions.* Princeton: Princeton University Press, 1983.

Stinson, John J. "Dualism and Paradox in the 'Puritan' Plays of David Storey." *Modern Drama* 20.2 (June 1977): 131–143.

Storey, David. *Early Days/Sisters/Life Class*. New York: Penguin, 1980.

———. *Home/The Changing Room/Mother's Day*. New York: Penguin, 1984.

———. *In Celebration/The Contractor/The Restoration of Arnold Middleton/ The Farm*. New York: Penguin, 1982.

ANOTHER STOREY:
A REAPPRAISAL OF *MOTHER'S DAY*

Phyllis R. Randall

Since it opened at the Royal Court in September 1976, David Storey's only produced farce, *Mother's Day*, has received little scholarly attention. Undoubtedly one reason it has been neglected is that it received not just negative but scathing reviews. Michael Billington denounced it as a "stinker," a "calculated exercise in bad taste comedy" (*Guardian* 8), while J. W. Lambert decided that it was out of Storey's range and belonged "in a wastebasket" (*Sunday Times* 35). Irving Wardle concurred, declaring Storey to be "wholly deficient in farcical talent" (*Times* 13).

The source of these criticisms is a play about a working-class family in the north of England, a family named Johnson that is long on ancestry (the husband claims descent from Samuel Johnson and the wife from a certain DeJohn, inventor of the toilet) but short on the attributes that constitute normality. They are, to use the current terminology, a dysfunctional family. The domineering mother is stingy and greedy and openly favors her younger son, Gordon. He is a preternaturally lascivious thug who "seduces" (a family word for any sex, including rape) every women who enters the house, including his sisters. The older son, Harold, a dim Royal Air Force mechanic who, after seventeen years has yet to win his first promotion, on a visit home decides, with parental consent, to marry his sister Edna. Sister Lily, even more dim-witted, is her mother's scapegoat for the family descent from its prestigious forebears; she spends most of her time in a closet.

+ water clo*set*

187

The father of this tribe is a house painter who won his bride many years before by seducing her as she lay "naked and inexperienced" on her bed (211; all references are to the Penguin edition of *Mother's Day*) but now must ask permission to get into their locked bedroom.

Into this den of depravity comes seventeen-year-old Judith Waterton, innocently running away from home with her seducer/husband Farrer, who, we learn later, makes a living by seducing gullible daughters of rich men and collecting ransom for their return. The play opens with Judy claiming the room her husband has booked for them in the Johnson house on their escape from her parents' home. Thereafter, it consists of unbridled libidos, mistaken identities, cross-dressing, talking at cross purposes, and a complicated plot—the typical fare of farces. All the while, Mrs. Johnson presides over this household with her own code of propriety and decorum. She will not tolerate a visitor's not removing his hat—or his gum—when he speaks to her.

Even with this brief summary, those familiar with David Storey will recognize typical Storey ingredients: the Northern England locale, a council house setting, the overbearing mother who has married beneath her, characters from different social classes. And even those early critics who deplored the play recognized that Storey was working on a familiar theme—the destructive family.

Much of the play, then, is familiar territory. What is so very different about this play is that it is a farce, a genre Storey had not attempted before and worlds apart from the realism and poetic naturalism of the plays that critics and public alike had responded to favorably. One problem that the critics had is that, expectations thwarted, they found "the wildly comic farce so uncharacteristic of Storey as to be unacceptable" (Free and Whittaker 163). According to J. L. Styan, farce is readily misjudged: "Perhaps because we have so much realistic dialogue and presentation today, judgments upon farce and artificial comedy inappropriate to these forms are easily made" (260).

Yet farcical elements can be found in any number of Storey's novels and plays, as both Kerensky (4) and Brown (35) have noted. The most pertinent to this play occurs in the otherwise sombre novel *A*

Temporary Life, especially in the scene in which art school teacher Freestone is invited to have dinner with the head of the school, Mr. Wilcox. Conned into paying for the gas to get them to the house, Freestone dines on a bowl of watery soup, an apple, and a shared piece of cheese, all the while listening to his host's zany ideas on nutrition. Bitterly cold, Freestone in desperation asks for some brandy, instead receiving a home-brewed fungi concoction, one sip of which makes him feel "as if my stomach's being removed . . . " (121).

This farcical scene from the novel is especially pertinent because the novel pairs with Storey's play *Life Class*,[1] and *Life Class* and *Mother's Day* were written within the same week (Norman 32). *Life Class* itself has many farcical elements, with mysteriously appearing limericks, and the discovery that Headmaster Foley stores bottles of his own urine on the shelves in his office, or that he steals coals from the school to take to his home, one coal at a time. Though farce as a genre was a departure for Storey, therefore, it hardly seems beyond his abilities.

Another source of disparagement of the play was the vulgarity of the language and behavior. The men rarely refer to seduction; instead, they "fuck," a word used so frequently for their triumphs that both it and the triumphs begin to lose their lustre, for some even their validity.[2] Both the bragging and the overuse of the vulgarity are exaggerations, gross but in keeping with the violence and "[o]utrage to family piety" that Eric Bentley says constitute farce (227).

Blind spots in judging Storey are not uncommon, even when it comes to his most successful plays. For example, Michael Billington found in his first review of *The Contractor* that "the demands of the work eliminated the human relationships" ("Guys Hold More" 14) and had to see it again before he found an "ineradicable image" in the tensions among and between the workers and family ("Dramatizing Work" 8). Albert Hunt judged the theme of *In Celebration* as "monumentally trivial" (681). Even *Home* was not immune from a critic's scorn: Walter Kerr found its "calculated stasis . . . both wearying and artificial" (18).

More positively, it should be noted that at least a few critics judged *Mother's Day* to be a fine play right from the start. Reviewing it in the *International Herald Tribune* (2 Oct. 1970), John Walker found it a "very funny and disquieting comedy. . . ." Clive Barnes also called it "very funny," with "riotously decadent humors" (54). Oleg Kerensky noted that the audience liked it when he saw it: "Personally, I found it more amusing and more theatrical than many of Storey's highly praised earlier efforts. If it had been a hitherto undiscovered piece by Orton, it would probably have been hailed as another of his comic masterpieces" (12).

Kerensky's point regarding audience approval corroborates Storey's own recollection that during the weeks of the play in preview, the audience "roared with laughter and thought it absolutely outrageously funny" (reported in Hutchings, 115). Only when the critics came on opening night did the audience clam up. Another corroboration: A local librarian told me he liked the play, that the audience "roared with laughter" the night he saw it. Like most of the world, I have not seen the play—the critics effectively silenced it—but I read it in manuscript before it was published and found it funny then, as I still do. Considering that some critics have taken a while to warm up to Storey's talents and considering that some of us have liked the play from the start, surely *Mother's Day* deserves another look.

A major source of the play's pleasure is its humor. It ranges from the broad humor typical of farce to insider humor—Storey's parody at the end of his earlier family play, *The Contractor*. The farcical fare of *Mother's Day* includes mistaken identities, disguises, and a complicated plot that intertwines greed, rape, incest, and an active Oedipal complex. Detective Peters, hired to find Judy, comes to the Johnson house disguised as Judy's mother, where "she" is accorded the usual Johnson male hospitality, a seduction—with both Gordon and Farrer presiding. Mrs. Johnson discovers Peters's disguise from, of all people, dim Lily, so that when the real Mrs. Waterton appears with Judy, she can handle with aplomb the mini-crisis as Gordon and Patrick come racing back to the living room with their "discovery." She calmly introduces the dishevelled Peters as her eccentric sister-in-law who delights in disguises, including one as a detective. The men catch on at once, and Peters must remain silent.

The humor encompasses slapstick comedy. Act III begins with a darkened stage, three mysterious figures creeping into the living room and hiding in various places, and finally a fight and a beating when the characters collide. Though the intended victim is Mr. Johnson—the Oedipal impulse is being acted upon by his son Gordon—it is Peters who is knocked out. In the resulting melee, when Peters awakes at an inconvenient time, he is hit over the head with a kettle to put him under again. To rectify his mistake, Gordon concocts a new plot. He will take advantage of Peters's amnesia by killing his father and blaming it on Peters. Peters, confused enough to believe he has murdered Mr. Johnson, is led to believe he is crazy when Johnson arrives to see what all the noise is about.

The comedy includes nonverbal routines as well, particularly with the tea things. Mrs. Johnson hides them so that the rest of the family cannot make tea, but she cannot remember where she put them. Others, of course, including Mrs. Waterton and Judy, unexpectedly find the hiding spot because they sit on the pillow that hides the pot.

Storey also includes one-liners and comic vaudeville-like exchanges. Farrer tells Judy they are safe in the Johnsons' house because it is off the beaten track where "people in our predicament might easily go." "There aren't many people in our predicament," she responds. "How can you say there's a beaten track?" (216). Another example reveals Mrs. Johnson's adroitness in keeping the upper hand:

MRS. JOHNSON: That child [Lily] would be a raving lunatic if I didn't watch her.
MR. JOHNSON: She is a raving lunatic.
MRS. JOHNSON: There: you see. All my care for nothing.

To assure Judy that she did indeed meet Farrer when he arranged for the room, Mrs. Johnson identifies him.

MRS. JOHNSON: Is he a well-built man?
JUDY: Medium.
MRS. JOHNSON: With sandy hair.
JUDY: Light-coloured.
MRS. JOHNSON: Name of Farrer.
JUDY: He's called Farrer.
MRS. JOHNSON: First name John.

JUDY: Patrick.
MRS. JOHNSON: That's the man. (181–82)

The character Judy herself is an interesting comic variation. Like the typical innocent ingenue, she walks into this trap of a home, frightened, alone, unsure of herself. After her "seduction," however, she feels more at home (as Farrer notes) and her lines, which still sound innocent on the surface, can be interpreted another way. When Gordon and Farrer take the real Mrs. Waterton up to "see the room" where Judy was held (where many seductions take place), Judy thinks that she "might go up as well." Mr. Johnson reminds her that she has not seen his room, and she responds, "Oh, I should so love to see the rest of the house" (265). Since we know that Mr. Johnson has tried to seduce Judy before, we can decipher what it is she would "so love to see."

The comedy of the play includes another level as well, for *Mother's Day* is a homecoming play gone wild.[3] After two years Harold comes home from the Royal Air Force, and his mother immediately suggests he could go back. What he finds at home is love and romance in the person of his sister Edna, and so he will stay. But strangers come home, too, and to a warmer welcome. Seducer Farrer, urged by Mrs. Johnson to make this house his home, does so to such an extent that Mrs. Johnson treats him as she does Gordon and accepts him as her nephew. (Originally he was designated a nephew to bypass the restrictions against renting rooms to strangers). She even assures Mr. Waterton that "there will always be a home for you here. And not only a home, but a hearth and bed" (247), though we do not learn if he will accept the offer. And certainly Judy comes home. In the last scene she returns with her mother to the home of "darling Mrs. Johnson" (259), where, as noted, she is eager to explore the rest of the house. Like Ruth in Pinter's *Homecoming*, she has found her niche.

The humor at the end of *Mother's Day* lies not only in the lines themselves but also in their reminding us of the end of Storey's earlier play, *The Contractor* (1969). In each the parents of the bride (and in *Mother's Day* the bridegroom as well!) come to terms with the new circumstances of their lives. In *The Contractor* Mr. and Mrs. Ewbank talk of the tent workers and autumn, literally as a season, but metaphorically as their lives. Ewbank wonders what will become of them. "You'd think you'd have something to show for it, wouldn't you. After all this time" (121), a sobering, even melancholy assessment of his life's work as tent contractor and as family man. Yet he has supervised the erection and taking down of the tent, Mrs. Ewbank has joined in its decorating, and the family has united to bring off the wedding. Now they leave the stage, arm in arm. "That's summat" (122), Ewbank concludes. The momentary union, brief as it is, is something to keep them going.

In his farce, Storey, with his penchant "to work the same thing from different angles" (Sage 64), presents a sharp contrast. The Johnsons also reflect on the past, especially their illustrious forebears, but they see each generation as better than the preceding one. Mr. Johnson says, "Gordon is up there seducing the eyeballs out of Judith. The son supercedes the father. It's the old, old story that history tells" (268–69). Mrs. Johnson agrees that they have had great good fortune; "unlike many families . . . whose names echo down the centuries of our glorious past—we have found our true vocation . . . a united family" (269). For, unlike the Ewbank family, which scatters after the wedding, leaving the parents alone, the Johnsons are together under one roof— their to-be-married daughter will still live at home, and they gain son Harold, who leaves the Air Force to marry. Moreover, they have added "nephew" Farrer. And who knows how long Judy will stay in this house she now finds agreeable? Self-satisfied, richer, many seductions later, with more going on above their heads at the moment they speak, with the approaching marriage of their son to their daughter, the Johnsons find the world a perfectly satisfactory place.

Of course, it is satisfactory only in the topsy-turvy world that Storey has created for this play. He aimed in *Mother's Day* for the kind of anarchy where "Everything which was against the rule and totally unacceptable in family life was the norm" (quoted in Hutchings 115). So where society establishes a strong taboo on incest, Storey establishes it as a norm for the family. Where society accepts the Oedipal complex as a metaphoric explanation for a stage of development, Storey establishes it as a literal goal—Gordon is out to kill his father, and Mr. Johnson accepts his impending death as normal. Even Harold, once his libido has been aroused by Edna, decides that he would like to kill his father. Where society expects the mother to nurture and nourish her children, Storey creates a mother who charges son Harold for taking up space and air and denies her daughter Lily food and a bed and locks her in a closet.

But Storey inverts more than the norms and taboos of society. He inverts the values he has created in his other plays. Where other plays establish the value of work, *Mother's Day* dismisses it in favor of the pleasure of play—seducing. Only Mr. Johnson's housepainting is made notable, and then to emphasize how worthless he is to the family since his working-class profession was the cause of Mrs. Johnson's disinheritance. Where other plays establish the value of ritual, in *Mother's Day* even the tea ceremony is impossible, since Mrs. Johnson hides the pot, the caddy, and even, apparently, the milk!

But there is one other inversion of values that Storey saves to the end. The one value Storey presents in *Mother's Day* as normal and desirable for these characters, cynical as it is, is one that an audience might also find acceptable. It is the value that all the seductions imply, indeed, are a metaphor for: It is better to get the other person before he gets you. Or, as Storey puts it, "Everybody involved in it is screwing everybody else, which is a reflection of the world we live in" (quoted in Kerensky 17).

Here the monster mother, who has played no part in the family seductions, proves herself a master. When she intuits Mr. Waterton's gullibility, she has no difficulty in getting him to go up from his original £250 ransom to £1000. (Peters will get none since he has told her the ransom was only £150.) Peters's purpose in returning in disguise as Judy's mother is to be able to claim some expense money. When Mrs. Johnson discovers his disguise, she goes into action again. Peters asks the real Mrs. Waterton for expense money. As gullible as her husband, she writes out a check for £1000, throwing in an extra £100 "in lieu . . . of interest that may have accrued in the time" (263). But Peters, in disguise as a woman, cannot give his own name, so Mrs. Johnson steps in with hers. Later Peters negotiates for a sum from the £2000 Mrs. Johnson has collected on this caper. She offers him the £150 he had offered her originally. Taking off his disguise, Peters threatens to call the police to report this "house of ill-repute" (265). In turn taking off her clothes, Mrs. Johnson threatens him: "I shall say you attempted to assault me. . . . I shall say you . . . endeavored to perform a variety of acts upon my person of which the constabulary itself may never have heard" (266–67). So Peters must settle for her top offer, £300, minus, of course, her customary charges for tea, heat, entertainments, and the anguish he has caused her by dressing as a woman: "Some of us, I can assure you, were brought up in environments where behaviour of that sort was not the custom" (267).

Beyond the laughs these lines and the actions of the play stir at this moment, however, is the disquieting realization that we tend to root for people like Mrs. Johnson who not only hoodwink the high-faluting Watertons but also outsmart the conniving detective. Yet we are torn, for everything else about this woman is anathema to us—not only what she believes but also how she behaves as wife and mother. No wonder Walker labeled this comedy "disquieting"; the anarchy of this system of values bodes ill. He noted in his review that the London critics "have not merely disliked" the play; "they have denounced it with such a sense of outrage, protesting so much, that I can only imagine that it has touched them on a raw nerve" (n.p.). Brown too felt the "critical herds' bellowing" excessive (36). Is it possible that a source of the outrage, the bellowing, was the difficulty of facing the double standard the Johnsons reveal in us?

A farce should end with everything turning out right side up for the characters, and it does. Mrs. Johnson has the money, the men—and presumably the women—their pleasure. But the right side up ending of this farce disturbs. We can laugh our way through the upside-down world until the last moment when we recognize the deeper truth about this monster mother and her monster family: Despite their exaggerations, they are much like us. Storey planned to show the Johnson family as "a microcosm of English domestic life with their delusions, illusions and fantasies, and their inveterate capacity to live in the past" (quoted in Kerensky 16–17). Surely our disquietude at the end is a measure of his success.

Unlike the protagonists of Storey's other plays, who go down in defeat at worst or in tenuous acceptance of life's terms at best, the Johnsons in *Mother's Day* end in triumph and assurance. They have achieved a united family—a family, as Mrs. Johnson notes at the end of the play, descended from two who formed "the great canopy of civilization: one the inventor of a book, and the other of a means whereby we might dispose of it." "Ah, yes," Mr. Johnson replies. So, Mrs. Johnson reasons, "With that behind us, what have we to fear of what lies ahead?" (269).

What indeed? With these representatives of humanity, the apocalypse is here in the family, just where Storey has been showing us it was all along.

Notes

1. See Randall for an analysis of Storey's penchant for pairing works.

2. Hutchings, one of the few scholars to take this play seriously, finds it significant that the sexual encounters may not actually take place (110–12). He points out that none is verified by the partner and that Mrs. Johnson comments on Gordon's imagination after he boasts about his prowess with Judy. Yet Mrs. Johnson's veracity, too, is in doubt—Edna asks at one point, "Are you telling the truth, then, Mother?" (181), and we already know that she is unreliable in her judgment of Gordon. Moreover, the humor disappears if the sex is in doubt. In farce, we accept the unacceptable. As Bentley puts it, in farce "we enjoy the privilege of being totally passive while on stage our most treasured unmentionable wishes are fulfilled before our eyes by the most violently active human beings that every [sic] sprang from the human imagination" (229). This description, it seems to me, perfectly fits Storey's farce.

3. Free and Whittaker analyze *Mother's Day* as one of Storey's intruder plays, noting that virtually all the intruders become assimilated. Since the newcomers do not alter the environment but are altered by it and since they come to make this house their home, as Mrs. Johnson frequently mentions, I think it is more in keeping with its farcical tone to consider it a homecoming play.

Works Cited

Barnes, Clive. "On the London Stage, King Comedy Reigns." *New York Times* 26 Sept. 1976: 54.

Bentley, Eric. "Farce." *The Life of the Drama*. New York: Atheneum, 1967. 219–56.

Billington, Michael. "Guys Hold More than Guyropes." *Times* (London) 21 Oct. 1969: 14.

————. "Dramatising Work." *Times* (London) 7 April 1970: 8.

————. "*Mother's Day.*" *Guardian* 23 Sept. 1976: 8.

Brown, Geoff. "*Mother's Day.*" *Plays and Players* 24 (Dec. 1976): 35–36.

Free, William J., and Lynn Page Whittaker. "The Intrusion Plot in David Storey's Plays." *Papers on Language and Literature* 18 (Spring 1982): 151–65.

Hunt, Albert. "Too Far above Ground." *New Society* 1 May 1969: 681.

Hutchings, William. *The Plays of David Storey: A Thematic Study*. Carbondale: Southern Illinois University Press, 1988.

Kerensky, Oleg. "David Storey." *The New British Drama: Fourteen Playwrights Since Osborne and Pinter*. New York: Taplinger Pub. Co., 1977. 3–17.

Kerr, Walter. "Like Pinter . . . Except." *New York Times* 29 Nov. 1970, sec. 2: 1+.

Lambert, J. W. "David Storey Week: Triumph and Disaster." *Sunday Times* (London) 26 Sept. 1976: 35.

Norman, Philip. "World without End." *Sunday Times* (London) 26 Sept. 1976: 3.

Randall, Phyllis R. "Division and Unity in David Storey." In Hedwig Bock and Albert Wertheim, eds. *Essays on Contemporary British Drama*. Munich: Hueber, 1981. 253–65.

Sage, Victor. "David Storey in Conversation." *New Review,* October 1976, 63–65.

Storey, David. *The Contractor*. New York: Random House, 1970.

————. *A Temporary Life*. New York: E. P. Dutton, 1974.

————. *Mother's Day*. In *Home, The Changing Room, and Mother's Day*. Harmondsworth: Penguin, 1978. 171–269.

Styan, J. L. *The Elements of Drama*. Cambridge: Cambridge UP, 1969.

Walker, John. "David Storey's Unsettling *Mother's Day*." *International Herald Tribune* 2 Oct. 1976: (page number deleted from a photocopy sent by IHT).

Wardle, Irving. "Unanswered Questions after Coming Home to the Finest Family in the Land." *Times* (London) 23 Sept. 1976: 13.

SPACE, LANGUAGE, AND ACTION IN
THE CONTRACTOR

William J. Free

David Storey sprang to international prominence as a playwright on the
basis of *The Contractor* in 1970. Although the plays that preceded *The
Contractor—The Restoration of Arnold Middleton* (1967) and *In
Celebration* (1969)—were modest critical and popular successes in
England, *The Contractor* brought Storey his first large-scale
international publicity and his "image" as an innovative force in the
modern theatre.

The originality of *The Contractor* comes from its arresting use of
stage space. The principal action of the play is the building of a tent on
stage during the first and second acts and the dismantling of it during
the third. *The Contractor* generates enormous audience appeal on the
immediate sensory level. Curiosity about the technical details of the
tent and how it is constructed is, as John Russell Taylor realized of the
original production, the vital part of the play (150). The attaching of
supporting poles and pulleys, the raising of the canvas, held the Royal
Court audience's attention to the point of threatening to overwhelm the
dialogue. What the actors said became far less meaningful than what
they did.

The innovative way Storey fills stage space in this play produces
several consequences both to the action of the play and to the
relationship of the action to the dialogue. The play presents not just one
image of space but several. This complex interaction of action and
space forces the audience to interpret the significance of the visible

action on-stage and dialogue by comparing it to other actions and spaces off stage. Playwrights frequently situate important events in an imagined elsewhere not represented on stage. The most obvious historical example is the locating of violence off stage in Greek drama and the related entrance of messengers with crucial information coming from some off stage place.

Both the presentation of past events (which obviously implies places other than the immediately visible stage) and the suggestion of off-stage space contradict the normal theoretical dictum that the theatre deals with an immediately present image. Charles R. Lyons states the received view: "No theatrical representation of human experience can be performed that does not exhibit a human figure in space . . . " (27). To be theatrical in this sense, the image of humanity in space must be present to the eyes and ears of the audience seated in a particular theatre in a particular city at a particular time. This real experience generates a powerful flow of energy among the actors, the spectators, and the inanimate objects on stage, and this energy flow defines the theatrical experience.

A second kind of mediated experience occurs in the imagination and memory.[1] This unseen experience is also temporal and spatial since "we cannot imagine a human figure fully removed from space and time" (Lyons, 31). The theatre presents this second reality absent to the immediate sensory experience through a variety of onstage signs. Hanna Scolnicov designates the two realities as "the theatrical space within" and "the theatrical space without," the space and time experienced as present and on stage and the space/time imagined as off stage, either present or past (14). The dynamic interaction between these two spaces expands the possibilities of theatrical representation beyond the immediately present in a number of ways limited only by the imagination of the playwright.

Describing this dynamic requires an elaborate definition of space. One such comes from Susanne K. Langer's description of architecture. A building, she contends, is more than just a container; it is an expression of what she calls an "ethnic domain." Following Heidegger's concept of place as space defined by the addition of human purpose,[2] Langer elaborates on the concept of architecture as follows:

"A place, in this non-geographical sense is a created thing, an ethnic domain made visible, tangible, sensible" (95). She goes on to characterize an "ethnic domain" as containing, in addition to space, physical objects, facial expression, posture, movement, and dynamics. The sum of this "physically present human environment . . . expresses the characteristic rhythmic functional patterns which constitute a culture" (96).

Langer's use of the word "domain" opens us to another set of terms. Christian Norberg-Schulz in *Existence, Space & Architecture* defines a place as a specific space contained within a domain, which is larger than a place and, therefore, can contain several places. Domains and places related to one another in a field/ground gestalt. Domains are "relatively unstructured 'ground[s]' against which places appear as more pronounced 'figures'" (23). But domains are only "relatively" unstructured. Man divides worlds into domains "as an expression of [his] general need for imagining his world 'as an ordered cosmos within an unordered chaos'" (23).

The descriptions of space provided by Langer and by Norberg-Schulz apply to the vocabulary of theatre description by elaborating the distinction between on- and offstage spaces. Places, in the sense described above, are always onstage. Domains can be on-stage provided there exist several onstage places contained within those domains. Domains can also be suggested as offstage spaces which ground the onstage places and give them meaning and significance.

Places and domains are connected, as Norberg-Schulz describes, by paths. Paths are means for moving from one place to the other within the realm of a domain. In the case of several on-stage places, paths may be simple movements crossing the stage. In the case of off-stage spaces, paths occur as entrances and exits. However, the possibility exists that no paths connect places either on or off stage, so characters cannot move freely from one place to the other. For example, in Chekhov's *Three Sisters* Moscow is an off-stage domain, but the sisters can find no path between themselves and the Russian capital.[3]

The vocabulary of space which I have just described—the ethnic domain (or places) of on-stage space, the larger domains offstage, and the paths connecting them—proves extremely useful in understanding the use of space in *The Contractor*. Storey manipulates inner and outer theatrical space as the play's principal structural feature by presenting experiences in which off-stage events and suggested off-stage spaces function to define the audience's understanding of the events depicted on stage more clearly than does the dialogue. Without the invisible context surrounding the action, the language being spoken on stage seems trivial or even absurd.

The *Contractor* represents or alludes to three layers of space and two dimensions of time. The place of the action represented during all three acts of *The Contractor* is the lawn of the Ewbank house, the lawn on which the tent is to be erected.

> The stage is set with three tent poles for a marquee, twenty or thirty foot high, down the center of the stage at right angles to the audience. The poles should be solid and permanently fixed, the ropes supporting them, from the top, running off into the wings. Each pole is equipped with the necessary pulley blocks and ropes, the latter fastened off near the base as the play begins. (9)

In addition to being physically present to the audience for the entire play, the tent is also the setting of the major off-stage event of the play, the wedding for which the tent is being erected. As is typical in Storey's plays, the central event of *The Contractor* occurs during the time gap between acts.[4] The wedding gets talked about throughout the play, and the audience sees its effect on the disheveled tent in Act Three, but its importance is only nominal. Emphasis on the wedding and attention to the process of tent building in a sense soften the audience's focus on the other events happening on stage, events which involve a complex dialectic of language and action, off- and on-stage spaces.

The focus on physical action as defining the on-stage space of *The Contractor* and the relationship of that action to the words being spoken on stage challenge the common understanding that in stage language "the words go somewhere, move towards a predetermined end . . . [and] advance the action" of the play (Styan, 12). Keir Elam, summarizing the consensus view of stage dialogue, writes that stage dialogue is distinguished from real talk by its greater syntactic orderliness and its informational intensity. Elam quotes Bronislaw Malinowski's definition of "phatic communion"—the use of words which "serves to establish bonds of personal union between people brought together by the need of companionship and does not serve any purpose of communicating ideas" (quoted in Elam, 180). In phatic language, the social function of language dominates over descriptive or informational functions. Elam continues:

> what is said is very often of less importance than the fact of saying something. . . . In the drama, on the contrary, the information-bearing role of language is normally constant: every utterance counts, everything said is significant and carries the action and 'world-creating' functions forward in some way (180).

The dialogue of *The Contractor* more clearly resembles Malinowski's phatic language than it does either Styan's or Elam's definitions of dramatic dialogue. In *The Contractor* language is a second action which parallels the main action indirectly rather than furthering it directly. Storey himself recognizes this division of action and dialogue. He states that "*The Contractor*'s such a physical thing that you can't really relate the text to it directly. The conception is more theatrical" (quoted in Hayman, 14). As the men build the tent they joke, banter playfully among themselves, and tease the retarded Glendenning. The following exchange typifies their conversation. Fitzpatrick enters eating a sandwich and carrying Marshall's shoulder bag. Marshall, Kay, and Ewbank are already on stage:

> FITZPATRICK: Is that a ton of lead you have in there, Marshy, or the latest of your mother's buns? (*He slings the bag to MARSHALL who misses it.*) He couldn't nick a tail off a chocolate mouse.
>
> MARSHALL: Nor a cold off a wet morning!
>
> (*They both laugh.*)
>
> FITZPATRICK: (*catching sight of* EWBANK). Oh, good Christ. Good morning. How are you? Good day. Good night . . .

(Mumbles on through a ritual of touching forelock, bowing, etc.)

EWBANK: Mind where you put your feet, Fitzpatrick,
                 or I'll have them bloody well cut off.
FITZPATRICK: Aaah! *(Steps one way then another. To*
                 MARSHALL) As long as it's my feet
                 only he's after.

(They both laugh.) (10)

Assuming that Kathleen George is correct in her assertion that the early scenes determine the rules that will govern the world of the play (13), the rules which the dialogue establishes to govern the ethnic character of this place are clownishness, jokes with sexual innuendo as a prime feature, and a breezy and relaxed atmosphere. This mode of dialogue continues throughout the play.

Overshadowing this casual dialogue is the purposeful business of building the tent, a labour in which the men cooperate with the same ease with which they banter with one another. Often the dialogue alludes to this action, as when the foreman, Kay, gives instructions or one of the men asks another for help, but more frequently the dialogue resembles the chit-chat which working men engage in to make the time pass more easily. However, this easy-going banter takes on greater significance when viewed within the context of the off-stage domain which surrounds the on-stage place.

Off-stage space interacts with the on-stage building of the tent in two layers. The nearer layer is the house owned by Ewbank, also the owner of the firm that builds the tent. Ewbank's daughter's wedding provides the occasion for building the tent. Three generations of the Ewbank family enter the stage space from the house and interact with the men on stage.

To appropriate the vocabulary of space which I have borrowed from Langer and Norberg-Schulz, the lawn on which the workers are erecting the tent is the place of *The Contractor* and the Ewbank's house is the domain within which the place is situated. At first glance, the relationship between place and domain is warm, friendly, and reciprocal. Ewbank admires and compliments the men's work, as does the bride-to-be Claire and her fiancé Maurice. The elderly Ewbanks visit the construction cite, he to amuse the men with his account of his one-time profession of rope making, she to keep him from being too much of a pest. Ewbank's son Paul even helps build the tent. Although the dialogue hints of generational conflict among the Ewbanks (a theme Storey had explored earlier in *In Celebration*), the Ewbanks' relationship with their workers seems untroubled and positive.

William Hutchings argues that "Through the ritual of tent-raising, the workmen . . . find a vital quality that the Ewbank family lacks: a sense of coherence, hierarchy, and unity, forged through common purpose and shared experience . . . " (170). It is equally possible to raise the question of whether this cohesion is rather an ideological illusion. A careful look at the relationship of on- and off-stage spaces in the play allows themes to emerge in the dialogue which undercut an optimistic view of the men's on-stage work.

A point worth noting is that the imaginary path linking the off-stage house and the on-stage action connects the two spaces in only one direction. The family come and go at ease, but the workers never exit the stage to the house. It is a territory closed to them, one which defines them in a conventional class structure. They are the workers, the Ewbanks are the bosses. The workers remain separate. Their banter, their work, may give the audience the impression that they are experiencing a bonding. But a careful look at their words might as well suggest a suppressed consciousness of their position as alienated from the off-stage world.

The workers' alienation never takes the form of direct confrontation. It exists, instead, as a series of themes which pop up again and again, embedded in their casual conversation. As such, it is a minor rather than dominant element. It does not negate Hutchings's idea of bonding as much as add a further dimension to it, emphasizing the fact that although the men form a coherent society when at work, they are isolated from membership in the other social structures off stage, structures to which they have no paths.

One such theme is desire for Ewbank's daughter Claire, the bride-to-be. Claire comes from the house to the tent location on numerous occasions and engages in the men's banter. But they know that she and her kind are inaccessible to them. All, that is, but the half-wit Glendenning. Glenny here functions rather like the fools in

Shakespeare: he thinks and speaks the forbidden. The men, picking up on the theme of marriage, tease Glenny that he needs a wife and suggest one of the four daughters of their foreman, Kay:

> GLENDENNING: Ah . . . I w,w . . . w,w . . . w,w . . .
>   wouldn't want one of Kay's lasses.
> MARSHALL: Which one would you like, Glenny?
> GLENDENNING: I w . . . w . . . wouldn't mind the one they
>   have in theer. (*Gestures at the
>   house.*) (*They laugh.*) . . .

When Bennett says she's spoken for, Glenny answers:

> (*carried away*) Th . . . th . . . th . . . there's many a slip twi
>   . . . twi . . . twi . . . twixt c . . . c . . . c
>   . . . cup and l . . . l . . . l . . . l . . . lip!
>   (28)

The men change the subject, but Glenny's gesture at the house underlines the futility of his wish. Glenny's desire to marry Claire is so preposterous that only a half-wit can have the innocence to articulate it.

The theme of the inaccessible Claire comes up again in Act Two. Maurice is asking Fitzpatrick why he doesn't marry. He replies, not to Maurice, but to Claire: "I could never find a lady, as beautiful as yourself, who'd be glad enough to have me" (68). Fitzpatrick's experience working on the tent is a constant reminder of the things that are out of his grasp—the absence of a path to the house.

A second theme undercutting the theme of workers' bonding is their frequent talk about their inability to leave Ewbank's employ, a theme Ewbank himself reiterates throughout the play: "I take on all those that nobody else'll employ . . . " he says. "Anybody who'll work. Miners who've coughed their lungs up, fitters who've lost their fingers, madmen who've run away from home" (38). Speaking of being employed by Ewbank, Fitzpatrick and Marshall repeat the idea, sharing the sentence "Some of course . . . Have no alternative . . . " (99). The presence of Paul, Claire, and Maurice, who come down the one-way path from the house, makes the theme more specific. Other professions are denied these men, as is the high-class education which opens the paths to those professions.

Fitzpatrick asks Paul if he's a college man. His answer is affirmative:

FITZPATRICK:	I've always fancied that, you know, myself. Books. Study. A pile of muffins by the fire.
MARSHALL:	A pile of what?

(*They laugh.*) (46)

Marshall's turning Fitzpatrick's daydream into an obscene joke shows how absurd it really is. When the men find out that Maurice is a doctor, the joking continues:

FITZPATRICK:	A doctor! By God.
MARSHALL:	Fitzie's always fancied himself as that.
FITZPATRICK:	Aye. The stethoscope is my natural weapon. There's not many a thing, now, that I couldn't find with that.

(*They laugh.*) (47)

Finding out that Claire is a nurse, Fitzpatrick aspires to a job in a hospital; but he finally admits to being a born and bred Irish working man. The theme continues in Act Two when Fitzpatrick fancies himself a criminal lawyer, but he admits he didn't study in school. "No, no," he tells his mates: "I'm too old now, to go to school, and too damn poor to bother" (63). Fitzpatrick plays the clown throughout the play, picking up themes from the snatches of casual dialogue and fantasizing on them. His wit is edged with realism, whereas Glenny's is the innocent product of his mental slowness. Fitzpatrick knows who he is, where he is, and what is closed to him.

A third theme that building the tent brings home to the men is the difference between their lodgings and their employer's. They are erecting on the lawn of the off-stage domain of Ewbank's house a tent to be used for one night of celebration. The temporary tent impresses the men as better than their homes:

MARSHALL:	Wouldn't mind living here meself.
FITZPATRICK:	You should see his bloody room.
MARSHALL:	A hovel.

| FITZPATRICK: | Pig-sty. |
| MARSHALL: | It is. He's right. (79) |

They're joking, of course, but the context of the joke makes a point—they are working for the pleasure of someone else. Ewbank constantly nagging them not to damage the grass reminds them and the audience that the men are not in "their" space.

The alienation between Ewbank and his men emerges clearly in Act Two. He enters drunk. He is unhappy about their work and climbs a ladder to do it himself. At this point, the split also applies to Paul, who has helped the men throughout the first act and has tried without much success to gain a rapport with them. When Fitzpatrick mocks Ewbank by singing "Somebody has had a tipple . . . /Somebody has had a drop . . . ," Paul corrects him sharply with "I think we've had enough of that" (73).

Act Three increases Ewbank's bad mood. He complains to the men about the quality of their work. At one point, he turns on Marshall, who is trying to make small talk:

MARSHALL:	The couple got off to a happy start, then Mr. Ewbank.
EWBANK:	What? . . .
MARSHALL:	The happy . . .
EWBANK:	Mind your own bloody business. Bennett, I don't call that working. (*To MARSHALL*) How the hell would you know that?
MARSHALL:	I . . . Me . . . We . . . (103)

Ewbank can be chummy with his men in the workplace, but they must not joke or make small talk about his private life. He reserves for himself the privilege of being critical or intimate about his children. In Act One he had joked about his future son-in-law Maurice: "He's so refined if it wasn't for his britches he'd be invisible" (38). But as the play goes on, his mood toward his workers is more strained and irritated. The audience may sympathize with Ewbank because of the stress he is under, but the separation between him and his workmen is clear. Like the path to the house, the workers' banter seems to have only one permissible direction.

A second off-stage domain presents a third perspective. This is the almost undefined space "out there" from which the men come to work and to which they go after work. The play offers no evidence that the man have any private relationship with one another after work hours. They inquire about and make jokes about each other's families and life-styles, but their banter does not have a relational function beyond passing the time of day. The space beyond also threatens the cohesiveness of the Ewbank family. The children and the old people will leave immediately after the wedding. Paul seems to drift from space to space without much purpose or direction. His participation in the tent building is a momentary whim, not an expression of a found purpose for his life. England, the space outside Ewbank's house and lawn, seems shadowy, undifferentiated, unorganized, a space where, to quote Heidegger, people and resources are just "lying around" in random order. This sense of the temporariness of any organized, purposeful human activity recurs in several of Storey's plays, most prominently in the football team in *The Changing Room* and the daughters of the household in *The Farm*.

In *The Contractor,* Storey offers a double vision of his subject. Looked at only from the standpoint of a single, on-stage place, the play does seem to present a positive and socially uplifting view of workers bonding and finding a common purpose in the work of erecting a tent. But viewing that action against the ground of the off-stage domain of Ewbank's house and the one-way path connecting it to the tent and the accessible but empty larger domain surrounding that, the play suggests a different theme. The rituals of work which connect these men (and the players in *The Changing Room* and the art students in *Life Class*) are temporary stays against the confusion of an alienated, disordered, and purposeless life.

Storey constructs his play so that these two views never confront one another openly. Ronald Hayman says of *Home*:

> *The fact of non-confrontation is made integral to the conception and to the nature of the characters. They have to be people who don't, who can't confront what there is to confront, and that's the subject, isn't it?* (16; italics Hayman's)

So it seems the subject of many of Storey's plays. The dramatic problem is how to create characters who do not have the consciousness to confront what there is to confront on the one hand and to situate them so that the audience can confront it on the other. Storey solves the problem in *The Contractor* by setting up a dialogue between on-stage and off-stage space. The dialogue is whispered, but it is audible to the attentive audience. By his shrewd solution to this problem, Storey adds another dimension to the continuing development of theatrical space and its uses.

Notes

1.   Kant introduces this distinction in the following passage from *The Critique of Judgement*:

> Every form of the objects of sense (both of external sense and also mediately of internal) is either *figure* or *play* [*gestalt* or *spiel*]. In the later case it is either play of figures (in space, viz, pantomime and dancing) or the mere play of sensation (in time). (Tr. J.H. Bernard, New York: Hafner, 1966, 61.)

The play of sensation in time includes music, voice and other sound. In its definition of objects present to the external sense, the passage describes the entire time/space continuum that is the aesthetic grounding of the theatrical experience in the first sense I described. But the passage also leaves open the possibility of invisible, inaudible experience mediated by some sign system that is present to the external sense. References to off-stage space can occur through any such sign that can be used as part of the theatrical experience—as Tennessee Williams frequently suggests off stage space through music.

2.   Heidegger's *Being and Time* presents a number of descriptions of space pertinent here. Most relevant to my discussion are:

> Equipment has its *place*, or else it 'lies around.' This must be distinguished in principle from just occurring at random in some spacial position. (136)

and

> A totality of equipment [is] constituted by various ways of
> the 'in-order-to. . . . ' (97)

The distinction here between a random, purposeless figuration of space as
opposed to one organized in order to do something describes both Langer's
description of a building existing in order to express an ethnic domain and my
description of theatrical space in what follows.

    3. I borrow this example from Stanley Longman, "The Spacial
Dimension of Theatre," *Theatre Journal*, March 1981, 46–59. He discusses the
importance of the off-stage space of Moscow to the on-stage action of
Chekhov's play, but he does not use the place/domain terminology I am using
here, nor does he speculate on the possibility of a path linking the two spaces.
Such a path may exist in the reality of Russian geography, but no such path is
possible for the sisters. Paths in the theatre space are possible only if defined as
possible within the play.

    4. Ronald Hayman first remarked on this feature of Storey's plays in
Playback when he remarked on the non-confrontational nature of Storey's
characters. Lynn Paige Whittaker and I find it as a nearly ubiquitous structural
pattern in the plays. Also see Hutchings, p. 150, for applications to other plays.

Works Cited

Elam, Kier. *The Semiotics of Theatre and Drama*. London: Methuen, 1980.

Free, William J., and Lynn Page Whittaker. "The Intrusion Plot in David
    Storey's Plays." *Papers in Language and Literature*, Spring 1982, 151–
    65.

George, Kathleen. *Rhythm in Drama*. Pittsburgh: University of Pittsburgh
    Press, 1980.

Hayman, Ronald. *Playback*. New York: Horizon, 1974.

Heidegger, Martin. *Being and Time*. Tr. John Macquarrie and Edward
    Robinson. New York: Harper and Row, 1962.

Hutchings, William. *The Plays of David Storey: A Thematic Study*. Carbondale:
    Southern Illinois University Press, 1988.

Langer, Susanne. *Feeling and Form*. New York: Scribner's, 1953.

Lyons, Charles R., "Character and theatrical space," *The Theatrical Space.* Cambridge: Cambridge University Press, 1987.

Norberg-Schulz, Christian. *Existence, Space & Architecture.* New York: Praeger, 1971.

Scolnicov, Hanna. "Theatre space, theatrical space, and the theatrical space without." *The Theatrical Space.* Cambridge: Cambridge University Press, 1987.

Storey, David. *The Contractor.* London: Cape, 1970.

Styan, J. L. *The Elements of Drama.* Cambridge: Cambridge University Press, 1960.

Taylor, John Russell. "David Storey." *The Second Wave: British Drama of the Sixties.* London: Eyre Methuen, 1971; rev. 1978.

THE MARCH ON RUSSIA

Kimball King

The March on Russia premiered in the Lyttleton Theatre of the Royal National Theatre complex on April 6th, 1989, eight years after Storey's last published play, *Early Days*, had been produced in the smaller Cottesloe Theatre in the same building. In 1983 Storey had commented to William Hutchings that most of his plays had been written for the Royal Court Theatre but that the Court had become "very parochial" and "preoccupied with politicizing drama. I find that a form of Philistinism" (*Plays of David Storey*, 181), while he claimed that the Court had veered from its original intent to be a writer's theatre. Storey had even harsher words for the National Theatre, which he considered a "complete anathema," adding that it was "an impresario's idea—a computer's idea—of a theatre, only for revivals and doing middle-class, middlebrow drama" (*Plays of David Storey,* 182).

Perhaps the intimacy and flexibility of the small Cottesloe with its fringe theatre atmosphere ultimately convinced Storey that it would be an appropriate setting for *Early Days*. Having seen the productions of *Early Days* in the Cottesloe and *The March on Russia* in the Lyttleton, I believe that the Cottesloe does generate the proper ambiance for the "poetic" and "realistic" qualities of the playwright, which director Lindsay Anderson has praised in his interview in this volume. The Lyttleton appeared to me to be too vast an arena for a sensitive but narrowly focused work like *The March on Russia*. Neither the setting nor the plot was sufficiently complicated to justify using the very technical resources of the Lyttleton, and the 1,200-seat auditorium tended to overwhelm the understated conversational nuances of the characters—children educated beyond the comprehension of their parents, an old couple constantly sparring in a believably ritualistic manner, at once abrasive and amusing. Anderson's insistence that Storey is primarily not a naturalist depends on the director's association of political determinism with that theatrical genre. All of Storey's novels and plays reveal his compassion for confused and imperfect people, and *The March on Russia* is especially evenhanded in its tender assessment of the foibles of individual characters. Anderson has noted that Storey's "action-scenario is rather like the pretext of a ballet" (Interview). The staging has to be "choreographic" rather than "naturalistic."

The structure of *The March on Russia* is familiar to admirers of the writer's earlier works. There is a gathering of family members for a particular event, as in plays from *The Contractor* to *Early Days*. However, the main event takes place off stage as if it were too emotionally taut to render without being melodramatic, or ultimately less significant than the events which preceded it or emanated from it. In this case the Pasmores' adult children have assembled to celebrate their parents' sixtieth wedding anniversary, in the manner of the Shaw family in *In Celebration*, who had been married for forty years. The anniversary dinner in both plays takes place at a restaurant where everyone, especially the children, has too much to drink. Following the celebration, the children scatter to their far-flung residences.

Storey is a keen observer of sociological changes in English family structure. Medical science has prolonged human life, and elderly people remain a burden to their children for a longer period of time, often dwelling in retirement communities or otherwise "artificial" surroundings. Senility or unresolved psychological conflicts are given more opportunity to surface. The dissolution of the "traditional" family often leaves longtime marriage partners confronting divorced or recently separated children. Although there is still a morbid national fascination with the old class system, class boundaries are less clearly delineated, and educational, economic, and social status may vary greatly from generation to generation. Family members are dispersed over a wider geographical range. The elderly Pasmores are working class, now living in an isolated Northern community in a retirement house provided by their son, Colin, a college teacher and author of a commercially successful history text. Both of their daughters are college graduates. One is wealthy, childless, and has been active in politics. Neither she nor her middle-class sister with two children is presently living with her husband. All the children blame themselves for failing to tend adequately to their parents' needs. Their lonely father has disgraced himself by shoplifting in the small community's only store. Like a bored child in an unfamiliar environment, he acted impulsively and now worries that his actions have sullied a lifelong reputation for honesty and hard work.

As Hutchings has indicated, their are numerous autobiographical allusions in Storey's plays and novels. An educated artist-son often contends with his coal-miner father, as did Storey. London seems to represent freedom and culture; Leeds is associated with repression and brutality. Protagonists often feel divided between their physical and intellectual selves. Storey had been both a rugby player and a painter. (Hutchings, 11). Furthermore, characters overlap from novel to novel to play: Ewbank, who is an employer in the novel, *Radcliffe*, is the dramatic protagonist in *The Contractor* (Hutchings, 12). The Pasmore family in *The March on Russia* was introduced in Storey's fourth novel in 1972, which was only part of a largely unpublished major work completed four years earlier.

The relationship between the 1972 novel and the 1989 play indicates Storey's passion for verisimilitude and his creation of characters who appear to live in time unmoored by specific fictional or dramatic settings. The protagonist of the novel, Pasmore, has suffered a nervous breakdown or severe "mid-life crisis" and has abandoned his wife and children. At the conclusion of the novel he returns to his family and his job. Eighteen years later in *The March on Russia*, he is still neurotic, still fighting off panic attacks and depression. But he is tenured, more prosperous, though not highly esteemed in academic circles. Furthermore, a third child has been born following his reconciliation to his wife, to whom Colin refers casually when he chats with his sisters. Colin's father, a recently retired collier, seems to have forgotten disowning his son at the time of his son's earlier breakdown and vents his pent-up bitterness on his recently divorced daughters. John Russell Taylor has pointed out that parents in Storey's work present the same personality profile: "Captious, bitter, impossible to satisfy . . . (they) represent some negation of individuality . . . they seem to want to punish their children for the hardships they themselves have gone through" (Taylor, 8–9).

In *The March on Russia* Storey demonstrates a greater compassion for unreasonable parents. The senior Pasmores are so fragile and vulnerable that their dilemma demands attention. Their house and means are more comfortable, one assumes, than what they have known in their youth. Ironically, the capitalist system has worked to their benefit in the sense that they have rest and attractive surroundings in their final years. But the deprivations of their early lives have left them without resources to face an unstructured and physically undemanding existence. For the first time they question the value of their lifetime experiences and approach the end with a sense of futility.

Like Chekhov, Storey can capture a personality without judgment and like his Russian predecessor he chooses not to endorse one point of view at the detriment of another. *The March on Russia* masterfully blends pathos with comedy in the manner of Chekhov's *The Cherry Orchard*. The audience is captivated by humorous verbal exchanges between the characters. Rightly or wrongly, one associates a greater degree of bickering and complaining with older people. Amused audiences watching *The March on Russia* in the Lyttleton were doubtless comparing the Pasmores' contretemps to similar dialogues between their own parents or grandparents.

Storey skillfully engages us with the "natural" humor of such exchanges but manages simultaneously to create an undercurrent of irony. For example, the Pasmores tease each other about the old man's interest in a twenty-five-year-old "back-fence" neighbor:

> MRS. PASMORE: Should hear him over the fence to Mrs. Halliday next door. She's twenty-five. You'd think *he* was twenty-seven.
> PASMORE: The spirit is all that counts.

MRS. PASMORE: Leaning on the fence to hold himself up.
You'd think he was trying to court her.
PASMORE: She knows a good-looker when she sees one.
MRS. PASMORE: You're old enough to be her father. (7)

This droll exchange takes place in front of Colin early in the play, but later Mrs. Pasmore confides to her daughter that Pasmore caused her grief by his womanizing when he was a younger man. What appeared at first to be good-natured teasing—almost comical considering each of the couple's advanced ages—becomes in retrospect a reminder of unforgiven dalliances which have left a bitter aftertaste. Storey the psychologist has also provided a family dynamic, which accounts in part for present frustrations. Mrs. Pasmore admits that she could never bring herself to "cuddle" Colin, and his father was overly severe with him. The girls idealize their father, as their mother idealized her own father ("He never complained. Not once. Never! He was a saint. A saint!" [45]), but she corrodes any sense of independence in Wendy as proof of a "vicious streak" (45) and expresses her ultimate disappointment in her eldest daughter, Eileen: "If you had a child, you'd understand" (50). But Storey never blames the marital failures of the Pasmore children or their drinking problems or their inability to cope professionally on their victimization within a dysfunctional family.

Rather, he places a particular English family, one biographically similar to his own, in the context of a disintegrating nation. There may be specific social ills or individual psychological pathologies which have affected the Pasmores, but these pale before the dark, defeating spectre of a crumbling world order. Although Storey distrusts a hierarchical class structure and expresses concern for the economically exploited, he focuses more on the psychological and social damage caused by the failure of governmental systems than on specific political issues. In *The March on Russia* he appears to find the roots of an unhealthy English body politic in the industrial revolution. He chooses as his spokesman Colin Pasmore, an historian and social scientist whose earliest intellectual inspiration was his reading of *The Prophecies of Jonathan Wroe*. Colin marvels: "It seemed remarkable (to me) that a product of the industrial revolution could see the consequences so far ahead, the disposition, the conformity, the dilution of feeling, the despiritualization—which has turned us into the people we are today" (21).

None of England's major political parties provide realistic solutions to the nation's malaise. Eileen Pasmore has been rejected by the Labour party because her ex-husband was a prominent businessman and she is presently registered as an "Independent." Colin and Wendy appear to be cynically apolitical, prevented as much by their intelligence as by their personal problems from finding a viable national agenda. Old Pasmore continues to vote for Labour (out of habit rather than conviction). But the elderly mother quite vehemently switches her allegiance from Labour to the Tories. She argues: "Socialism's worn out—there has never been such a gutless generation—but makes me weep to see well-fed, well-clad people with subsidized housing and a national health with state benefits pension, complaining that they've never had a chance" (19). She also identifies with Mrs. Thatcher's relentless work ethic and no-nonsense style, although the former prime minister's name is not invoked.

The playwright has moved beyond blaming specific offenders to examining the consequences of failed ideologies. No solutions are offered—only an admonition that we recognize widespread dissatisfaction in contemporary English life. Religious belief is not seen as a panacea; however, the absence of spiritual commitment contributes to the individual characters' sense of emptiness. It is not unusual for elderly people to avoid discussions of death, and yet the Pasmores' denial of the inevitable defines their lives to an extent. Their boasting about their ability to survive a life of self-denial and to preserve a marriage marred by poverty and disappointment belies their fear that everything that they have lived for has been pointless. Mrs. Pasmore disapproves of swearing on the Sabbath, yet she notes that "Every day is alike up here," except Sunday, which is only different because there is "no milkman." She notes matter-of factly that the church she was married in is now a bowling alley. Such information contains no apocalyptic significance, but clearly the world Storey describes has been diminished by the passing of spiritual values and a commitment to marriage, as well as increased political cynicism.

Storey has expressed irritation at being compared to D.H. Lawrence on the basis of the two artists both being miners' sons. Storey's novels were more directly influenced by Wyndham Lewis's, a comparison which Hutchings has recently explored. (*The Plays of David Storey*, 16). The stage plays, however, are reminiscent of Eugene O'Neill. Storey's dialogue is more natural and persuasive than O'Neill's, while his dramatic crises are less powerful and more inconclusive. Nevertheless, the dynamics of the family in the works of the two writers are similar: an older married couple is often bound together despite mutual feelings of resentment; sibling rivalry remains unresolved in middle age; with drinking comes moodiness, accusations, and eventually remorse. Both writers have used the device of a child who died young to raise issues of guilt and repressed anger. Mary Tyrone, in *Long Day's Journey Into Night*, blames Jamie for having exposed baby Eugene to a fatal case of the measles. The Shaws of *In Celebration* have also lost a child whose memory haunts the entire family. *The March on Russia* also reminds me to a degree of O'Neill's *The Iceman Cometh*. Hickey's "pipe dreams" and the fantasies of other denizens of Harry Hope's bar are similar to the delusions which sustain several members of the Pasmore family. The older sister, Wendy, cherishes her father as a symbol of working-class nobility, the source of her political commitment to the underprivileged. Her younger sister, Colleen, escapes into clichés of "finding herself" at forty-plus and Colin settles for the outward appearance of domestic and professional stability. The mother remains more realistic than the others, although she takes excessive pride in the hardness of a life which younger generations cannot understand.

Intellectually and emotionally the most bankrupt, Pasmore Senior holds on to a fantasy of heroic episodes which date back to the Crimean War. Repeatedly he offers fragments from his supposedly Halcyon days as a sailor, and, when he is disgraced in front of his children, his cantankerous wife ultimately leads him back to his sustaining myth by prodding him to "Tell me—that time—when you marched in Russia." The telling of this elusive and possibly fabricated tale has become a ritual of their marriage, very like the story which the old lady prods her husband to retell in Ionesco's *The Chairs*. When the latter demurs, Ionesco's old woman asserts with unintentional irony that she never tires of the story: "it fascinates me, it is your whole life." Now, consoling, Mrs. Pasmore hopes that her husband's narrative will restore his wounded self-esteem. As in most of Storey's plays (and novels), there is a hint of regeneration at the conclusion, a low-key optimism oddly juxtaposed against a sense of sadness and loss, the ubiquitous contrarities of hope and despair.

Works Cited

Anderson, Lindsay. Interview in this volume.

Hutchings, William. *The Plays of David Storey: A Thematic Study*. Carbondale: Southern Illinois University Press, 1988.

Taylor, John Russell. *David Storey*. Writers and their Work 239. Ed. Ian Scott-Kilvert. London: Longman, 1974.

BIBLIOGRAPHY

Primary Sources

I. INDIVIDUAL PLAYS

The Changing Room. London: Jonathan Cape, 1972.

——. New York: Random House, 1973.

——. Harmondsworth: Penguin, 1973.

——. With intro. by E. R. Wood. London: Heinemann, 1977.

The Contractor. In *Plays and Players* December 1969: 63–86. London: Jonathan Cape, 1970.

——. New York: Random House, 1970.

——. Harmondsworth: Penguin, 1971.

Cromwell. London: Jonathan Cape, 1973.

The Farm. London: Jonathan Cape, 1973.

Home. London: Jonathan Cape, 1970.

——. In *Plays and Players* August 1970: 61–77.

——. New York: Random House, 1971.

——. In *Plays of the Year* [1971]. Vol. 41. Ed. J. C. Trewin. London: Elek Books, 1972.

In Celebration. London: Jonathan Cape, 1969.

——. New York: Grove Press, 1969.

———. In *Plays of the Year* [1969]. Vol. 38. Ed. J. C. Trewin. London: Elek Books, 1970.

———. Harmondsworth: Penguin, 1971.

———. With intro. by Ronald Hayman. London: Heinemann, 1973.

Life Class. London: Jonathan Cape, 1975.

The March on Russia. London: Samuel French, 1989.

Mother's Day. In *Home, The Changing Room, and Mother's Day*. Harmondsworth: Penguin, 1978.

The Restoration of Arnold Middleton. London: Jonathan Cape, 1967.

———. In *Plays of the Year* [1967]. Vol. 35. Ed. J. C. Trewin. London: Elek Books, 1968.

———. In *New English Dramatists* 14. Harmondsworth: Penguin, 1970.

Sisters. In *Early Days/Sisters/Life Class*. Harmondsworth: Penguin, 1980.

II. COLLECTED PLAYS

The Changing Room, Home, and The Contractor: Three Plays by David Storey. New York: Bard-Avon, 1975.

In Celebration and The Contractor. Harmondsworth: Penguin, 1977.

Home, The Changing Room, and Mother's Day. Harmondsworth: Penguin, 1978.

Early Days/Sisters/Life Class. Harmondsworth: Penguin, 1980.

In Celebration, The Contractor, The Restoration of Arnold Middleton, and The Farm. Harmondsworth: Penguin, 1982.

III. OTHER WORKS

NOVELS

Flight into Camden. London: Longman, 1960.

———. New York: Macmillan, 1961.

———. Harmondsworth: Penguin, 1976.

Pasmore. London: Longman, 1972.

————. New York: E. P. Dutton, 1972.

————. New York: Avon, 1975.

————. Harmondsworth: Penguin, 1976.

Present Times. London: Jonathan Cape, 1984.

————. Harmondsworth: Penguin, 1986.

A Prodigal Child. London: Jonathan Cape, 1982.

————. Harmondsworth: Penguin, 1984.

Radcliffe. London: Longman, 1963.

————. New York: Coward-McCann, 1963.

————. New York: Avon, 1965.

————. Harmondsworth: Penguin, 1977.

Saville. London: Jonathan Cape, 1976.

————. New York: Harper & Row, 1976.

————. Harmondsworth: Penguin, 1978.

————. New York: Avon, 1978.

A Temporary Life. London: Allen Lane, 1973.

————. New York: E. P. Dutton, 1974.

————. New York: Avon, 1975.

————. Harmondsworth: Penguin, 1978.

This Sporting Life. New York: Macmillan, 1960.

————. London: Longman, 1960.

————. New York: Avon, 1975.

————. Harmondsworth: Penguin, 1976.

————. Intro. by the author and commentary and notes by Geoffrey Halson. London: Longman, 1978.

CHILDREN'S LITERATURE

Edward. Illus. Donald Parker. London: Allen Lane, 1973.

FILM AND TELEVISION ADAPTATIONS

Early Days. London Weekend Television, 1981.

Home. Public Broadcasting Service, 1973.

In Celebration. American Film Theatre, 1975.

This Sporting Life. Continental, 1963.

TELEPLAY

"Grace," from the short story by James Joyce. 1974.

DOCUMENTARIES DIRECTED

"Death of My Mother" (on D. H. Lawrence), 1963.

"Portrait of Margaret Evans," 1963.

ARTICLES, ESSAYS, AND REVIEWS

"Cells." *New Statesman* 19 April 1963: 612.

"Journey through a Tunnel." *Listener* 1 August 1963: 159–61.

Letter. *Times* (London), 15 February 1974, 15.

"Marxism as a Form of Nostalgia." *New Society* 15 July 1975: 23.

"Ned Kelly on Film." *Manchester Guardian* 7 February 1963: 7.

"Nolan's Ark." *New Statesman* 31 May 1963: 840–41.

"On Lindsay Anderson." *Cinebill: The American Film Theatre—The Second Season*. New York: AFT Distributing Corp., 1975.

"Passionate Polemics." *New Society* 28 January 1967: 137–38.

"Robert Colquhoun." *New Statesman* 12 October 1962: 500–501.

"What Really Matters." *Twentieth Century* 172 (Autumn 1963): 96–97.

"Which Revolution?" *The Guardian* 18 October 1963. Review of Alan Sillitoe's *The Ragman's Daughter*.

"Working with Lindsay." *At the Royal Court: 25 Years of the English Stage Company*. Ed. Richard Findlater. New York: Grove Press, 1981. 110–15.

POETRY

"Blake." In the program accompanying the production of *The Restoration of Arnold Middleton*, Royal Court Theatre, 1967. London: G. J. Parris, 1967. [12].

"Grandfather." In the program accompanying the production of *The Contractor*, Royal Court Theatre, 1969. London: G.J. Parris, 1969. [6].

"Miners." In *Playbill* accompanying the production of *The Restoration of Arnold Middleton*, Criterion Theatre, 1967. London: Playbill, Ltd., 1967. [14].

IV. SECONDARY SOURCES

Anderson, Lindsay. "The Court Style." *At the Royal Court: 25 Years of the English Stage Company*. Ed. Richard Findlater. New York: Grove Press, 1981. 143–147.

Although this is primarily a reminiscence of the early years of the English Stage Company, Anderson concludes it with his personal regret that George Devine (its founder, who died in 1966) never saw one of Storey's plays—though he would surely have approved "their poetry, their realism uncluttered by naturalism, . . . [and] their vision of society untouched by the crudity of propaganda."

———. "On David Storey." *Cinebill: The American Film Theatre—The Second Season*. New York: AFT Distributing Corp., 1975.

In this brief tribute (published in the program that accompanied the "second season" of the American Film Theatre series, which included Anderson's film of *In Celebration*), Lindsay Anderson describes Storey as "one of the most profound, poetic and *feeling* writers of our time," who creates "a deeply human art, one that questions and consoles. It is in the great tradition, very rare today."

Ansorge, Peter. "The Theatre of Life." *Plays and Players* 20 (September 1973): 32–36.

In this interview-based article, Ansorge explores Storey's transition from novelist to playwright and from idealist to pragmatist. Storey discusses *Cromwell* in particularly useful detail and asserts that "life has got[ten] far too complex for making political gestures anymore [sic]. They don't work. . . . To look for vague unifying political gestures is romanticism."

Browne, Terry W. *Playwrights' Theatre: The English Stage Company at the Royal Court Theatre*. London: Pitman Publishing Co., 1975.

This short history of the English Stage Company includes a brief account of the productions of Storey's works. An appendix lists all plays produced season by season at the Royal Court, with their opening dates, authors, and directors; a second appendix records specific financial details, including grants support, the number of performances of each play, its production costs, box office takings, and the percentage of seats sold.

Bygrave, Mike. "David Storey: Novelist or Playwright?" *Theatre Quarterly* 1.2 (April–June 1971): 31–36.

Bygrave argues that Storey's novels are more important than his plays, and that many of the themes of the plays are the themes of the novels, reworked and extended. He discusses Storey as an "apocalyptic" writer and considers *Radcliffe* "his key work." *Arnold Middleton* is deemed "one long tinkering theory ending with the simple admission that life goes on," while *The Contractor* is "a study of corruption."

Cave, Richard Allen. "Poetic Naturalism: David Storey." *New British Drama in Performance on the London Stage, 1970–1985*. Buckinghamshire: Colin Smythe, 1987. 133–174.

Cave's commentary on Storey's plays combines literary analysis and details of performance. He characterizes Storey as an artist "seeking to shape life-experience into art without destroying its essential randomness and autonomy by moulding it to fit some impersonal theory or interpretation. . . . The presentation of experience allows several possible interpretations to come into play in his audiences' minds (as likely as not of a conflicting nature), yet each is true to the event and each is felt to be right." Cave discusses Storey's lesser-known "literary" plays at length, praising *Cromwell* in particular as "a radical development of the history play [which] made for superb poetic theatre."

Cox, Frank. "Writing for the Stage: Keith Dewhurst, Peter Nichols and David Storey Talking to Frank Cox." *Plays and Players* 14 (September 1967): 40–42, 50.

In this interview-based article, Storey discusses in detail the pre-production history of *The Restoration of Arnold Middleton*, the play's thematic relationship to his novels and his own life, and the ways in which he learned the "technical business of playwrighting" (including "the technicalities of dramatic dialogue") while writing scenarios for two films.

Craig, David. "David Storey's Vision of the Working Class." *The Uses of Fiction: Essays on the Modern Novel in Honour of Arnold Kettle*. Ed. Douglas Jefferson et al. Milton Keynes, England: Open University Press, 1982. 125–38.

In his overview of Storey's novels (through *Saville*), Craig emphasizes that "Storey's style *shows*, with the physical salience and exactitude of Conrad, though he is very different from Conrad in that he often works with deep-seated upsets of a psychological kind rather than with dilemmas of work or duty or other social bonds." He emphasizes that Storey's characters struggle to "preserve their vital selves" and discusses their "torn feelings" on separating from their family origins in the working class—aspects of his work that also recur in the plays.

Duffy, Martha. "An Ethic of Work and Play." *Sports Illustrated*, 5 March 1973: 66–69.

Duffy's article includes an extensive biographical profile of Storey, along with many details of the difficulties of producing *The Changing Room*, a section of which also appears in the issue.

Dutton, Richard. "*Home* by David Storey." *Modern Tragicomedy and the British Tradition: Beckett, Pinter, Stoppard, Albee, and Storey*. Norman: University of Oklahoma Press, 1986. 151–61.

Dutton assesses *Home* as an absurdist tragicomedy, placing it within the context of works of Beckett and Pinter as "a tissue of innuendo and suggestion" and "an open-ended social allegory."

Ecker, Gisela. "David Storey: *Home*—'schones Wetter heute' oder Strukturen des 'small talk.'" *Englishes Drama von Beckett bis Bond*. Munich: Wilhelm Fink, 1982. 250–71.

Ecker's remarkably thorough analysis of *Home*—the most comprehensive and detailed assessment of any of Storey's individual works—is divided into five sections, whose subjects are: (1) the absence of a traditional plot; (2) differences in class and gender among the characters, whose series of on-stage combinations gives the play a sonata-like form; (3) the unreliability or unverifiability of much that the characters alleged about themselves or others, despite the play's appearance of realism and accessibility; (4) conversation analysis according to communication orientation theory, including characteristic patterns of the spoken dialogue (e.g., the use of ellipses, evasion, omission of subject or object in individual lines), speaker-hearer interaction, and thematic variations; (5) an overview of the large number of divergent interpretations that the play has evoked. In German, with quotations in English.

Flatley, Guy. "I Never Saw a Pinter Play." *New York Times*, 29 November 1970, sec. 2: 1, 5.

This joint interview with Storey and Lindsay Anderson occurred at the time of the New York premiere of *Home*. During the banter-filled conversation, Storey insists that there are "no symbols" in *Home* and maintains that he is "not so sure they [the characters] are where they say they are [since he] can't believe *anything* they say" (Anderson disagrees with both remarks). Storey also denies any knowledge of Harold Pinter's works and discusses having written the play in two days (along with a second and "completely different" play, also called *Home*, which "was about a mental institution"). He also recounts his involvement in a brawl with students at the school in the East End of London where he was teaching immediately before winning his first major literary prize. Given the tone of the conversation, Flatley's final (unanswered) question is apropos: "you two aren't putting me on, are you?"

Free, William J. "The Ironic Anger of David Storey." *Modern Drama* 16.3–4 (December 1973): 306–17.

Free contrasts Storey's first four plays with works by Harold Pinter, John Osborne, Arnold Wesker, and John Arden, contending that "Storey's sense of outrage is more restrained and his sense of irony more biting than Osborne's," for example. Despite his stylistic differences from the others, Storey is said to be "almost archetypally" a "Royal Court dramatist."

———— and Lynn Page Whittaker. "The Intrusion Plot in David Storey's Plays." *Papers on Language and Literature* 18 (Spring 1982): 151–65.

Free and Whittaker discuss Storey's characteristic dramatic structure as "a variant of the well-made play which Girdler Fitch identified in 1948 as the 'intrusion plot,'" wherein an outsider is introduced into a homogenous social group and thereby "forces an adjustment which either accommodates or rejects him." A heuristic is also provided for this pattern which, although it "may not be fully present in any given play[,] . . . provides a point of reference from which to understand the unique themes and structures of each of them."

Gibb, Frances. "Why David Storey has got it in for academics, the critics, and 'literary whizz-kids.'" *Times Higher Education Supplement*, 4 February 1977, p. 9.

> In addition to being "on record as saying that half the English literature departments in the country should be closed" and that "they are one cause of the present malaise of the English novel," Storey here comments on many of his literary contemporaries—one of the very few occasions on which he has done so. Among the novels he admires are Saul Bellow's *Herzog*, Gunter Grass's *The Tin Drum*, Alexander Solzhenitsyn's *Cancer Ward*, and V. S. Naipaul's *A House for Mr. Biswas*; however, he dismisses the fiction of Margaret Drabble and John Fowles as "completely artificial pseudo-writing . . . a box of tricks." He characterizes playwright Tom Stoppard as "the John Fowles of the intellectual world . . . all whizz-kid undergraduate kind of writing." He also contends that the English novel "has not the future—the present— of films and theatre," in which he sees "more potential."

Gindin, James. "David Storey." *British Dramatists since World War II, Part II: M–Z*. Vol. 13 of *Dictionary of Literary Biography*. Detroit: Gale Research Co., 1982. 501–13.

> This thorough overview of Storey's life and works concludes that "it is in Storey's capacity to create terse yet profoundly revealing verbal structures for [his] characters and situations, to build a moving portrait of a person or an occupational segment of experience from a fragmented and carefully controlled dialogue or monologue, that his intensely dramatic talent resides."

Gray, Nigel. "Show Them You Can Take It." *The Silent Majority: A Study of the Working Class in Post-War British Fiction*. New York: Barnes & Noble–Harper & Row, 1973. 133–59.

> Gray's detailed analysis of *This Sporting Life* includes extensive quotations from the novel; its analysis of characters "who had been fucked over by a violent corrupt system since they were born" and whose "only hope was to stop feeling, to become deadened or to die" is in some ways pertinent to the plays as well.

Gussow, Mel. "To David Storey, A Play is a 'Holiday.'" *New York Times*, 20 April 1973, 14.

This interview-based biographical profile of the playwright accompanied the Broadway opening of *The Changing Room*. Storey contends "that his works were not specifically drawn from his own life" but are based on "imagined experience based on general knowledge based on things I've seen—and lived through"; he also contrasts the years that he spends laboring on his novels against the quick and spontaneous writing of the plays.

————. "When Writers Turn the Tables Rather Than the Other Cheek." *New York Times*, 16 July 1989, 5–H.

This humorous account of animosities between playwrights and critics includes an account of an incident in which Storey, after reading Michael Billington's negative review of *Mother's Day*, "cuffed" (i.e., struck) the reviewer in the bar of the Royal Court Theatre. Billington later called a press conference, to which "Storey, a rugged ex-rugby player, responded by saying that critics should be in better physical shape if they planned to challenge playwrights in print."

Hayman, Ronald. *British Theatre since 1955: A Reassessment*. Oxford: Oxford University Press, 1979. 55–58.

Hayman maintains that "Storey has repeatedly gone back to naturalism, after repeatedly falling out of love with it"; in *Home*, "avoidance of confrontation" is both the play's theme and its central dramatic technique.

————. "Conversation with David Storey." *Drama* 99 (Winter 1970): 47–53.

Here Storey discusses his start in the theatre, his working relationship with Lindsay Anderson, his method of writing, and the nature of his "plays of understatement" as well as the reasons why he considers himself "more a novelist than a playwright." He also criticizes the reviewers of *Home* for "having done a disservice to the play in saying that it was about a nuthouse."

————. *Playback*. London: Davis-Poynter, 1973. New York: Horizon, 1974. 7–20. Reprint of the above interview from *Drama*.

Heiney, Donald, and Lenthiel H. Downs. "David Storey." *Contemporary British Literature*. Vol. 2 of *Essentials of Contemporary Literature of the Western World*. Woodbury, N.Y.: Barron's, 1974. 208–14.

Storey's best-known plays put theatergoers "back in Beckett no-action territory" although "the magic of characterization and theme" make them successful; brief biography is accompanied by discussion of *This Sporting Life, The Contractor,* and *Home.*

Hennessy, Brendan. "David Storey in Interview with Brendan Hennessy." *Transatlantic Review* 33–34 (1969): 5–11.

In addition to extensive remarks on his novels, Storey here discusses what Hennessy terms the theme of "the difficulty of loving in our time" and offers his view of the poem that is read aloud in *Middleton.* He also remarks that the character of Joan is "so profoundly underwritten that it depends almost entirely on the temperament of the actress what she turns out like" and insists that "An artist doesn't experiment; this is something technicians do. . . . It's a form of sentimentality to assume that art, or 'the theatre,' is something that can be 'experimented' in."

Hilton, Julian. "The Court and Its Favours." *Stratford-upon-Avon Studies 19: Contemporary English Drama.* Ed. Malcolm Bradbury and David Palmer. London: Edward Arnold, 1981. 139–155.

This brief assessment of Storey's first five plays suggests that "one of the keys to understanding his highly distinctive blend of the poetic and the naturalistic, and his concern for communal acts of a physical kind . . . lies in the Nietzschean model" of tragic drama as a synthesis of Apollonian and Dionysian forces, as described in his study entitled *The Birth of Tragedy.*

———. "The Court and Its Favours: The Careers of Christopher Hampton, David Storey, and John Arden" in *Modern British Dramatists: New Perspectives.* Ed. John Russell Brown. Englewood Cliffs, N.J.: Prentice-Hall, 1984. 50–74.

This is a reprint of the above article.

Hutchings, William. "'Invisible Events' and the Experience of Sports in David Storey's *The Changing Room." Proteus: A Journal of Ideas* 3.1 (Spring 1986): 1–7.

Hutchings analyzes the formation and dissolution of the team bond in *The Changing Room* as a paradigm of the experience of sports; he also discusses Storey's doctrine of "invisible events" in theatre and in life.

———. "'Much Ado About Almost Nothing' Or, The Pleasures of Plotless Plays." *Within the Dramatic Spectrum.* Ed. Karelisa V. Hartigan.

Comparative Drama Conference Papers 6. Lanham, MD: University Press of America, 1986. 107–114.

This is a discussion of the nature of minimalism and the alleged "plotlessness" of *The Changing Room* and *The Contractor* as well as Samuel Beckett's "dramaticule" *Breath*.

———. *The Plays of David Storey: A Thematic Study*. Carbondale: Southern Illinois University Press, 1988.

Hutchings assesses the plays in terms of the devaluation of traditional ritual, desacralization, and the disintegration of the family, comparing Storey's works to those of Chekhov, Beckett, Brecht, and others. The book includes an extensive interview with Storey, conducted in August 1983; the bibliography lists numerous reviews of individual productions as well as primary and other secondary sources.

———. "'Poetic Naturalism' and Chekhovian Form in the Plays of David Storey." *The Many Forms of Drama*. Ed. Karelisa V. Hartigan. Comparative Drama Conference Papers 5. Lanham, MD: University Press of America, 1985. 79–85.

This essay defines Storey's "poetic naturalism" and relates it to the Chekhovian tradition.

———. "The Work of Play: Anger and the Expropriated Athletes of Alan Sillitoe and David Storey." *Modern Fiction Studies* 33.1 (Spring 1987): 35–47.

This comparison of Sillitoe's *The Loneliness of the Long-Distance Runner* and Storey's *This Sporting Life* also includes some discussion of *The Changing Room*; it emphasizes the nature of economic exploitation and expropriation of athletes in both writers' works.

Joyce, Steven. "A Study in Dramatic Dialogue: A Structural Approach to David Storey's *Home*." *Theatre Annual* 38 (1983): 65–81.

By applying the principles of the Prague school of literary criticism (particularly the theories of Jan Mukarovsky and Jiri Veltrusky), Joyce contends that "Storey explores the possibility of meaning existing in non-language, that is, in the delicate psychological interstices where 'being' is contingent upon the establishment of communicative ties with fellow humans. This language of absence is crucial to understanding the drama," as he contends in his ensuing analysis of *Home*. He places Storey's dramas "somewhere between the Osborne tradition of the 'angry young men' and the Pinter tradition of exhuming the psychological remains of broken lives by means of manipulating subtext."

Kalson, Albert E. "Insanity and the Rational Man in the Plays of David Storey." *Modern Drama* 19.2 (June 1976): 111–128.

Kalson analyzes the fact that in six of Storey's first seven plays "at least one character is on the verge of insanity, an idiot or a certifiable lunatic" and considers it as "an artist's attempt to reconcile himself to a bewildering universe where the line between sanity and insanity is often invisible. . . . For some of them, to lose the mind is to gain the self."

Kerensky, Oleg. "David Storey." *The New British Drama: Fourteen Playwrights Since Osborne and Pinter*. London: Hamish Hamilton; New York: Taplinger Publishing Co., 1977. 3–17.

Kerensky alleges that Storey "gave up anything like a plot" in *The Contractor*, in which "thoughts are never developed, and the play's rather obvious social themes are only gently touched upon"; the content of *The Changing Room* is said to be "even more elusive." *Mother's Day*, however, is described as "more amusing and more theatrical" than his earlier works, most of which are briefly discussed.

Knapp, Bettina L. "David Storey's *In Celebration* and Gabriel Cousin's *Journey to the Mountain Beyond*: From 'Maw' to Mater Gloriosa." *Theatre Annual* 33 (1977): 39–55.

Knapp considers both *In Celebration* and Cousin's *Journey to the Mountain Beyond* (the stage adaptation of the Japanese novel *Mayarana* by Schichiro Gukazara). She considers both works "therapeutic in their grandeur" and "as potent in their cleansing capacity as a Euripides tragedy," wherein "the action is simple and no outside event intrudes to detract from the march of an inexorable fate," but she contends that they "dramatize two attitudes toward life" in their characterizations of mothers. Storey's Mrs. Shaw is said to be "a destructive and sterile force," whereas Cousin's character O Rin is "a positive stalwart and courageous mother figure."

Loney, Joseph. "Shop Talk with a British Playwright: David Storey Discusses *Home* and Other Scripts." *Dramatists Guild Quarterly* 8 (Spring 1971): 27–30.

When asked about the "Pirandellian riddle" he has posed in *Home* ("just
what *Home* can possibly mean—and *who* the enigmatic characters
really are and *where* they are"), Storey insists that he has "never seen
those characters particularly as mad" and that "quite easily they could
have been anywhere else"; he also discusses his "feeling that the play
has an organic life of its own" which "has to be allowed to exist without
any impositions from any direction." He also comments briefly on the
central metaphor of *The Contractor* and on what he considers "the basic
tragedy" of *In Celebration*, that "education had alienated *all* of [the
sons] rather than enhancing their lives."

Morgan, Margery. "David Storey." *Great Writers of the English Language:
    Dramatists*. Ed. James Vinson. London: Macmillan, 1979. New York:
    St. Martin's, 1979. 556–558.

Morgan contends that it is impossible to say whether Storey is primarily
a novelist or primarily a dramatist, and she notes that his concern with
social class is essentially moral and cultural rather than political. She
likens his repeated reworking of specific incidents to a graphic artist's
use of idiosyncratic motifs in a number of paintings, while "his most
distinguished plays suggest a structuralist model in the kind of
integration they achieve."

Morley, Sheridan. *Review Copies: Plays and Players in London, 1970–1974*.
    London: Robson Books, 1974.

This compilation of reviews contains a number of brief comments on
Storey's plays: *The Contractor* is "well-constructed" but "lacks the
solid foundation of the tent and is altogether less satisfactorily built";
Home is "a shapeless, aimless and ultimately hopeless" play in which
"language is . . . governed by rhythm and economy rather then [sic]
intelligibility"; *The Changing Room* is praised for its documentary
effectiveness; and *Cromwell* is said to be "an undoubtedly major if
flawed play" comparable to Edward Bond's *Lear*.

Nightingale, Benedict. "David Storey." *Contemporary Dramatists*. Ed. James
    Vinson. 2nd ed. London: St. James Press, 1977. 763–766.

In this brief overview, Nightingale compares Storey's works to those of
fellow Yorkshireman and playwright David Mercer, finding Storey's
the more universal. He emphasizes Storey's recurrent theme of the
power that the past has over the present and assesses the effects of
"social, topographical, intellectual, and (perhaps) moral uprooting" as

well as the division of "mind from emotion and hands from mind." He also notes the "resilient Stoicism" of Storey's characters.

————. "Everyman on His Uppers." *New Statesman*, 19 April 1974: 558–59.

In this review of *Life Class*, Nightingale deftly and concisely defines the typical Storey protagonist, though he considers the characters from whom his composite is drawn to be a "pretty sorry lot"—among whom Allott is "a voyeur who passes his working days instructing other voyeurs" as well as "Storey man on his existential uppers." However, the play is also said to be "at least as rich as *The Changing Room*" and asserts that audiences "who are prepared to do a little homework in the stalls . . . will leave the theatre feeling that a good deal more has occurred than they can remember having actually seen and heard on stage."

Pearce, Howard D. "A Phenomenological Approach to the *Theatrum Mundi* Metaphor." *PMLA* 95.1 (January 1980): 42–57.

This essay discusses the tent in *The Contractor* as "a stage within a stage" with "its opening, toward the audience, corresponding precisely to the non-existent fourth wall of dramatic realism." Pearce also establishes "a parallel between tent and stage [and between] the contractor Ewbank's celebration and the playwright Storey's play." He then examines "the perennial *theatrum mundi* metaphor" which suggests "worlds in relationship to one another and may represent the ontological pole of the theatre-dream topos." Storey's characters, he notes, are "most of them rootless . . . [and] incomplete beings," though the play "declares the worth of the artist's triumph even in the face of confused values and the chaos of existence. . . . Entertainment and laughter are [seen as] the fundamental response to life."

Porter, James E. "*The Contractor*: David Storey's Static Drama." *University of Windsor Review* 15.1–2 (1979–80): 66–75.

Porter considers *The Contractor* a celebration of "the new privileges attained by the British working class and the productive, 'convivial' relationship that class has established with the higher classes on the labour scale." As such, it is an advance over earlier plays in which adversarial labor-management relationships and rigid class distinctions are displayed.

Quigley, Austin E. "The Emblematic Structure and Setting of David Storey's Plays." *Modern Drama* 22 (September 1979): 259– 276.

Focusing on "the pattern of artificial occasionality in the events which bring about character interaction" in Storey's plays (the wedding, the rugby match, the art class), Quigley assesses Storey's originality as a dramatist as a result of "his ability to transform conventional technical devices into structural images which control the thematic implications of the plays."

Randall, Phyllis R. "Division and Unity in David Storey." *Essays on Contemporary British Drama*. Ed. Hedwig Bock and Albert Wertheim. Munich: Hueber, 1981. 253–65.

Randall's analysis of Storey's oeuvre emphasizes the interrelatedness of his novels and plays, both in terms of their themes—particularly the disintegration of the family and "the disintegration of the individual personality, often into madness." She also points out that his works "are, while not precisely autobiographical, heavily reliant on the circumstances and activities of Storey's own life" and finds the major source of unity in his works to be the division Storey has felt within himself—between artist and athlete, the physical and the spiritual, the external and internal aspects of human existence. A heuristic showing the interrelationships of the novels and plays is also included.

Reinelt, Janelle. "The Central Event in David Storey's Plays." *Theatre Journal* 31 (1979): 210–20.

Reinelt analyzes Storey's attempts "to define a style which suits his material while avoiding the traditional solutions to problems of form provided by preceding generations." She contends that he achieves this by depicting "a series of private or minimally shared realities which exist on the basis of intentional participation."

Ridley, Clifford A. "Oops—The British Are Coming." *The National Observer*, 2 November 1974: 23.

Ridley's review of *The Farm* typifies complaints about Storey's alleged plotlessness, contending that it is essentially "a play in which nothing happens. And in the theatre, something *ought* to happen. That . . . is what theatre means." Nevertheless, Ridley concludes, "if *The Farm* isn't theatre, exactly, it's an interesting something-or-other."

Roberts, Philip. "David Storey's *The Changing Room*." *The Royal Court Theatre, 1965–1972*. London: Routledge & Kegan Paul, 1986. 107–20.

Roberts's extensive account of the Royal Court's production of *The Changing Room* offers particularly detailed reminiscences that are unavailable elsewhere: members of the original cast recall the auditions, the play's unorthodox rehearsal process (including "a very rough, enthusiastic, unskilled, and mercifully fairly short" rugby match), and the ways in which they accustomed themselves to the play's requisite on-stage total nudity. Comments by Storey and Lindsay Anderson are also included.

Rosen, Carol. *"Home." Plays of Impasse: Contemporary Drama Set in Confining Institutions*. Princeton: Princeton University Press, 1983. 128–46.

Rosen discusses *Home* as "a play about killing time"—"a naturalistic study of psychic hibernation" as well as "a theatrical dead end . . . [whose] listless people no longer want things to happen"; their "inner freedom to remember and to imagine [is] checked by an outer world of restrictions." Storey's characters, she contends, "are subordinated to an environment which defines as well as supports their action." Like Peter Weiss's *Marat/Sade* and Friedrich Dürrenmatt's *The Physicists* (discussed in the same chapter), *Home* explores the concept of madness "as a central myth of our neoromantic age."

———. "Symbolic Naturalism in David Storey's *Home*." *Modern Drama* 22.3 (September 1979): 277–89.

Rosen analyzes the ways in which *Home* "works metaphorically as a model of modern life and . . . concretely as a close-up of the private world of five mental patients." She also notes that Storey goes beyond Chekhov in his insistence on the illusion of the everyday.

Ryan, Paul. "Author and Director." In the program accompanying the National Theatre production of *The March on Russia*. London: The National Theatre, 1989. [11, 13, 15, 17].

Ryan discusses the thirty-year collaborative relationship between Storey and Lindsay Anderson. He also describes the playwright's "Pauline conversion to the power of art" on hearing the first verse of Paul Verlaine's *Chanson d'Automne*, which, Ryan suggests, "could stand as an epigraph for the text of *Home*"; "for a man who admits to being tone deaf," he also remarks, "Storey is an exceptionally musical writer whose plays have a truly poetic rhythm."

Sage, Victor. "David Storey in Conversation." *New Review*, October 1976: 63–65.

This is in many ways Storey's most candid and self-critical interview, providing lengthy and often surprising reassessments of his novels and plays. He describes "intellectualism" as "the English disease" and "self-protective bullshit most of the time"; he also discusses "working-class puritanism" and repudiates his novel *Radcliffe* as "too pretentious." In assessing the influences on his work, he expresses his admiration for Wyndham Lewis (especially *Rude Awakening*) but describes D. H. Lawrence as "a prick, actually, and the more he went on the more of a prick he showed himself to be"—adding that "after *Sons and Lovers* it's all rubbish."

Shelton, Lewis E. "David Storey and the Invisible Event." *Midwest Quarterly* 22 (Summer 1981): 392–406.

Shelton identifies Storey's doctrine of "invisible events" as "a consistent characteristic of Storey's dramatic mode" and assesses "four distinct applications of the term" in *Life Class*, relating it to other examples from both the novels and the plays.

Shrapnel, Susan. "No Goodness and No Kings." *Cambridge Quarterly* 5 (Autumn 1970): 181–87.

Shrapnel discusses "the meticulously, pessimistically and yet warmly observed behaviour of apparently unremarkable people" as the primary characteristic of *The Changing Room, Home, The Restoration of Arnold Middleton*, and *In Celebration*. She studies changes in Storey's use of language in particular, noting that the language of *In Celebration* and *Arnold Middleton* is commensurate to the exposure of domestic relations, while in *The Contractor* and *Home* the language is deliberately incommensurate with the tragedy of human experience that the plays portray.

"Speaking of Writing, II—David Storey." *The Times* (London), 28 November 1963, 15.

In this interview-based essay by "our special correspondent" (otherwise unidentified), Storey discusses the background of *This Sporting Life*, *Flight into Camden*, and *Radcliffe*, and he identifies D. H. Lawrence and Wyndham Lewis as "opposite poles of my temperament, both with qualities I admire and would like to emulate." Having scripted the film version of *This Sporting Life*, Storey became "more conscious of a feeling that the novel is really the form of a century ago," though he had not at this time begun writing for the theatre.

Stinson, John J. "Dualism and Paradox in the 'Puritan' Plays of David Storey." *Modern Drama* 20.2 (June 1977): 131–43.

Stinson presents an overview of the themes and motifs of Storey's plays, which are considered "more fully developed and extended" in his novels. He assesses the importance of the "puritan ethic" of work and its consequences when Storey's characters who are educated "professionals" transcend their working-class backgrounds.

Taylor, John Russell. "British Dramatists: The New Arrivals, No. 3. David Storey: Novelist into Dramatist." *Plays and Players* June 1970: 22–24.

Taylor outlines Storey's early works in chronological order, incorporating a number of quotations from him on the advantages of working within a number of art forms—novels, plays, films, painting; he also discusses Storey's methods of writing, notes his unhappiness with the reception of some of the novels, and praises "the intensity with which [the plays] summon up one man's vision of the world."

———. *David Storey*. Writers and their Work 239. Ed. Ian Scott-Kilvert. London: Longman, 1974.

This thirty-page pamphlet provides a cogent overview of Storey's novels and plays, emphasizing that he is "emphatically not a gentlemanly writer" but one whose writings are "patently, even obsessively, autobiographical." Another "obsessive theme in Storey's work [is] mental and emotional breakdown."

———. "David Storey." *The Second Wave: British Drama of the Sixties*. London: Eyre Methuen, 1971; rev. 1978. 141–54.

This is a reprint of the *Plays and Players* article cited above.

Thomann, Claus. "David Storey. *Cromwell*." *Englische Literatur der Gegenwart, 1971–1975*. Ed. Rainer Lengeler. Dusseldorf: Bagel, 1977. 107–116.

The first half of Thomann's essay provides a deft overview of Storey's novels and plays through *Saville* and *Mother's Day* (1976), emphasizing the interrelatedness of many of his works, their recurrent themes, their autobiographical motifs, and their characteristic form (described as a concentratedness of time, place, and action). *Cromwell* is then discussed not only as an apparent anomaly among Storey's works (with its multiple locales, manifold dramatic actions on stage, etc.) but also as a play that shows significant continuity with his other works in important but less apparent ways. *Cromwell*'s political themes are also carefully and eloquently set forth. In German, with quotations in English.

Weaver, Laura H. "The City as Escape into Freedom: The Failure of a Dream in David Storey's Works." *West Virginia University Philological Papers* 28 (1982): 146–53.

Weaver's analysis focuses on the city as a means of transcendence for Storey's characters, who hope to find there "a release from repressive families and communities," though such geographical flight typically fails to provide psychological freedom. Discussion focuses on the novels *Flight into Camden* and *Pasmore* plus two autobiographical essays.

———. "Rugby and the Arts: The Divided Self in David Storey's Novels and Plays." *Fearful Symmetry: Doubles and Doubling in Literature and Film*. Ed. Eugene J. Crook. Tallahassee: University Presses of Florida, 1981. 149–62.

Weaver discusses Storey's "personal experience of family- and community-induced division [which] has led him to a consistently dichotomous vision manifested even when he writes about the creative process and when he evaluates the arts." She focuses particularly on the rhetoric of his theorization about artistic activity, citing his essays on British painters, his discussion of his relationship with Lindsay Anderson, and his drama and book reviews.

Willet, John, et al. "Thoughts on Contemporary Theatre." *New Theatre Magazine*, 7:2 (Spring 1967): 6–13.

This is a transcript of a panel discussion featuring Storey, Edward Bond, Ronald Bryden, and others. It includes Storey's most theoretical comments ever on the theatre, as he assesses its "evolution from romance to ritual" in the preceding ten years as well as the "sort of introversion" wherein the essential "problems" of life have come to be seen as fundamentally "within us and not without."

Wimmer, Adolf. "David Storey." *Pessimistisches Theater: eine Studie zur Entfremdung im englischen Drama, 1955–1975*. Salzburg: Institut fur Anglistik and Amerikanistik, Universitat Salzburg, 1979. 116–30.

In this chronological overview of Storey's plays through *Life Class*, Wimmer emphasizes the recurrent theme of despair and "deep hopelessness" that is most fully expressed in *Home*; it is also evident, he contends, in Arnold Middleton's unduly high expectations of the modern world and its inhabitants, in the fragility and futility of the tent constructed in *The Contractor*, and the acute loneliness of the workers, teachers, and rugby players in his plays. Storey is deemed a "connecting link" between the generation of "Angry Young Men" and subsequent playwrights whose works supplant anger with despair. In German, with quotations in English.

Worth, Katharine J. *Revolutions in Modern English Drama*. London: Bell, 1973. 26–30 and 38–40.

Worth notes that Storey "moves between novel and drama with Maugham-like ease" and relates his "gentle conversational forms of realism" to "the N.C. Hunter/ Priestley mode" of the 1930s. She also praises the the naturalistic qualities of his plays, their lyricism, and his sense of timing.

Young, B. A. *The Mirror Up to Nature: A Review of the Theatre, 1964–1982*. London: William Kimber, 1982. 71–73.

In this brief discussion of *Home*, Young suggests that with this play Storey "has begun to work quite independently of any stage conventions generally accepted," creating a work that "does not develop but is slowly unveiled as a whole that was whole when the house-lights first went down." Storey is termed "a true original, sensitive and poetic and constantly aware of a dramatist's responsibility towards his audience."

CONTRIBUTORS

LINDSAY ANDERSON has directed many of David Storey's plays in their initial productions at the Royal Court Theatre and the National Theatre in London; he also directed the screen adaptations of Storey's *This Sporting Life* (1963) and *In Celebration* (1975) as well as the television versions of *Home* (1973) and *Early Days* (1981). His other films include *If. . .* (1969), *O Lucky Man!* (1973), *Britannia Hospital* (1982), and *Glory! Glory!* (1989).

RUBY COHN, Professor of Comparative Drama at the University of California (Davis), has published widely on contemporary American, English, and French drama, as well as a book on *Modern Shakespeare Offshoots*. An editor of several journals, she has written three books on the works of Samuel Beckett: *Samuel Beckett: The Comic Gamut*, *Back to Beckett*, and *Just Play: Beckett's Theatre*.

WILLIAM J. FREE teaches Modern Drama and Shakespeare at the University of Georgia and is Artistic Director of the Partly Free Theatre Cooperative. He has published two books and over thirty articles on drama, film, literary and dramatic theory, and literature, including two previous articles on David Storey. His third book, *Christopher Hampton: An Introduction to His Plays*, is scheduled for fall publication in the Milford series.

WILLIAM HUTCHINGS is an Associate Professor of English at the University of Alabama at Birmingham. His book entitled *The Plays of David Storey: A Thematic Study* was published by Southern Illinois University Press in 1988; he is now completing a book-length study of the novels of Alan Sillitoe.

KIMBALL KING is Professor of English at the University of North Carolina and is General Editor of Garland Publishing's Casebooks on Modern Dramatists series. He has published books and articles on modern British, Irish, and American drama and has been a member of the Modern Language Association's Executive Committee on Drama.

D. S. LAWSON is Assistant Professor of Humanities at Lander College in Greenwood, South Carolina. He has read papers on modern British drama at MLA, NEMLA, and the annual University of Florida Comparative Drama Conference. He is currently at work on a book on Joe Orton for Greenwood Press.

ADA BROWN MATHER lives in New York and worked as a director and teacher of acting. Her teaching has included the Meadowbrook Theatre and a training school at Oakland University, Rochester, Michigan, the Juilliard School, New York University, Playwrights' Horizons, and others; for the last two years she has run a Shakespeare Programme at the Avignon Theatre Festival.

LOIS MORE OVERBECK is Research Associate with the Graduate School of Emory University, Atlanta. She is Associate Editor of *The Correspondence of Samuel Beckett*, and co-editor of *Intersecting Boundaries: The Theatre of Adrienne Kennedy* (University of Minnesota Press, forthcoming in 1992).

PHYLLIS R. RANDALL, professor of English at North Carolina Central University, has published articles on Caryl Churchill, Sam Shepard, and David Storey, and edited *Caryl Churchill: A Casebook* (1989). An Assistant Editor of *American Speech*, she has also published on language and gender, including *Women Speaking: An Annotated Bibliography of Verbal and Nonverbal Behavior, 1970–1980* (1982, with Mary E. W. Jarrard).

JANELLE REINELT, Professor of Theatre Arts at California State University at Sacramento, has published numerous articles on critical theory, feminism, and performance. She is currently at work on a book on the influence of Bertolt Brecht on contemporary British drama.

SUSAN RUSINKO, Chair of the English Department at Bloomsburg University (Pennsylvania), is the author of *Terence Rattigan, Tom Stoppard, and British Drama, 1950 to Present: A Critical History*; her articles and book reviews on modern drama have appeared in *The Shaw Review*, *Modern Drama*, and *World Literature Today*.

PATRICIA TROXEL is an Assistant Professor of Dramatic Literature at California Polytechnic State University in San Luis Obispo. She has published articles on topics ranging from ancient Greek to modern theatre, with particular emphasis on contemporary British and continental playwrights. She is presently completing a manuscript on the plays of David Hare and also works as a director and dramaturge.

LAURA H. WEAVER is an Associate Professor of English at the University of Evansville (Indiana). Her areas of publication are drama (two articles on David Storey, a bibliographic essay on Arthur Kopit, two articles on theatre history), the divided-self theme in literature and composition, and ethnic autobiography/ biography.

INDEX